Yo Soy Así

Third Edition

Virgil Blanco
Juan Saborido
Leonard Gallo

Kendall Hunt
publishing company

Pak ISBN: 978-1-7924-4122-6
Text Alone ISBN: 978-1-7924-4123-3

Published in the United States of America

Contents

Introduction

The objective of this project is to develop a ***student-centered*** elementary Spanish textbook for English speaking college students. The student is the constant variable; therefore the other factors must adjust and adapt to the learner. Given this approach, this textbook will assist the instructor in fulfilling his/her three primary teaching responsibilities: modeling providing examples, coordinating learning activities and evaluating progress.

Language acquisition requires that learning must take place at three different levels: cognitive, affective and psychomotive. Therefore the student must not merely pronounce well, but he must understand what he/she is saying and when and in what context to use it. This book proposes to provide the student with a variety of correct models, which he/she can imitate through a number of drills. The drills are designed for repetition, recognition, individual production and thoughtful reproduction or adaptation. Syntax and morphology will be acquired through especially designed exercises which will facilitate cognitive inductive learning through contrasts, comparisons, patterns, and analogies. Situational learning within real cultural settings will enable the learner to emote in the target language at the proper stimuli. Group work is an essential component of our student-centered approach. Therefore, *YO SOY ASI* provides numerous exercises and activities that facilitate a group-work approach.

Grammatical explanations presented deductively will serve only to reinforce that which had been previously adopted inductively through a variety of exercises. The sequence of learning activities and exercises have been designed to allow the instructor for quick diagnostic evaluation of the learners' progress and skills Development: repeating, recalling, understanding the spoken word, understanding the written word, applying the rules, synthesizing previously learnt material, and creating his/her own sentences.

Without an understanding of the culture of the speakers of the target language, language learning is completely meaningless. It becomes a system of meaningless symbols and sounds. Research demonstrates that students who are interested in a given culture are more motivated to learn the language, and are more apt to succeed. This textbook will provide instructors with the elements necessary to interest students in the variety of cultures existing in the Spanish speaking world. A reliance of English or cognates will enable students to begin their journey exploring the many countries and people that comprises the Hispanic World.

Culture will be presented in such a way as to appeal to students, focusing on the positive rather than controversial or divisive issues.

For our purpose, culture refers to the artistic accomplishment of people, as well as the intricate system of inter-personal and intra-personal relationships that govern group behavior. Therefore, we will provide samples of both at the end of every chapter. Additionally, students will be referred to existing web sites, interesting movies, and absorbing readings that will familiarize them with *El Mundo Hispano*.

The workbook was designed to allow the student to create/his/her own scrapbook/ portfolio in Spanish describing his/her world in the target language. The workbook will provide examples and patterns to help the student describe his/her environment, his/her life, his/her thoughts, his/her feelings to an imaginary speaker of the target language. It will serve as a consulting reference manual in Spanish for the student. It will also aid instructors *diagnosing* difficulties the student might be encountering in the target language, since students will be recording their own experiences. This will also enable the instructor to *prescribe* appropriate activities to improve performance.

El Español

Cultura

Spanish, the Spanish World and You

You are studying Spanish because it is a very important language from a political, economic, and cultural perspective. It is one of the most spoken languages in the World. Spanish is spoken by about 500 million native speakers and by an even larger number of people who speak it as a second language or as a foreign language. There are approximately about 50 million Spanish speaking people in the United States. It is spoken in Europe, Africa, Asia, North America and South America. It is even spoken in Antarctica where Chile and Argentina claim territorial sovereignty, maintaining research and military stations there. Spanish is also important from a business perspective as Spanish speakers are one of the best consumers of American products. Latin American countries are also very rich in natural resources of all different types. For example, most of U S imported oil comes from Spanish countries not from the Middle East, as many Americans erroneously think. Spanish culture with its millennial traditions in the arts, sciences, music, literature, sports, cuisine, fashion, and every human endeavor will enrich your life as you learn more about it and the language you are starting to learn.

The Spanish world is known for its great diversity. It is so diverse that some people question its very identity. Is it a linguistic unit?—Is it an ethnic group, a people, a race,

a nation?—It is difficult to define because it defies any definition. Many Spaniards question the very notion of Spain, as many Latin Americans question the very notion of the terms *Latin American, Hispanic,* or *Latino.* Let's review the facts and you can come up with your own definition.

The Iberian Peninsula was inhabited about 35,000 years ago by the first Europeans. We do not know whether they came from North Africa or from Asia Minor. During the last glacial age about 15,000 years ago, most northern Europeans took refuge in Spain. The first Iberians were followed by the Celts, Greeks, Phoenicians, Carthaginians, Romans, Jews, Germanic tribes, Moors, Arabs, Syrians, and Gypsies.

Although there was extensive intermarriage, some of these groups ended up more isolated than others in a very mountainous area. Therefore, people in some areas developed their own language, customs, and identity. Thus, there are millions of Spaniards who are bilingual and whose second language is Spanish.

When the Spaniards conquered parts of Africa, Asia, and the Americas, they found well-established civilizations that had developed different languages and customs. Therefore, there are countries such as Peru where many people speak Quechua as their first language and Spanish as a second language. The same is true of Paraguay where many people speak two languages, Guarani and Spanish. There are also Spanish countries where there are many people who do not speak Spanish. That is the case of Mexico. The Spaniards were in the Philippines for 400 years. They left their language, their religion, and their customs. However, nowadays, Tagalog replaced Spanish as the first language in the Philippines.

Millions of immigrants flocked to Latin America during the nineteenth century from countries as diverse as Japan, China, Lebanon, Italy, Germany, Ireland, Wales, Russia, and Eastern Europe. They brought their customs and their language. Most of them integrated into the Latin America melting pot; others preferred to remain separated, preserving their language and customs. There were Welch, German, Scottish, Croatian, Japanese, and many other communities in many parts of Latin America. The big influx of African slaves to the Spanish colonies came during the nineteenth century as well. They were brought primarily to the Caribbean area to harvest sugar and other crops. Some of them ran away, forming their own communities; others were integrated into the new nations forged out of former Spanish colonies. Three quarters of the land of the continental United States was once Spanish territory. Such American legends as Daniel Boone, Sam Austin, and Admiral David Farragut are part of that heritage.

Geographically as well, the Spanish world extends from places of perennial snow in Antarctica to tropical paradises in the Caribbean or the Pacific Ocean, from places where it never rains in North Africa or South America, to places where it always rains in northern Spain or Southern Chile.

Can you now define that which is Hispanic?

Diálogos

Lea y repita los siguientes diálogos. Trate de imitar estos diálogos. Practique los diálogos sin leer el libro, con un compañero de clase

<u>El professor Pacheco se presenta a su nueva clase de español.</u>

El profesor Pacheco –

Muy buenos días. Soy el Profesor Pacheco.

Soy de Chile, soy chileno.

Esta es la clase de español elemental.

El libro que usamos es "Yo soy así".

Es un libro interesante y práctico.

Ahora quiero saber quién es usted.

Los estudiantes se presentan al profesor Pacheco.

- Buenos días, profesor Pacheco, yo soy Sofía y soy de New Jersey.

- Yo soy Miguel y éste es mi amigo Daniel, somos de California.

- Yo soy Raquel y soy de New York.

- Yo soy Samuel y soy del Canadá.

Los estudiantes se presentan y se conocen en la clase.

Sofía—Hola, buenos días, me llamo Sofía, y tú. ¿Cómo te llamas?

Arturo—Buenos días. Yo me llamo Arturo. Mucho gusto.

Sofia—Encantada. ¿De dónde eres?

Arturo—Soy de Michigan, y tú.

Sofía—Yo soy de New Jersey.

Luisa—Hola que tal. Yo soy Luisa y éste es mi amigo David.

Mateo—Hola Luisa, Yo soy Mateo. Mucho gusto.

David—El gusto es mío.

Más Diálogos

Una Llamada Telefónica

Begoña—Hola, Pepe, ¿Qué tal? ¿Cómo estás?

Pepe—Muy bien, ¿Qué tal? ¿y tú?

Begoña—Muy bien. Soy estudiante del profesor Pacheco. ¿y tú?

Pepe—Soy estudiante del Profesor Pacheco tambien.

Begoña—Sí, él es muy simpático.

Pepe—Sí, y muy inteligente también.

En el Aeropuerto

Policía—Su nombre, por favor.

Turista—Yo soy José Pacheco López.

Policia—¿Nacionalidad?

Turista—Yo soy Chileno

Policia—¿Destino?

Turista—Río de Janeiro, Brasil

Policia—Gracias, buen viaje.

Turista—De nada, adiós.

Preguntas del Diálogo

Piense, Pregunte y Conteste

1. ¿Cómo se llama el profesor?

2. ¿Cómo se llama el libro?

3. ¿Es de noche/ por la mañana/ por la tarde? (In Arturo's dialogue)

4. ¿Cómo se llama el doctor?

5. ¿Qué clase es?

Vocabulario

*** De Lecturas**

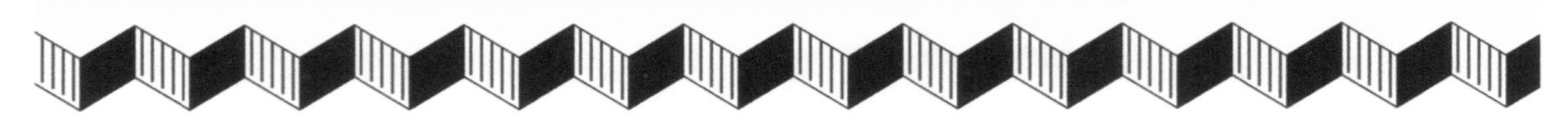

Expresiones de Saludo

When greeting people we often use the following expressions:

Hola	Hello, Hi
Buenos días	Good morning
Buenas tardes	Good afternoon
Buenas noches	Good evening
	Good night

Expresiones de Despedida

When saying "goodbye" we may use the following expressions:

Adiós	Goodbye
Hasta pronto	See you soon
Hasta luego	See you later
Hasta mañana	See you tomorrow
Chao	Chao
Hasta la vista	See you around

Otras Expresiones

¿Qué tal?	What's up?
¿Cómo estás?	How are you?
¿Cómo está usted?	How are you?
(Muy) bien	(Very) well
(Muy) mal	(Very) bad
Excelente	Excellent
Terrible	Terrible
Así así	So so
Mucho gusto/un placer	My pleasure
Encantado(a)	Delighted
El gusto es mío	The pleasure is mine
Gracias	Thank you

De nada	You're welcome
No hay de qué	You're welcome

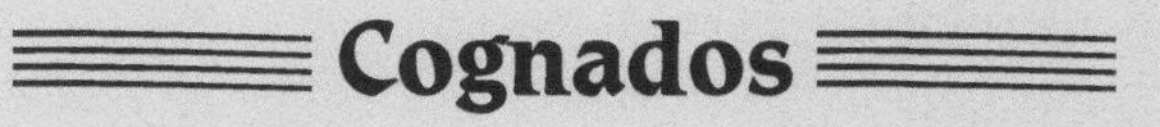

Cognados

One way of increasing your vocabulary in Spanish is by using cognates—words in different languages, having similar meanings, with the same linguistic root. Study the following groups of cognates and then add other words to the lists.

Words ending in *—or*

actor
calculador
color
doctor
factor
moderador
motor
profesor
radiador
regulador
tractor

Words ending in *—al*

actual
canal
carnal
casual
lineal
manual
marcial
parcial
potencial
puntual
sensual
visual

Words ending in *—sión*

admisión
decisión
mansión
misión
omisión
pasión
televisión
tensión
visión

Words ending in *—ción*

atracción
contracción
dirección
elección
lección
producción
reacción
relación
traducción

Cognados

Words ending in *–dad*

Calidad
Cantidad
Ciudad
Generalidad
Libertad
Movilidad
Personalidad
Universidad
Vecindad

Words ending in *–able*

aconsejable
amable
disponible
favorable
probable
soluble

Adjetivos terminados en E

1. amable
2. independiente
3. imprudente
4. prudente
5. agradable
6. inteligente
7. paciente
8. impaciente
9. importante
10. brillante
11. sociable
12. dominante
13. elegante
14. variable
15. cobarde
16. valiente
17. humilde
18. Insoportable
19. alegre
20. amigable
21. competente
22. responsable

Adjetivos terminados en Z

1. feliz
2. capaz
3. tenaz
4. audaz
5. veloz
6. eficaz
7. sagaz

Adjetivos acabados en l

1. sentimental
2. especial
3. juvenil
4. vil
5. imbécil
6. fácil
7. difícil
8. frágil
9. volátil
10. sutil
11. vital
12. fácil
13. difícil
14. frágil
15. volátil
16. sutil
17. musical
18. genial
19. leal
20. cruel

Gramática

El Alfabeto en Español (The Spanish Alphabet)

Las Cinco Vocales (The Five Vowels)

The sounds of the vowels in Spanish are crisper and shorter than the sounds produced in the English language. Each vowel produces only one distinguishable sound and when a syllable contains a diphthong, each vowel is pronounced independently from the other. Imitate carefully the sounds of the vowels in Spanish:

a as in *father*
Ana mamá sala ama

e as in *net*
Elena Pepe peso tele

i as in *see*

Inés Pili sí siglo

o as in *no*

Paco no dos dónde

u as in *ruler*

Rufo ruso Cuba tú

When a weak vowel (**I** and **U**) and a strong vowel (**A**, **E**, and **O**) are used in the same syllable, the natural phonetic emphasis falls on the strong vowel. There is no need to use an accent mark:

Alicia seis nueve cuatro agua siete biblioteca Lourdes Miami

When two weak vowels form a diphthong, the emphasis falls on the second vowel:

Luisa viudo fui

When two vowels follow each other, an accent mark is used to break the diphthong:

Sofía García

Las Consonantes (The Consonants)

There are twenty-two consonants in the Spanish alphabet (one more consonant than in the English alphabet).

b (be)
c (ce)
d (de)
f (efe)
g (ge)
h (hache)
j (jota)
k (ca)
l (ele)
m (eme)
n (ene)
ñ (eñe)
p (pe)
q (cu)
r (ere)
s (ese)
t (te)
v (ve)
w (uve doble)
x (equis)
y (i griega)*
z (zeta)

*The **y** also functions as a vowel when it is found at the end of a word, having the same sound as the vowel **i**, such as: *muy*.

The phonetic sounds of most consonants in Spanish produce the same sound as those in the English language. The consonants **l**, **f**, **p**, **m**, **n**, **t**, and **s** have similar sounds; however, a breath of air as in English does not accompany the p and t consonants:

lata monta notable tomate patos fotos

The **d,** although resembling the English **d,** is pronounced harder when found at the beginning of a word, and somewhat softer in a middle of a word:

Diego dame domingo desatar disco

nudo candidato capacidad emotivo inodoro

There are other variations of the **d** depending on the regions where the language is spoken. For example, it is common to pronounce a final **d** similar to a *th* sound in areas of Spain. Thus, *madrileños* (residents of Madrid) may be heard saying "*Madrith.*" Likewise, in other areas, the sound of the final **d** may be silent and now becomes "*Madrí.*"

The **ñ,** the extra consonant, produces a sound similar to the English words *onion* and *canyon.* The sound is reminiscent of the French ***-gn*** combination:

caña cañada caño cañería Ñico

The **h** is never pronounced in Spanish:

hola alcohol hablo Humberto

The words *hola* and *ola,* although having different meanings, are pronounced the same.

The **j** takes the English sound of the **h:**

jamón jerez jinete jornada Julio

The **c** and the **g** consonants have two distinct sounds, depending on the immediate vowel following them in a syllable. With the vowels (**a, o,** or **u**) they produce the same hard sound as in English:

casa cola Cuzco concha cubo
gallo gota gusto goma gato

When followed by the vowels (**e** or **i**) the **c** produces the same sound as the **s:**

cero cielo celos cifra cilantro

In certain areas of Spain, in particular the northern regions, the **c** is pronounced similar to a soft ***th*** sound in English. Likewise the ***th*** sound is found in the *-za, -zo,* or *-zu* combinations in the same areas of Spain. The **z** is never used with the vowels **e** or **i.** Thus the plural of *luz* becomes *luces.*

The letter **k,** although included in the Spanish alphabet, is only used with words borrowed from other languages. To attain the English **k** sound with the vowels **e** or **i,** remember to use the **-que** or **-qui** combination: *Quito* or *queso.*

It is then possible to achieve the hard **c** sound this way: ca que qui co cu.

The **g** has the same sound as the English **h** when it is followed by the vowels (**e** or **i**). It is similar to the **j** sound:

gente gitano
jefe jirafa

However, the vowel **u** is not pronounced if found between the **g** and the vowels **e** or **i.** In this case the **g** has a hard sound, similar to the (**ga, go,** or **gu**) combinations:

guerra guitarra

Then, it is possible to achieve the hard **g** sound with all five vowels:

ga gue gui go gu

If the **u** carries the *diérisis* **ü** in the same combination of letters, then it is pronounced independently, similar to the sound *–gua* in the words *agua, aguacate,* or *guacamole:*

Güines nicaragüense cigüeña cigüeñal

The letters **b** and **v** have similar sounds in Spanish. Their sound is closer to the English **b.** There is no phonetic difference between the following words:

bacalao Benito bingo bonito burro
vaca venado vino volar vulgar

Until recently the Spanish alphabet included the following consonants: **ch, ll,** and **rr.** Although they are still used in Spanish, they are merely considered double consonants. The sound produced by the combination **ch** is found in words like *cha cha cha, che, chino.*

The **ll** is pronounced like the **y** in most parts of the Spanish-speaking world. Thus the words *gallo, gallina,* and *gallego* are pronounced similar to the words *yanqui, yerba,* and *yo.*

The **rr** combination is pronounced as a trilled sound and is never found at the beginning of a word or after the consonant **n.** The sound of the **r** is equally strong when found as the initial letter in a word; thus, *ferrocarril, cigarro, perrito, refresco, Roberto,* and *Enrique* have similar **rr** or **r** sounds.

If the consonant **r** is used within a word, then it carries a weaker-trilled sound, as in the words: *María, arena, parabrisa,* and *morena.*

The letter **w** has limited uses. Just like the **k,** it is used in commonly non-Spanish words: *whisky, windsurf, waterpolo, Walkman,* among others.

The **x** is pronounced similar to the English **x** if found between two vowels. If it is followed by a consonant, it is often pronounced like an **s**:

examen próximo exacto
extraordinario expedición explosión

Acentuación (Accent Marks)

Not all words in Spanish need an accent mark or *tilde*! Generally, the accent mark denotes the phonetic emphasis on a given syllable if the word does not follow the natural stress on that particular syllable. In other words, an accent mark expresses an exception to the following rules.

Words ending in any of the five vowels or the consonants **n** or **s** carry the stress on the next to the last syllable:

*mu**cha**cho E**le**na ele**fan**te **ca**qui **Car**men mu**cha**chos*

All other words ending in a consonant (except **n** or **s**) are stressed on the last syllable:

*ron**car** apti**tud** Bra**sil** fri**jol** Inter**net***

Then, if a word carries the stress on a different syllable, it must show the accent mark on the vowel of the syllable that is stressed:

*in**glés** **glán**dula **pá**jaro glo**tón** **clí**max*

All words in Spanish that are stressed on the third (*esdrújulas*) or fourth (*sobresdrújulas*) syllables must be written with an accent mark:

*Cu**én**tamelo cen**tí**metro **cláu**sula **lám**para en**tré**gaselo*

There is a final use of the *tilde* or accent mark. Certain words have the same spelling, but have different meanings. Then, an accent mark is used to differentiate their meanings:

él = he	el = the
tú = you	tu = your
sí = yes	si = if
más = more	mas = but
sólo = only	solo = alone
aún = moreover	aun = even
té = tea	te = you (object pronoun)

Cardinal Numbers

0 cero

1 uno

2 dos

3 tres

4 cuatro

5 cinco

6 seis

7 siete

8 ocho

9 nueve

10 diez

11 once

12 doce

13 trece

14 catorce

15 quince

16 diez y seis (dieciséis)

17 diez y siete (diecisiete)

18 diez y ocho (dieciocho)

19 diez y nueve (diecinueve)

20 veinte

21 veinte y uno (veintiuno)

22 veinte y dos (veintidos)

23 veinte y tres (veintitres)

24 veinte y cuatro (veinticuatro)

25 veinte y cinco (veinticinco)

26 veinte y seis (veintiseis)

27 veinte y siete (veintisiete)

28 veinte y ocho (veintiocho)

29 veinte y nueve (veintinueve)

30 treinta

31 treinta y uno (una)

40 cuarenta

50 cincuenta

60 sesenta

70 setenta

80 ochenta

90 noventa

Subject Pronouns

Singular	Plural
Yo, I	**Nosotros (as),** We
Tú, You (fam.)	**Vosotros (as),** (fam.)
Usted, You (pol.)	**Ustedes,** You (pol.)
El, he	**Ellos,** They (masc./mix)
Ella, she	**Ellas,** They (fem.)

The English subject pronoun ***it*** has no counterpart in Spanish; it is understood.

Es una clase muy interesante.
It is an interesting class.

The Verb *Ser*

Spanish uses two verbs to express "to be." Although these verbs have specific uses and can't be interchangeable, we will only learn the verb "ser" in this unit. The present tense of "ser" is irregular, and it must be learned by itself.

Ser	Ser	
Yo soy	Nosotros/as	Somos
Tú eres	Vosotros/as	Sois
Él, Ella es	Ellos/as	Son
Usted	Ustedes	

1. *Ser* is used to identify the subject.

   Yo soy Roberto Sandoval.
   Ella es Teresa Molina.

2. *Ser* describes characteristics that are viewed as inherent qualities of the subject.

   Mi hermano es simpático y divertido.
   Teresa Molina es muy estudiosa.

3. *Ser* states origin and nationality.

   El Doctor Blanco es de Cuba.
   Él es cubano.

4. *Ser* is also used to tell time and to express dates.

¿Qué hora es?	*What time is it?*
Son las dos de la tarde.	*It is two o'clock in the afternoon.*
Hoy es el 22 de noviembre.	*Today is the 22nd of November.*

5. With the preposition ***de*** to express ownership and to indicate what things are made of.

   El carro no es de Teresa; es de Carlos.
   It is not Teresa's car; it is Carlos'.

   La casa de los González no es de madera; es de adobe.
   The González's house is not (made of) wood; it is made of adobe.

6. To form impersonal expressions like: es necesario, es importante, es imposible, es probable, and so on.

   Es necesario estudiar para sacar buenas notas.
   It is necessary to study in order to get good grades.

   Es importante hablar español en la clase.
   It is important to speak Spanish in class.

¿Qué hora es?

Las horas del día

In order to ask "*What time is it?*", Spanish uses the expression:
¿Qué hora es?
To respond, use "**Es la + time**" when the hour is "**una**" *(one)*.

Es la una de la tarde.	It is 1:00 P.M.
Es la una y uno de la mañana.	It is 1:01 A.M.

Notice that the hour *one* is feminine (*una*), while the minute *one* is masculine (*uno*). Use "*y*" to separate hours and minutes.

Use **"Son las + time"** when the hour is higher than one.

Son las dos de la tarde.	It is 2:00 P.M.
Son las nueve y cuarenta y cinco de la mañana.	It is 9:45 A.M.
Son las doce y cuarto de la tarde.	It is 12:15 P.M.
Son las cuatro en punto.	It is exactly 4:00.

Use "**media**" to express ½ *past the hour*, and "**cuarto**" to express ¼ *past the hour*.

Son las siete y media de la mañana.	It is 7:30 A.M.
Es la una y cuarto de la tarde.	It is 1:15 P.M.

Noon may also be expressed as "**Es el mediodía**". (the use of the articles el, la is optional)
Midnight as **"Es la medianoche".**

To express the minutes after the half hour subtract the minutes left until the next hour. Instead of using "**y**", use "**menos**". For example:

Son las once **y** cincuenta de la noche.	It is 11:50 P.M.
Son las doce **menos** diez.	It is 10 minutes until 12.
Es la una **y** cincuenta y cinco.	It is 1:55.
Son las dos **menos** cinco.	It is 5 minutes to 2.

A. State the appropriate greeting depending on the given time: Buenos días, Buenas tardes, or Buenas noches.

1. 8:05 P.M.	**2.** 12:15 P.M.	**3.** 10:00 A.M.
4. 4:00 P.M.	**5.** 11:25 A.M.	**6.** 7:30 P.M.
7. 1:00 A.M.	**8.** 1:00 P.M.	**9.** 12:00 A.M.

B. Give the correct time for the following items.

1. 5:15 P.M.	**2.** 11:20 A.M.	**3.** 1:40 P.M.
4. 6:55 A.M.	**5.** 7:00 P.M.	**6.** 1:00 P.M.
7. 8:30 A.M.	**8.** 4:45 P.M.	**9.** 12:00 A.M.
10. 3:30 P.M.	**11.** 10:15 A.M.	**12.** 12:00 P.M.

Questions

Including an interrogative pronoun that specifically asks for some type of information may also form questions. The most common question words are:

¿Qué?	What?
¿Por qué?	Why?
¿Quién(es)?	Who?
¿Con quién(es)?	With whom?
¿Para quién(es)	For whom?
¿Cómo?	How? / What like?
¿Cuál(es)?	What? / Which?
¿Dónde?	Where?
¿Adónde?	Where to?
¿De dónde?	From where?
¿Cuándo?	When?
¿Cuánto(a)?	How much?
¿Cuántos (as)	How many?

Placing the interrogative pronoun first followed by the verb and then by other words in the question is the standard syntax.

¿Quién enseña la clase de español?	*Who teaches the Spanish class?*
¿Dónde trabaja él?	*Where does he work?*

Ejercicios

Deletreo (Spelling)

1. You are leaving a message in your professor's answering machine. Greet him, say your full name, spell your last name for him, and give your phone number, your e-mail address, and your course title. End the message saying "por favor, llámeme" (please, call me).

2. Spell these following nouns. Ejemplo: Juan *jota,u,a,ene*

María	correo	profesor
Smith	teléfono	estudiante
Días	encantado	Universidad

3. Accent marks to differentiate meanings.

From ____________ you ____________ he ____________

The (masc. sing.) ____________ if ____________

Your ____________	tea ____________	only ____________
Even ____________	yes ____________	moreover ____________

Drills

A. Start a conversation with your students using the following drill:

"Buenos días (tardes, noches). Me llamo Profesor Saborido. ¿Y usted?

¿Cómo se llama?"

— ANSWER

"Mucho gusto (un placer, encantado)."

B. Same thing but in a familiar way.

"Buenas tardes. Soy Pedro. ¿Y tú? ¿Cómo te llamas?"

Diálogos

Matching.

A. Buenas tardes.	**1.** Sí, de Nueva Jersey.
B. ¿Cómo te llamas?	**2.** Bien.
C. ¿Qué tal?	**3.** Buenas.
D. Mucho gusto.	**4.** Me llamo Pedro.
E. ¿Eres americano?	**5.** El gusto es mío.

Fill in the blanks in the following conversations.

A. Hola, me llamo José Antonio. ¿Y tú?

- Me llamo ____________. Mucho ____________.

- Un ____________.

- ____________ luego.

- Adiós.

B.

Buenas tardes. Mi ____________ es Doctor Blanco. ¿ ____________ se llama usted?

- Buenas ____________. Me ____________ ____________.

- ____________ gusto, María Luisa.

- ____________, Doctor Blanco.

C.

Hola, soy Oscar. ¿Y tú? ¿Cómo te ____________?

- ____________ llamo Lupe. Encantada.

- ____________. Hasta ____________.

- Chao. Adiós.

D.

____________ días, clase. Soy el Profesor Gallo.

- Buenos ____________, Profesor.

- ¿Cómo te llamas tú?

- Mi ____________ es Pedro. Mucho ____________, Profesor.

- ____________ Pedro. Adiós, clase.

-____________ luego, Profesor.

Las Conversaciones de los Estudiantes

Keep up with these two conversations. ¡Ojo! One is formal, the other one familiar.

Profesor: Hola, buenos días.

Estudiante: ____.

Profesor: Soy el Profesor Saborido. ¿Cómo se llama usted?

Estudiante: ______________________________.

Profesor: Encantado.

Estudiante: ______________________________.

Profesor: Hasta mañana.

Estudiante: ______________________________.

Oscar: Hola, buenas noches.

Tú: ______________________________.

Oscar: Me llamo Oscar. ¿Y tú?

Tú: ______________________________.

Oscar: Un placer. Adiós.

Tú: ______________________________.

Ejercicios De Gramática

A. Give the correct time for the following items.

1. 5:20 P.M.	**2.** 11:20 A.M.	**3.** 1:25 P.M.
4. 6:30 A.M.	**5.** 7:10 P.M.	**6.** 1:55 P.M.
7. 8:00 A.M.	**8.** 1:05 P.M.	**9.** 12:05 P.M.
10. 3:15 P.M.	**11.** 10:35 A.M.	**12.** 12:00 A.M.

B. Little Ana can't tell time yet and is always asking **what time it is.** Express the time according to the model.

MODELO: 8:25 a.m. Son las ocho y veinticinco de la mañana.

1. 12:45 p.m. ______________________________
2. 11:05 a.m. ______________________________
3. 1:15 p.m. ______________________________

4. 9:30 a.m. ______________________________

5. 7:15 p.m. ______________________________

C. Complete these questions and statements with the appropriate form of **SER (to be).**

1. Usted __________ profesor y yo __________ estudiante.
2. Sofía, ¿ __________ (tú) estudiante?
3. Señor y señora López, ¿ __________ ustedes de España?
4. Nosotros __________ de Costa Rica.

D. Complete these questions and statements with the appropriate form of **SER (to be).**

1. Ustedes __________ estudiantes y yo __________ profesor.
2. José, ¿ __________ (tú) estudiante?
3. Señores Pérez, ¿ __________ ustedes de España?
4. Nosotros __________ de Nueva York.
5. Ellos __________ de Puerto Rico y usted __________ peruano.
6. Ella y yo __________ mexicanos.
7. ¿ __________ tú de Puerto Rico?
8. Ella __________ María López.

E. Fill in the blank with the appropriate form of the verb Ser and the corresponding adjective.

inteligente elegante musical leal sentimental audaz veloz independiente agradable pobre leal sociable insoportable dominante variable competente prudente responsable alegre

1. Yo __________ __________
2. Mi hermano __________ __________
3. Mi amiga __________ __________

4. Mis amigos y yo ____________ ____________
5. Tu y tus amigos ____________ ____________
6. Julian y Pedro ____________ ____________
7. Tu ____________ ____________
8. Tu y yo ____________ ____________
9. Elena ____________ ____________
10. El Sr. Lopez y el Sr. Ramirez ____________ ____________

F. Conteste a las siguientes preguntas.

1. ¿Qué actriz es bonita??
2. ¿Qué actor es guapo?
3. ¿Qué cantante es famosa?
4. ¿Quién es cómico?
5. ¿Quién es muy inteligente?
6. ¿Quién es muy creativo?
7. ¿Qué edificio es muy alto?
8. ¿Qué carro es muy rápido?
9. ¿Qué película es muy romántica?
10. ¿Qué comida es deliciosa?

G. Haga la pregunta correcta para la contestación escrita.

1. ____________. Es una regalo.
2. ____________. Para mi amiga.
3. ____________. Son chocolates.
4. ____________. Son chocolates de Suiza.
5. ____________. Son doce chocolates.
6. ____________. Son deliciosos.

Proverbios y Dichos

Sayings are part of the cultural heritage of Spanish-speaking people. Some sayings are hundreds of years old. They reflect the thinking and the experience of a whole nation.

Para Practicar la R rr

R con R cigarro,
R con R barril,
Rápido corren los carros
Por los rieles del ferrocarril.

Sabiduría Popular

No hay peor sordo que el que no quiere oir.
He who does not want to hear is worse than deaf.

Ojos que no ven corazón que no siente.
Out of sight out of mind.

Yo Soy Así

that an argument is an opinion
by reasons and/or facts
a. All young people should go to school until

Monólogos

The purpose of this exercise is to listen, observe, and mimic your instructor who is serving as a role model. These monologues contain patterns or speech frequently used in the Spanish world. After you have mastered each one of the model phrases, you may adapt them to your own needs, changing some words that you will find in the vocabulary section on the back of the book or in a dictionary.

Escuche, Observe e Imite

Haciendo Nuevos Amigos

Me llamo José Antonio.
Soy de Madrid.
Vivo en el barrio de Salamanca, en la
Calle Goya.
Trabajo en un banco.
Estudio inglés y economía.
Me gusta charlar con mis amigos, tocar la guitarra y cantar.
También me gusta esquiar, nadar, practicar el inglés y bailar.
Soy práctico y simpático.

Me llamo María Luisa.
Soy de La Habana.
Vivo en Miami, en la Calle Ponce de León.
Trabajo en un hotel.
Estudio hostelería e idiomas.
Me gusta hablar con los turistas, tocar el piano, y escuchar música moderna.
También me gusta patinar, montar en bicicleta y jugar al tenis.
Soy idealista, romántica y un poco soñadora.

Me llamo Oscar.
Soy de Mendoza.
Vivo en Buenos Aires, en la Calle Florida.
Soy realista y amable
Trabajo en el aeropuerto.
Estudio ingeniería mecánica.
También estudio italiano.
Me gusta montar a caballo los fines de semana y jugar al fútbol con los amigos.
También me gusta dibujar y pintar.

Me llamo Lupe.
Soy de México.
Vivo en la Colonia La Florida, en la Calle Rosas.
Trabajo en un colegio.

Me gusta viajar, cocinar platos típicos, platicar con mis amigas, enseñar a los niños pequeños y escuchar música.

Me gustan las fiestas.

Soy divertida, alegre y no soy pesimista.

Preguntas del Monólogo

Piense, Pregunte y Conteste

1. ¿Quién es de México? – lupe
2. ¿Dónde trabaja Oscar? el aeropuerto
3. ¿Quién trabaja en el aeropuerto? oscar
4. ¿De dónde es José Antonio? madrid
5. ¿De dónde es Oscar? mendoza
6. ¿Quién es de la Habana? maria
7. ¿Qué le gusta a José Antonio? charlar con mis amigos
8. ¿Qué le gusta a María Luisa? tocar el piano
9. ¿A quién le gusta cocinar? lupe
10. ¿Quién trabaja en un banco? jose
11. ¿Quién es argentino? oscar

12. ¿Quién es español? Jose

13. ¿Dónde vive María Luisa? Miami

14. ¿Quién es romántico? Maria

15. ¿Quién es práctico? Jose Antonio

16. ¿Cómo es Lupe? alegre

17. ¿Cómo es Oscar?

18. ¿Cómo es José Antonio? practico y simpatico

19. ¿Qué instrumento toca María Luisa?

20. ¿Qué instrumento toca José Antonio?

Vocabulario

De Lecturas

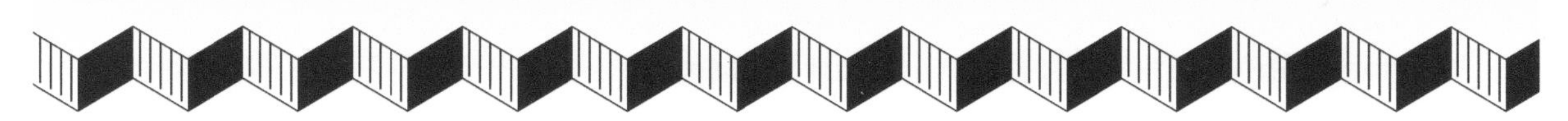

Sustantivos

El apellido	last name
El barrio	neighborhood
El caballo	horse
El colegio	school
El licenciado	professional title
El respeto	respect
El trato	treatment
El valor	value
La burla	ridicule
La calle	street
La economía	economics
La falta	lack of
La gente	people
La hostelería	hotel management
La ingeniería	engineering
Las fiestas	parties
Las mujeres	women
Las palabrotas	curse words
Las preguntas	questions
Los abogados	lawyers
Los amigos	friends
Los mayores	elderly
Los niños	children
Los países	countries
Los platos	dishes

Adjetivos

Algunos	some
Divertido	fun loving
Pequeños	small
Práctico	practical
Simpático	nice
Soñadora	dreamer
Terco	stubborn
Típicos	typical

Cognados

Words ending in *–dad*

Calidad
Cantidad
Ciudad
Generalidad
Libertad
Movilidad
Personalidad
Universidad
Vecindad

Words ending in *–able*

aconsejable
amable
disponible
favorable
probable
soluble

Vocabulario Práctico

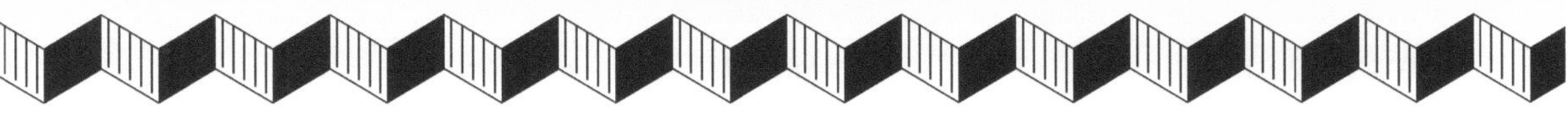

List of regular —*ar verbs*

Amar	to love
Ayudar	to help
Bailar	to dance
Buscar	to look for
Caminar	to walk
Cantar	to sing
Charlar	to chat
Cocinar	to cook
Comprar	to buy
Contestar	to answer
Coaversar	to converse, to have a conversation
Cuidar	to take care of
Desayunar	to have breakfast
Descansar	to relax
Desear	to wish
Dibujar	to draw
Enseñar	to teach
Escuchar	to listen
Esperar	to hope / to wait
Esquiar	to ski
Estudiar	to study
Hablar	to speak
Indicar	to indicate
Llamar	to call
Llegar	to arrive
Manejar	to drive
Mirar	to look at
Montar	to ride

Nadar	to swim
Necesitar	to need
Participar	to participate
Patinar	to skate
Pintar	to paint
Platicar	to talk
Practicar	to practice
Preguntar	to ask
Preparar	to prepare
Regresar	to return
Respetar	to respect
Tocar	to play (not sports) / to touch
Tomar	to take
Trabajar	to work
Usar	to use
Viajar	to travel
Visitar	to visit

Adjetivos descriptivos

Aburrido	*boring*
Alto	*tall*
Ambicioso	*ambitious*
Antipático	*not nice*
Atlético	*athletic*
Bajo	*short*
Bonito	*pretty*
Cínico	*cynical*
Cómico	*funny*
Creativo	*creative*
Dedicado	*dedicated*
Divertido	*amusing*
Dramático	*dramatic*
Egoísta	*selfish*
Estupendo	*stupendous*
Exótico	*exotic*

Expresivo	*expressive*
Fantástico	*fantastic*
Feo	*ugly*
Gracioso	*witty*
Guapo	*handsome*
Idealista	*idealist*
Misterioso	*mysterious*
Moreno	*brunet*
Nervioso	*nervous*
Pesimista	*pessimist*
Práctico	*practical*
Realista	*realist*
Rico	*rich*
Ridículo	*ridiculous*
Romántico	*romantic*
Rubio	*blond*
Simpático	*nice*
Soltero	*single*
Tacaño	*cheap*
Terco	*stubborn*

Adjetivos de nacionalidad

Alemania	alemán(es)*	alemana(s)
Australia	australiano(s)	australiana(s)
Austria	austriaco(s)	austriaca(s)
Bolivia	boliviano(s)	boliviana(s)
Brasil	brasileño(s)	brasileña(s)
Canadá	canadiense(s)	
Chile	chileno(s)	chilena(s)
China	chino(s)	china(s)
Colombia	colombiano(s)	colombiana(s)
Costa Rica	costarricense(s)	
Cuba	cubano(s)	cubana(s)
Ecuador	ecuatoriano(s)	ecuatoriana(s)
Egipto	egipcio(s)	egipcia(s)

El Salvador	salvadoreño(s)	salvadoreña(s)
Escocia	escocés(es)*	escocesa(s)
España	español(es)	española(s)
Filipinas	filipino(s)	filipina(s)
Francia	francés(es)*	francesa(s)
Guatemala	guatemalteco(s)	guatemalteca(s)
Grecia	griego(s)	griega(s)
Haití	haitiano(s)	haitiana(s)
Hungría	húngaro(s)	húngara(s)
Holanda	holandés(es)*	holandesa(s)
Honduras	hondureño(s)	hondureña(s)
Irak	iraquí(es)	
Irlanda	irlandés(es)*	irlandesa(s)
Israel	israelí(es)	
Italia	italiano(s)	italiana(s)
Jamaica	jamaiquino(s)	jamaiquina(s)
Japón	japonés(es)*	japonesa(s)
La India	hindú(es)	
Los Estados Unidos	estadounidense(s)	
Corea	coreano(s)	coreana(s)
México	mejicano(s)	mejicana(s)
Nicaragua	nicaragüense(s)	
Paraguay	paraguayo(s)	paraguaya(s)
Perú	peruano(s)	peruana(s)
Portugal	portugués(es)*	portuguesa(s)
República Dominicana	dominicano(s)	dominicana(s)
Rusia	ruso(s)	rusa(s)
Suiza	suizo(s)	suiza(s)
Venezuela	venezolano(s)	venezolana(s)
Uruguay	uruguayo(s)	uruguaya(s)

*Any adjective of nationality ending in (-és) or (-án) in its masculine singular form drops the accent mark in all other forms:

alemán	alemanes	alemana	alemanas
irlandés	irlandeses	irlandesa	irlandesas
francés	franceses	francesa	francesas

Gramática

The Present Tense

The Spanish present tense reports actions or events that take place in present time. It can also be used to report activities in progressive and/or emphatic ways.

Yo trabajo { I work / I am working / I do work

Spanish has three families of verbs. We recognize them by the three infinitive endings: *-ar, -er* and *–ir.* In this unit we will learn the pattern for regular *–ar* verbs only. To form the present tense, we first remove the *–ar* infinite ending and add the following pattern.

Yo	o
Tú	as
Ud., él, ella	a
Nosotros(as)	amos
Vosotros(as)	áis
Uds., ellos, ellas	an

	Trabajar	**Hablar**	**Cantar**
Yo	trabajo	hablo	canto
Tú	trabajas	hablas	cantas
Ud., él, ella	trabaja	habla	canta
Nosotros(as)	trabajamos	hablamos	cantamos
Vosotros(as)	trabajáis	habláis	cantáis
Uds., ellos, ellas	trabajan	hablan	cantan

As you will see, it is not necessary to use subject nouns or pronouns to express actions in Spanish. They can be used to create emphasis and/or to avoid lack of clarity.

The verb forms can tell us when the action is taking place (present, past, future) and who is performing the action. For example:

Nosotros trabajamos is translated as: *We work.* But the same action can be expressed simply as: *trabajamos.*

In order to form a negative statement, Spanish uses the word ***no*** in front of the verb:

*Nosotros **no** trabajamos.*
***No** trabajamos.*

One way of forming questions in Spanish is by switching the position of the verb or by adding a trigger expression at the end of a statement.

El Profesor Saborido enseña español.	¿Enseña español el Profesor Saborido?
Professor Saborido teaches Spanish.	El Profesor Saborido enseña español, ¿no?
	El Profesor Saborido enseña español, ¿verdad?

Nouns and Articles

All nouns in Spanish have gender. They are either masculine or feminine.

A. Masculine nouns: Nouns that end in *–o* are generally masculine. All nouns that refer to a male person are also masculine.

el libro	the book
el cuaderno	the notebook
el hombre	the man
el Papa	the Pope
el padre	the father

Exceptions: la mano — the hand

B. Most nouns that end in *–a* are feminine. All nouns that refer to a female person are feminine.

la libreta	the notebook
la escuela	the school
la mujer	the woman
la madre	the mother

Exceptions:

el día	the day
el mapa	the map
el planeta	the planet
el sofá	the sofa, the couch

C. Nouns that end in ***–dad, -tad, –tud,*** and ***-umbre*** are feminine.

la universidad	the university
la dificultad	the difficulty
la multitud	the gathering
la muchedumbre	the gathering

D. All nouns end in "-ión" are feminine with the exceptions of "camión" (truck) and "avión" (plane)

la canción	the song
la lección	lesson
la explicación	explain
la comunicación	communication
la nación	nation

E. For the correct gender of nouns that end in other consonants or vowels, one must consult a dictionary.

el lápiz	the pencil
la luz	the light
el tren	the train
la pared	the wall

F. To form the plural of nouns ending in a vowel, we add an (*s.*) If the noun ends in a consonant add *-es.*

el libro	los libros
la escuela	las escuelas
el profesor	los profesores
la universidad	las universidades
la nación	las naciones

If a noun ends in *–z,* to form the plural it is necessary to change the *–z* to a *–c* before adding ***–es.***

la luz	las luces
el lápiz	los lápices

G. As you may have observed in all the previous examples, nouns in Spanish must be preceded by an article, either definite or indefinite, that translates the English article ***the, a,*** or ***an.***

	Singular	Plural
Masculine	*el*	*los*
Feminine	*la*	*las*

The English singular indefinite articles ***a*** or ***an***, and their plural ***some***, ***a few***, are formed as follows:

	Singular	**Plural**
Masculine	*un*	*unos*
Feminine	*una*	*unas*

el profesor	los profesores
un profesor	unos profesores
la profesora	las profesoras
una profesora	unas profesoras

Descriptive Adjectives and Adjectives of Nationality

Descriptive adjectives are generally placed after the nouns they modify, and they must be in agreement (gender and number) with those nouns.

A. Descriptive adjectives ending in ***–o*** in the masculine singular form have four forms: ***-o***, ***-a***, ***-os***, and ***–as***.

Un alumno serio	Una alumna seria
Dos alumnos serios	Dos alumnas serias

B. Descriptive adjectives ending in ***–dor*** also have four forms: ***-dor***, ***-dora***, ***-dores***, and ***-doras***.

Un alumno trabajador	Una alumna trabajadora
Dos alumnos trabajadores	Dos alumnas trabajadoras

C. Descriptive adjectives ending in ***-ón*** have four forms as well: ***-ón***, ***-ona***, ***-ones*** and ***-onas***.

Un amigo comilón	Una amiga comelona
Unos amigos comilones	Unas amigas comelonas

D. Adjectives of nationality ending in a consonant also have four forms.

Un profesor español	Una profesora española
Dos profesores españoles	Dos profesoras españolas

E. Other adjectives have the same form for both masculine and feminine, but they must show number (singular or plural). If they end in a vowel, you must add an **-s.** If they end in a consonant, you must add **-es.**

Un profesor popular	Una profesora popular
Dos profesores populares	Dos profesoras populares

Summary of gender and number of adjectives

Descriptive adjectives ending in:	-o 4	-dor 4	ón 4	other 2
Adjectives of nationality ending in:	-o 4	consonant 4		other 2

Joselito es estudioso, trabajador y muy popular. Él no es dormilón.

Juanito y Joselito son estudiosos, trabajadores y muy populares. Ellos no son dormilones.

Carmen es estudiosa, trabajadora y muy popular. Ella no es dormilona.

Carmen y Luisa son estudiosas, trabajadoras y muy populares. Ellas no son dormilonas.

Joselito no es cubano ni español. Él es costarricense.

Juanito y Joselito no son cubanos ni españoles. Ellos son costarricenses.

Carmen no es cubana ni española. Ella es costarricense.

Carmen y Luisa no son cubanas ni españolas. Ellas son costarricenses.

The Verb *Gustar* and Encantar

To express the meaning of "to like," Spanish uses the verb ***gustar,*** which literally means "to be pleasing to." The subject of the verb is then what "is pleasing or are pleasing to," and the indirect receiver becomes the indirect object of the verb. Consequently, *gustar* can only be conjugated in its third person singular or plural (*gusta* or *gustan.*) Note the following sentences.

¿Te gusta la clase de español?	Sí, me gusta mucho.
¿Te gustan todas las clases?	No, no me gustan todas. Solamente me gusta la clase de español.

Gustar can be followed by another verb in the infinitive to express what one likes to do:

¿Te gusta hablar español?	Sí, me gusta mucho.

Note also that to state what one does not like, the negative word ***no*** must be placed before the indirect object pronoun.

¿Te gusta cantar? No, no me gusta cantar.

Other ways of expressing "what is pleasing to" with other indirect object pronouns:

Singular		Plural	
me	to me	**nos**	to us
te	to you	**os**	to you
le	to you, to him, to her, to it	**les**	to you, to them

Le gusta estudiar. He likes to study. (Studying is pleasing to him.)
She likes to study. (Studying is pleasing to her.)
You like to study. (Studying is pleasing to you.)

No nos gustan los vegetales. We don't like vegetables. (Vegetables are not pleasing to us.)

The Verb *ENCANTAR*

Similar to ***gustar, encantar*** is used to imply a higher degree of "to like". It is used to express the English idea of "to love things" and "to love to do things" Just like ***gustar,*** it is conjugated only in its third person singular or plural (*encanta* or *encantan*). Also an indirect object pronoun, instead of a subject pronoun must be used with this verb. Remember to use a verb in its infinitive to describe activities that one loves to do.

Me gusta cantar pero me encanta bailar.
I like to sing but I love to dance.

To express "to love" people or pets, one must use the verb ***amar,*** a regular ***-ar*** verb. (See page 45.)

The days of the week—Los días de la semana

In order to express today's day we ask: ¿Qué día es hoy?
To respond, we say:

Hoy es lunes. *Today is Monday.*
Hoy es martes. *Today is Tuesday.*

The days of the week are not capitalized in Spanish. In Spanish the first day of the week is lunes (Monday).

lunes, martes, miércoles, jueves, viernes, sábado y domingo.

¿Qué día es mañana? Mañana es miércoles.
What day is tomorrow? Tomorrow is Wednesday.

The months of the year—Los meses del año

FEBRERO						
lunes	**martes**	**miércoles**	**jueves**	**viernes**	**sábado**	**domingo**
1	2	3	4	5	6	7
8	9	10	11	12	13	14
15	16	17	18	19	20	21
22	23	24	25	26	27	28

To express today's date, say: ¿Cuál es la fecha de hoy?
The response is usually:

Hoy es el 15 de febrero. *Today is the fifteenth of February.*

Same as the days of the week, the months are not capitalized either.

MESES DEL AñO

enero, febrero, marzo, abril, mayo, junio, julio, agosto, septiembre, octubre, noviembre y diciembre.

Notice that with the exemption of the first (el primero) of any month, Spanish uses cardinal numbers (uno, dos, tres, etc.).

Hoy es el primero de enero.
Mañana es el dos de enero.
El miércoles es el tres de enero.

The seasons — Las estaciones

el otoño

el invierno

la primavera

el verano

Ejercicios

Drills

A. Conversation with your students. Formal drill:

"Buenos días. Me llamo Juan Saborido. Soy profesor. Soy de España y trabajo en la universidad de Middlesex ¿Y usted?

¿De dónde es?"

— ANSWER

"Mucho gusto. ¿Estudia usted aquí (here) en la Universidad de Middlesex?"

— ANSWER

B. Same thing but in a familiar way.

"Buenas tardes. Soy Pedro. Soy estudiante y soy puertorriqueño. Estudio en la universidad de Middlesex. ¿Quién eres y dónde estudias?"

— ANSWER

"¿De dónde eres?"

— ANSWER

"¿En dónde trabajas?"

— ANSWER

Piense y conteste. (Think and answer.)

1. ¿Cómo te llamas?
2. ¿De dónde eres?
3. ¿Dónde trabajas?
4. ¿Qué te gusta hacer (to do)?
5. ¿Qué clases tomas?
6. ¿Qué te gusta cocinar?

Diálogos

Matching.

A. ¿Quién eres tú?

B. ¿Estudias en Middlesex?

C. ¿De dónde eres?

D. ¿Trabajas? ¿dónde?

E. ¿Te gusta estudiar aquí?

1. Sí, en la librería de la universidad.
2. Sí, me gusta muchísimo.
3. Me llamo Juan.
4. Soy de Edison, Nueva Jersey.
5. Sí, tomo cuatro clases este semestre.

Fill in the blanks in the following conversations.

A. Hola, me llamo José Antonio. Soy de Nueva Jersey.

- Hola, ____________ Pedro. ____________ de Manhattan, Nueva York.

- ¿ ____________ tú un estudiante en esta (this) universidad?

- Sí, ____________ cuatro clases este (this) semestre.

B.

- Buenas tardes. ____________ Doctor Blanco. ¿ ____________ es usted?

- Hola. Me ____________ María y ____________ una estudiante de español en su (your) clase Spa 121.

- ¡Ah! ¿De dónde eres, María?

- ____________ ____________ New Brunswick.

C.

- Hola. Soy el Profesor Gallo. ____________ su (your) profesor de español este semestre. ¿Les ____________ hablar español?

- Sí, nos ____________ mucho la lengua española.

- ¿Cuántas clases ____________ ustedes este semestre?

- ____________ cuatro.

- ¿Son ustedes de Nueva Jersey?

-Sí, todos nosotros ____________ de Nueva Jersey.

Ejercicios de Gramática

I. Articles.

A. Complete by writing the appropriate indefinite article **(un, una, unos, unas).**

____________ (1) barrios, ____________ (2) caballo, ____________ (3) burla, ____________ (4) planetas y (5) ____________ mapa.

B. Write the appropriate form of the definite article **(el, la, los, las).**

____________ (1) fiesta, ____________ (2) cuaderno, ____________ (3) colegio, ____________ (4) mano y ____________ (5) libros.

II. Complete by writing the appropriate articles.

____________ (1) libros (some books), ____________ (2) pluma (the pen), ____________ (3) broma (a joke), ____________ (4) avión (a plane), ____________ (5) problema (the problem).

III. Complete using the **present tense of the verbs** in parentheses.

1. Yo____________ música popular. (escuchar)
2. Ella ____________ administración de negocios. (estudiar)
3. Los amigos ____________ (conversar) y ellos ____________ (tomar) café.
4. Ustedes ____________ (bailar) muy mal pero (but) ____________ (cantar) mejor.
5. ¿Qué ____________ él? (mirar)
6. Yo ____________ mucho el fútbol. (practicar)
7. Tú y yo ____________ bien (nadar)
8. ¿ ____________ tú mucho? (trabajar)

IV. Fill in the blank with the correct form of the **adjective**.

1. La casa es ____________ (alto) y ____________ (bonito).
2. Los muchachos son ____________ (fuerte) y ____________ (trabajador).
3. Las chicas son ____________ (moreno) y ____________ (delgado).
4. El libro es ____________ (grande) y ____________ (rojo).
5. Lupe es ____________ (pequeño) y ____________ (guapo).
6. Oscar es ____________ (egoísta) y ____________ (antipático)
7. María Luisa es ____________ (soñador).
8. Mi amiga María es ____________ (inteligente) y ____________ (cómico).
9. José Antonio es ____________ (simpático) y____________ (práctico).
10. Yo soy ____________ y ____________.

V. Fill in the blanks with the correct conjugation of the verb.

1. Yo ____________ (tomar) cuatro clases este semestre.
2. Mis amigos ____________ (trabajar) en el centro comercial (mall).
3. Tú ____________ (hablar) español muy bien.

4. Ustedes ____________ (desear) trabajar aquí.

5. Ellas ____________ (esperar) a su amiga.

6. Nosotros ____________ (bailar) en las fiestas.

7. Ella ____________ (comprar) ropa en la tienda.

8. Usted ____________ (estudiar) con su amiga en la biblioteca.

9. Vosotros ____________ (necesitar) más dinero.

10. Nosotras ____________ (cantar) canciones mexicanas.

VI. **Present tense of "ar" verbs.** Complete using the present tense of the verbs in parentheses.

1. Tú ____________ música. (escuchar, trabajar, hablar) (to listen to)
2. Nosotros ____________ español. (trabajar, esperar, estudiar)(to study)
3. Ellos ____________ café. (bailar, hablar, tomar) (to drink)
4. Usted____________ muy mal. (necesitar, bailar, desear)(to dance)
5. Ellos ____________ la televisión (mirar, bailar, esperar) (to look)
6. Yo ____________ muchos deportes. (bailar, tomar, practicar)(to practice)
7. Tú ____________ en la cafetería (desear, charlar, tomar) (to chat)
8. ¿____________ tú en Sears? (necesitar, cocinar, trabajar) (to work)
9. Ustedes ____________ la lección. (desear, bailar, preparar)(to prepare)
10. Yo ____________ por el parque. (caminar, necesitar, ayudar) (to walk)

VII. Constructions with **gustar** and **encantar.**

1. Yo/ **gustar** la clase de español.

____

2. Ella/ no **gustar** bailar tango.

____

3. Nosotros/ **encantar** este restaurante.

___

4. Tú/ no **gustar** los exámenes.

___

5. Ellos/ **encantar** el buen tiempo.

___

VIII. Answer the questions using ***gustar, encantar*** or ***amar.***

1. ¿Te gustan más las novelas románticas o las de misterio?

___

2. ¿Qué te gusta hacer (*to do*) en una fiesta?

___

3. ¿A quién amas más en este mundo *(in this world)*?

___

4. Durante el verano *(During the summer). ¿Que te encanta hacer?*

___

5. Pregúntale a tu profesor(a). *(Ask your professor).* ¿Qué le gusta hacer los fines de semana? *(week ends).*

___

IX. ¿Qué día/fecha es? Write the following days/dates in Spanish.

MODELO: Thursday, May 5th Jueves, el cinco de mayo.

1. Tuesday, November 25th ___
2. Sunday, January 10th ___
3. Saturday, March 1st ___

4. Monday, October 2nd ____________________

5. Wednesday, May 30th ____________________

X. Complete

¿Cuál es la fecha de hoy? ____________________

¿Qué día es hoy? ____________________

¿Qué día es mañana? ____________________

¿Cuándo es tu cumpleaños? ____________________

XI. Give the dates for the following holidays.

1. Halloween
2. The discovery of America
3. Thanksgiving Day
4. Last day of classes
5. Christmas
6. Independence Day

Charlando

Lupe y Adriana se Encuentran en la Piscina

Lupe—Hola, Adriana ¿Cómo estás?

Adriana—Bien, ¿y tú, en la piscina?

Lupe—Me gusta mucho nadar después de correr.

Adriana—Yo nado en la playa después de tomar el sol. Siempre camino por la playa. Me gusta mucho.

Lupe—¿Qué clases tomas este semestre?

Adriana—Tomo español dos con el profesor Gallo. No es muy difícil.

María Luisa Estudia en su Casa con su Mejor Amiga Gisela

María Luisa: Deseo que me presentes a tu primo Ernesto. Creo que es muy guapo y muy simpático.

Gisela—Sí, es guapo pero es muy antipático. Cree que es el mejor en todo. Vive en uno de los mejores barrios, estudia mucho, practica béisbol, nada, levanta pesas, esquía, toca la batería, baila, habla tres idiomas, y viaja todos los veranos.

María Luisa—¿De verdad? Es un chico muy interesante. Deseo conocerlo (meet him).

Gisela—Bueno, un día de estos los invito a mi casa.

Oscar Trata de Convencer a su Padre, Don Ernesto.
Su Novia, Laura Está Buscando Empleo

Oscar—Papá, mi amiga Laura desea trabajar en tu empresa.

Don Ernesto—¿Cómo es Laura? ¿Qué estudia? ¿En qué desea trabajar?

Oscar—Laura estudia comunicaciones. Desea ser publicista. Es inteligente, trabajadora, alegre, inteligente, práctica, y es morena con ojos verdes.

Don Ernesto—¡Que suerte tienes! Deseo conocerla. ¿Cuándo me la presentas? Tenemos un puesto perfecto para una chica joven como ella.

Cultura

La Rosa Blanca

Poesía escrita por el escritor y prócer cubano José Martí sobre la amistad.

Cultivo una rosa blanca
En julio como en enero
Para el amigo sincero
Que me da su mano franca.

Y para el cruel que me arranca
El corazón con que vivo,
Cardos ni orugas cultivo,
Cultivo una rosa blanca.

1. ¿Qué cultiva el poeta?
2. ¿Para quién la cultiva?
3. ¿Qué da el amigo?
4. ¿Quién es el enemigo?
5. ¿Qué no cultiva para el enemigo?
6. ¿Qué cultiva para sus enemigos?
7. ¿Qué quiere decir el poeta?

La Personalidad y el Respeto

El respeto es un valor muy importante en el mundo hispano. Se respeta a las mujeres y los hombres cuidan lo que dicen delante de ellas, por supuesto no se dicen palabrotas. También hay que respetar a los mayores. Hay que tratarlos de usted. El tú es para hablarle a los amigos y a la gente más joven. En algunos países hispanos la gente contesta a los señores con un "Sí, señor" o un "No, señor" o un "Sí, señora" o un "No, señora". También uno llama a personas mayores que merecen respeto con un "Don" o "Doña" delante del primer nombre. Es una forma menos formal que llamarlos por su apellido, o sea "Señor Pereira" o "Señora González". No importa la situación económica o social de una persona, aún le llaman "Don Fulano" o "Doña Fulana". El hacer muchas preguntas a otra persona se considera una falta de respeto. La sátira y la burla también son consideradas falta de respeto. A los profesores se les llama "Profesor", a los abogados se les llama "licenciado" y a los médicos se les llama "médico". Hay países donde les llaman "doctor" a los abogados y a los profesores. Lo importante es indicar respeto en el trato con otras personas.

Preguntas

1. ¿Cómo demuestran los hombres respeto a las mujeres?
2. ¿Cómo demuestran los jóvenes respeto a los mayores?
3. ¿Cómo se contesta a un señor para demostrar respeto?
4. ¿Cómo se contesta a una señora para demostrar respeto?
5. ¿Cuándo se utiliza el "Don"?
6. ¿Qué forma de llamar a alguien es más formal que "Don"?
7. ¿Cómo se considera la sátira?
8. ¿A quién se llama "doctor" en algunos países hispanos?
9. ¿Es importante indicar respeto en la cultura hispana?

Proverbios

En la unión está la fuerza.
Mas vale pájaro en mano que ciento volando.

Capítulo Tres

Mi Casa y Mi Barrio

Monólogos

Soy José Antonio

Vivo en un piso. El piso tiene 250 metros cuadrados.

El piso es grande y antiguo. Tiene un salón de estar, un comedor, cuatro dormitorios, dos baños, una cocina, una terraza y una pequeña habitación de servicio. Está en la quinta planta, a la izquierda.

Está en el barrio de Salamanca, en Madrid, en la Calle de Ortega y Gasset, muy cerca del Parque del Retiro. Cerca de mi casa hay muchos restaurantes, peluquerías, tiendas, cafeterías, bares, almacenes, galerías de arte, clínicas y muchos comercios. Está en un sitio muy céntrico. (place)

Soy María Luisa

Vivo en una casa en la Calle Ponce de León, en Coral Gables. Es una casa moderna de una sola planta. Está lejos del centro. Tiene una sala-comedor, tres habitaciones, tres baños, cocina, patio y una piscina. También tiene un garaje para dos carros.

Soy Lupe

Vivo en una casa adosada (Townhouse) en la Colonia La Florida. Es una casa en la Calle Las Rosas. La Florida es uno de los barrios satélites de la ciudad de México, Distrito Federal. Es una casa que tiene cochera para estacionar dos coches. La colonia tiene una alberca para todos los vecinos. La casa tiene un muro (wall) muy alto. Tiene dos plantas. Las cuatro alcobas están arriba. En la planta baja está la sala, el comedor, la cocina, la habitación de servicio, una biblioteca y un patio interior.

Preguntas de los Monólogos

Piense, Pregunte y Conteste

1. ¿Dónde vive José Antonio?
2. ¿Es un piso amplio?
3. ¿En dónde vive María Luisa?
4. ¿Cuántos baños tiene la casa de María Luisa?
5. ¿Tiene un garaje pequeño o grande?
6. ¿En dónde vive Lupe?
7. ¿Qué tipo de casa tiene Lupe?
8. ¿Cuántas plantas tiene la casa?
9. ¿Dónde están las alcobas?
10. ¿Tiene Lupe una biblioteca en la casa?

Vocabulario

De Lecturas

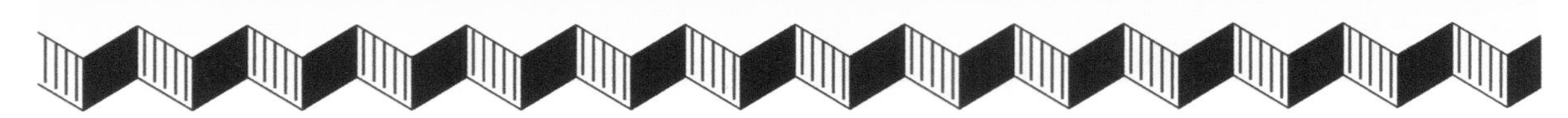

Sustantivos

El barrio	neighborhood
El centro	center of town
El comedor	dining room
El comercio	business
El muro	wall
El parque	park
El piso	apartment
El salón de estar	family room
El sitio	place
El techo	roof
La alberca/La piscina	swimming pool
La biblioteca	library
La calle	street
La casa	house
La cochera/El garaje	garage
La cocina	kitchen
La colonia	neighborhood
La gente	people
La habitación de servicio	laundry room
La izquierda	left
La lavandería	laundromat
La madera	wood
La parrillada	barbecue
La planta	floor
La sala-comedor	living-dining room
La terraza	terrace
La tía	aunt
Las clínicas	clinics
Las galerías de arte	art galleries

Las habitaciones/Las alcobas	bedrooms
Las huertas	vegetable gardens
Las losetas	tile floors
Las peluquerías	hair salons
Las puertas	doors
Las rejas	window bars
Las tejas	roof tiles
Las tiendas	stores
Las ventanas	windows
Los abuelos	grandparents
Los almacenes	department stores
Los baños	bathrooms
Los bares	bars
Los carros	cars
Los dormitorios	bedrooms
Los incendios	fire
Los jardines	flower gardens
Los ladrillos	bricks
Los ladrones	thieves
Los lugares	places
Los metros	meters
Los pisos	floors
Los restaurantes	restaurants
Los sitios	places
Los vecinos	neighbors

Verbos

Cambiar	to change
Comer	to eat
Conocerse	to know each other
Cultivar	to cultivate
Durar	to last
Estacionar	to park
Estar	to be

Gustar	to like
Haber (hay)	There is/There are
Mantenerse	to maintain
Poner	to put
Protegerse	to protect
Recibir	to receive
Reunirse	to gather
Saludar	to greet
Tener	to have
Vivir	to live

Adjetivos

Adosada	adjoining
Alto	high
Amplio	large
Antiguo	old
Baja	lower
Cara	expensive
Céntrico	central
Construidas	built
Estrechas	close
Muchos	many
Quinta	fifth
Sola	only
Soltera	single/not married
Todo	every

Vocabulario Práctico

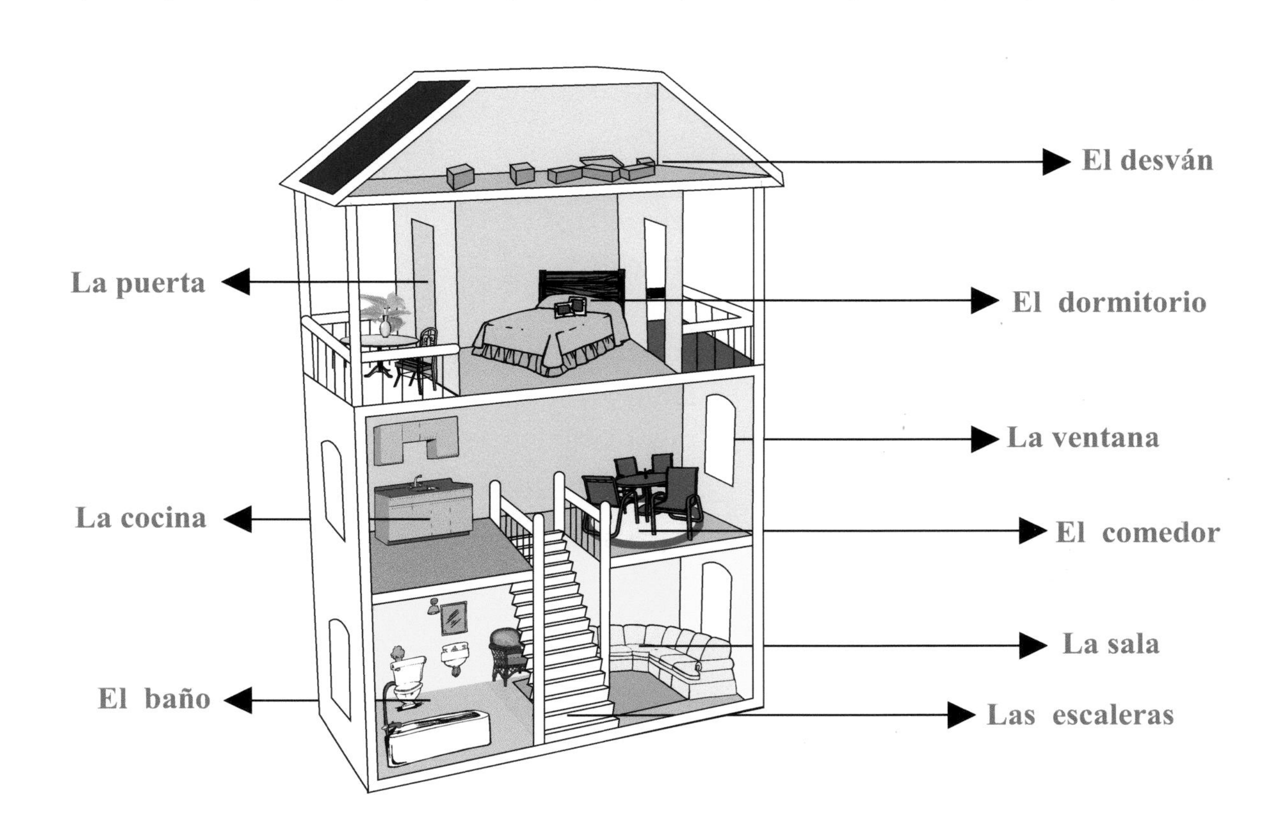

El armario	closet
El balcón	balcony
El dormitorio	the bedroom
El escritorio	desk
El fregadero	kitchen sink
El garaje	garage
El inodoro	toilet
El lavamanos	bathroom sink
El lavaplatos	dishwasher
El salón de estar	family room

La alcoba	bedroom
La alfombra	rug
La ducha	shower
La bañadera	tub
La cama	bed
La cómoda	chest of drawers
La estufa	stove
La habitación de servicio	laundry room
La lámpara	lamp
El pasillo	hallway
El piso	floor / apartment
El refrigerador	refrigerator
El sillón	armchair
El sofá	sofa
El sótano	basement
La mesa	table
La mesita de noche	night table
la piscina	swimming pool
La planta	floor
La silla	chair

Vocabulario Práctico

List of regular *–er* and *–ir* verbs.

–er verbs

Aprender	to learn
Beber	to drink
Comer	to eat
Comprender	to comprehend
Creer	to believe
Deber + inf.	should
Deber	to owe
Defender	to defend
Depender	to depend
Leer	to read
Vender	to sell
Ver*	to see

–ir verbs

Abrir	to open
Asistir a	to attend
Compartir	to share
Decidir	to decide
Discutir	to discuss
Escribir	to write
Insistir en	to insist
Permitir	to allow
Recibir	to receive
Subir	to go up
Sufrir	to suffer
Vivir	to live

1 Estas iapicas son amarilla

2 Estas hamburguesas son deliciosas

3 Esta bandera es grande

4 E~~st~~ Coche es

5 Estas gollos es bonito

- esas namburguesas son deliciosas
- ~~esa bandera es~~
  Aquella bandera es granda
- estos lapices son afilados
- Aquellos gallos ~~es~~ son bonito

Gramática

venti-uno

Demonstrative Adjectives

Demonstrative adjectives are used to state the position of people or things to which the speaker is referring. They must agree with the gender and number of the noun they modify. In English we use *this* or *these* to indicate that the object is near the speaker, and *that* or *those* to indicate that the object is at some distance from the speaker. Spanish also uses a third adjective to distinguish between the distance of two or more nouns that relate to the speaker or the listener.

Masculine	Feminine	
Este coche **Ese** coche **Aquel** coche	**Esta** casa **Esa** casa **Aquella** casa	This That That (far)
Estos coches **Esos** coches **Aquellos** coches	**Estas** casas **Esas** casas **Aquellas** casas	These Those Those (far)

It is also common to use the adverbs ***aquí*** (*here*), ***allí*** (*there*), and ***allá*** (*over there*) with demonstrative adjectives to further emphasize the distance.

Este coche aquí es barato, pero ese coche allí es caro.
This car is cheap, but that car is expensive.

Aquellos coches allá son los más caros.
Those cars over there are the most expensive.

Demonstrative Pronouns

Spanish demonstrative adjectives agree in number and gender with the modified noun. Let's review again:

this	**este** apartamento	*these*	**estos** apartamentos
(near)	**esta** casa		**estas** casas
that	**ese** apartamento	*those*	**esos** apartamentos
(closer)	**esa** casa		**esas** casas
that	**aquel** apartamento	*(far)*	**aquellos** apartamentos
(far)	**aquellas** casas	*those*	**aquellas** casas

Spanish uses **aquel** / **aquella** / **aquellos** / **aquellas** to show objects farther away from other objects previously mentioned or to the persons spoken to:

Esta casa es grande.
This house is big.

Esa casa es más grande.
That house is bigger.

Aquella casa es la más grande.
That house (over there) is the biggest.

Demonstrative constructions are usually accompanied by the following emphatic adverbs: **aquí** (*here*), **allí** (*there*), and **allá** (*over there*).

Voy a comprar ese apartamento que esta allí, aunque me gusta más aquel apartamento que está allá.

I am going to buy that apartment, although I like that one over there much better.

In order to avoid repetition, we can replace the demonstrative adjective with a pronoun. These pronouns carry an accent mark to distinguish them from the adjective forms:

Esta casa es grande.
This house is big.

Ésa es más grande.
That one is bigger.

Aquélla es la más grande.
That one (over there) is the biggest.

¿Cuál te gusta más? ¿Ésta, ésa o aquélla?
Which one do you like better? This one, that one, or that one over there?

Esto, eso, and **aquello** also function as pronouns. However, they only refer to abstract concepts, ideas, or nonspecific objects. Notice that in their neuter forms these pronouns do not carry an accent mark and are only used in the singular form.

Esto es muy importante.
This is very important.

No repitas eso.
Don't repeat that.

¿Qué es aquello?
What is that over there?

Cardinal Numbers

100 cien, ciento
101 ciento uno (una)
200 doscientos, doscientas
300 trescientos, trescientas
400 cuatrocientos, cuatrocientas
500 quinientos, quinientas
600 seiscientos, seiscientas
700 setecientos, setecientas
800 ochocientos, ochocientas
900 novecientos, novecientas

1.000 mil
2.000 dos mil
10.000 diez mil
100.000 cien mil
1.000.000 un millón (de)
2.000.000 dos millones (de)

In most Spanish-speaking countries a comma is often used to separate whole numbers and decimals.

¿Cuánto cuesta este libro? $42,50
How much is that book?

Ciento is shortened to **cien** before nouns and when followed by the numbers **mil** and **millones.**

Cien dólares
Cien mil dólares
Cien millones de dólares

Ordinal Numbers

Unlike cardinal numbers used to indicate quantities, ordinal numbers express the order of nouns in a given set. They must agree in number and gender with the modified noun. **Primero** (first) and **tercero** (third) are shortened to **primer** and **tercer** before a masculine singular noun. In most instances ordinal numbers are only used through *tenth;* afterward cardinal numbers are preferred and are always masculine since they refer to the noun **número.**

Primer (o/a)	First	**Sexto (a)**	Sixth
Segundo (a)	Second	**Séptimo (a)**	Seventh
Tercer (o/a)	Third	**Octavo (a)**	Eighth
Cuarto (a)	Fourth	**Noveno (a)**	Ninth
Quinto (a)	Fifth	**Décimo (a)**	Tenth

Observe the following spelling changes:

El primer presidente de los Estados Unidos fue Jorge Washington.
The first president of the United States was George Washington.

Carlos Primero fue un poderoso monarca español.
Charles the First was a powerful Spanish monarch.

La primera dama de los Estados Unidos es Michelle Obama.
The first lady of the United States is Laura Bush.

"El tercer siglo" but "el siglo tercero."
The third century.

La tercera calle a la izquierda.
The third street on the left.

La Quinta Avenida es muy elegante.
Fifth Avenue is very elegant.

Vivimos en el siglo veintiuno.
We live in the twenty-first century.

The Use of the Preposition *de* to Show Possession

Spanish does not recognize the "apostrophe s" to show ownership. Instead, the preposition "*de*" (of) is used:

La casa de José Antonio está en el barrio de Salamanca, en Madrid.
José Antonio's house is located in the Salamanca neighborhood, in Madrid.

Ese carro verde es de la Sra. Pasos.
That green car belongs to Mrs. Pasos.

Remember that when the preposition *de* is followed by the definite article *el* (the) the two words are contracted to form one word *del* (of the):

El despacho del Doctor Blanco está en el primer piso.
Dr. Blanco's office is on the first floor.

Los despachos de los Profesores Saborido y Gallo están en el segundo piso.
Professors Saborido and Gallo's offices are on the second floor.

The Present of *–er* and *–ir* Ending Verbs

In Capítulo Dos we learned the present tense of *–ar* verbs. There are two other families of verbs in Spanish: *–er* and *–ir.* Notice the new pattern for these two families of verbs. Before we add the endings we must also remove the infinitive endings **–er** and **–ir.** Note that the patterns are the same, except for the *nosotros* and *vosotros* forms.

	-er	**-ir**
Yo	-o	-o
Tú	-es	-es
Ud., él, ella	-e	-e
Nosotros(as)	-emos	-imos
Vosotros(as)	-éis	-ís
Uds., ellos, ellas	-en	-en

	Comer	**Vivir**
Yo	como	vivo
Tú	comes	vives
Ud., él, ella	come	vive
Nosotros(as)	comemos	vivimos
Vosotros(as)	coméis	vivís
Uds., ellos, ellas	comen	viven

Verbo Especial

The verb ***ver*** "to see" follows the regular pattern of ***–er*** infinitives. However, the "***yo***" form is slightly irregular.

Ver (To see, to watch)

Yo	veo
Tú	ves
Ud., él, ella	ve
Nosotros(as)	vemos
Vosotros(as)	veis
Uds., ellos, ellas	ven

The Expression *Acabar de* + Infinitive

A very useful expression that conveys a recent completion of an action can be formed by conjugating the verb **acabar** "to end" in the present tense, followed by the preposition ***de*** and a verb in the infinitive. This expression can be translated as "to have just done something."

Yo	acabo de llegar a casa.	*I have just arrived home.*
Tú	acabas de comer.	*You have just eaten.*
Ud., él, ella	acaba de entrar.	
Nosotros(as)	acabamos de escribir una carta.	
Vosotros(as)	acabáis de ver un programa interesante.	
Uds., ellos, ellas	acaban de leer el libro.	

The Expression *Hay*

Hay can be translated as *there is* or *there are.* It is often used with indefinite articles "*un, una, unos, unas,*" quantitative adjectives (*muchos, pocos*), or cardinal numbers (*uno, cinco, once . . .*). ***Hay*** is both singular and plural.

Hay un excelente restaurante español en Fords.
There is an excellent Spanish restaurant in Fords.

Hay muchos edificios modernos en la ciudad de Nueva York.
There are many modern buildings in New York City.

The Verb *Estar*

In the previous chapter you learned the formation and the specific uses of the verb **ser.** Now we will study the verb **estar,** the other Spanish verb that is also translated as *"to be."* Let's first learn the present tense:

Yo	estoy
Tú	estás
Ud., él, ella	está
Nosotros(as)	estamos
Vosotros(as)	estáis
Uds., ellos, ellas	están

1. *Estar* is used to indicate the location of the subject at any given time.

Cancún está en la Península de Yucatán.
Cancún is in the Yucatan peninsula.

Madrid está en España.
Madrid is in Spain.

Los estudiantes están en la sala de clase.
The students are in Spanish class now.

2. *Estar* is used to express an emotion or a condition of the subject.

Los estudiantes están contentos (tristes).
The students are happy (sad).

El Profesor Gallo está cansado porque trabaja mucho.
Professor Gallo is tired because he works a lot.

Mi amiga Julia está enferma (no está bien).
My friend Julia is sick (she is not well).

3. *Estar* is used to show the result of an action.

Los libros están abiertos.
The books are opened.

La puerta está cerrada.
The door is closed.

4. *Estar* is used to express actions in progress. The present progressive tense is formed using the present tense of *estar* and present participle of the main verb (the **-ing** ending in English). The present participle is formed by dropping the *–ar* infinitive ending and replacing it with *–ando.*

Most *–er* and *–ir* ending verbs take the *–iendo* to form the present progressive.

Infinitive	Tomar	Vender	Vivir
-ing	tomando	vendiendo	viviendo

Nosotros estamos escuchando al profesor.
We are listening to the professor.

Estamos aprendiendo español en la clase.
We are learning Spanish in class.

En este momento mi novia está trabajando.
At this moment my girlfriend is working.

¿Por qué no estás escribiendo?
Why aren't you writing?

The following verbs have irregular present participles:

Creer	creyendo	(believing)
Leer	leyendo	(reading)
Oír	oyendo	(hearing)
Traer	trayendo	(bringing)
Caer	Cayendo	(falling)

Ahora estoy leyendo un libro muy interesante.
I am now reading a very interesting book.

Estamos oyendo un programa musical muy bonito.
We are now listening to a very pretty musical program.

Ser and *Estar* contrasted

Ser	*Estar*
1. Identification	1. Location
2. Characteristics / qualities	2. Emotions / conditions
3. Origin / nationality	3. Results of actions
4. Time / date	4. Actions in progress
5. Ownership / material	
6. Impersonal expressions	

Ser

1. La Dra. Barrios es profesora.
2. Ella es muy popular.
3. La Dra. Barrios es chilena; es de Santiago de Chile.
4. Hoy es el 22 de febrero. Son las 3:15 de la tarde.
5. Esa casa es de la familia Castro. La casa es de adobe.
6. Es importante estudiar para sacar buenas notas.

Estar

1. Ahora estamos en la clase de español.
2. Estoy muy cansado.
3. El libro está abierto.
4. Estamos aprendiendo mucho en la clase de español.

Ejercicios

A. Conversation with your students:

Hola ¿Dónde vives?

— ANSWER

"¿Escribes mucha tarea en tu clase de español?"

— ANSWER

"¿Lees mucho en la clase?"

— ANSWER

"¿Lees muchos periódicos en inglés?"

— ANSWER

"Por las mañanas ¿bebes café?"

— ANSWER

"¿Qué comes generalmente en la cafetería?"

— ANSWER

"¿Comes mucho en restaurantes con tu familia?"

— ANSWER

"¿Cuál es tu restaurante favorito?"

— ANSWER

"¿Qué comes allí?"

— ANSWER

Piense y conteste. (Think and answer.)

1. ¿Dónde vives?
2. ¿Escribes bien en español?
3. ¿Bebes café en las mañanas o té?
4. ¿Qué comes cuando vas (you go) a la cafetería?
5. ¿Qué periódicos (newspapers) lees?
6. ¿Dónde vive tu mejor amigo?
7. ¿Escribes tu tarea (homework) por las mañanas o por las noches?

Matching

A. ¿Escribes en el pupitre?	**1.** Sí, en mi restaurante preferido.
B. ¿Comes hamburguesas?	**2.** Poemas de amor (love poems).
C. ¿Qué lees?	**3.** Jugo de naranja.
D. ¿Dónde vives?	**4.** No, en el cuaderno.
E. ¿Qué bebes?	**5.** Vivo en Edison, Nueva Jersey.

Ejercicios de Gramática

A. Complete the sentences with the most appropriate conjugation. One in each blank please.

bebemos escribe leo comprendemos reciben

vivimos bebes come leemos escribo viven

1. María escribe su tarea para la clase de matemáticas.
2. Nosotros vivimos en Nueva Jersey.

3. Yo leo una novela de ficción.

4. Ellos reciben cartas (letters) de sus amigos.

5. Nosotros comprendemos la lección de español.

6. Él come una hamburguesa y papas fritas.

7. Pedro y yo leemos la explicación en el libro.

8. Yo no escribo con bolígrafo rojo.

9. ¿ viven ustedes en esta casa?

10. Tú bebes jugo de naranja.

B. Choose the correct verb and then conjugate it.

1. Yo escribo (vivir, escribir, sufrir) mi tarea para la clase de español.

2. Ellos comen (comer, leer, comprender) las hamburguesas.

3. Tú lees (comer, leer, vender) unos poemas de amor.

4. Ustedes escriben (vivir, escribir, sufrir) cartas (letters) para sus amigos.

5. Ellas comprenden (comer, leer, comprender) la lección de español.

6. Nosotras comemos (comer, leer, comprender) una hamburguesa y papas fritas.

7. Pedro y mi amiga viven (decidir, vivir, escribir) en Nueva Jersey.

8. Nosotros no escribimos (decidir, vivir, escribir) con lápiz.

9. ¿ comen (comer, leer, comprender) ustedes en la cafetería o en el restaurante?

10. ¿Tú bebes (leer, beber, vender) jugo de naranja o refresco?

Demonstrative adjectives.

C. Use the correct form of *este, ese, or aquel.*

1. __esta__ novela que yo estoy leyendo es muy interesante y __estoy__ novela que tú estás leyendo es más interesante. Pero __aquel__ novela que ellos allá están leyendo es la más interesante.

2. __estos__ apartamentos que tú ves aquí son muy grandes y __esos__ apartamentos allí son más grandes. Pero __aquelios__ apartamentos allá son los más grandes.

3. Me gusta mucho __este__ disco compacto que estamos escuchando ahora pero __aquel__ nuevo disco compacto de Daniel Powder que ellos están escuchando es más popular.

4. __estos__ profesores aquí son muy populares con los estudiantes y __esos__ profesores allí son más populares. Pero __aquelios__ profesores allá son muy terribles.

5. Acabo de comprar __esta__ casa aquí. Mi hermana acaba de comprar __esa__ casa allí y mis padres acaban de comprar __aquella__ casa allá.

D. Translate the demonstrative adjective in parentheses.

1. Julia desea comer en __aquel__ *(that over there)* restaurante. – masculine
2. ¿Por qué no escribes con __este__ *(this)* lápiz? – masculine
3. Pedro y yo no comprendemos __esas__ *(those)* lecciones en __ese__ *(that)* libro.
4. Estamos estudiando mucho en __esta__ *(this)* clase.
5. ¿Quién es __aquella__ *(that over there)* profesora que está hablando con __aquellas__ *(those over there)* estudiantes?

E. Complete the sentences with the demonstrative adjective in parentheses.

1. María escribe __________ (this) tarea para la clase de español.
2. José no habla __________ (that) lengua (language).
3. Yo leo __________ (these) periódicos.
4. Ellos escriben __________ (those) cartas (letters).
5. Nosotros no comprendemos __________ (this) lección.

6. Él come ____________ (that) hamburguesa.

7. Pedro y yo no comprendemos ____________ (this) explicación.

8. Yo no escribo con ____________ (those over there) plumas rojas.

9. ¿Viven ustedes en ____________ (that over there) apartamento?

10. Tú bebes ____________ (this) refresco.

F. Complete the sentences with the **conjugation of the present tense and the demonstrative adjective in parentheses.**

1. María ____________ ____________ (ver/this) programa de televisión todos los lunes.

2. José ____________ mucho en ____________ (comer/that) restaurante griego.

3. Yo ____________ ____________ (escribir/those) cartas (letters).

4. Nosotros ____________ ____________ (leer/these) novelas de ficción.

5. Tú ____________ ____________ (comer/that) hamburguesa.

6. En la librería, ellos ____________ ____________ (vender/that) libro.

7. Pedro y yo no ____________ ____________ (comprender/this) explicación.

8. Yo no ____________ con ____________ (escribir/those over there) lápices.

9. ¿ ____________ ustedes en ____________ (vivir/that over there) casa?

10. Tú ____________ ____________ (beber/this) jugo de naranja.

G. Demonstratives.

Choose the response with the appropriate form of the demonstrative.

1. — ¿Te gusta esta película?

   — Sí, pero me gustó más **(that one)** ____________ .

2. — ¿Estuviste alguna vez en esta cafetería?

   — No, pero si estuve en **(that one over there)** ____________ .

3. — ¿Te gustó la discoteca de anoche?

   — Sí, me encantó. Pero **(this)** ____________ disco-pub no está mal tampoco.

4. — ¿Es moderno ese teatro?

— No, es antiguo, perio **(those over there)** aquellos cines son muy modernos.

5. — ¿Qué te parece este restaurante?

— Bien, pero **(that one)** ese me parece mejor.

H. Change the following actions to the **present progressive tense.**

MODELO Yo **escribir** mi tarea para la clase de español . ***estoy escribiendo.***

1. Ellos ***comer*** hamburguesas. comenuendo
2. Tú ***leer*** unos poemas de amor. leyendo
3. Mi papá ***vivir*** aquí. vive viviendo
4. Yo ***Estudiar*** mucho para el examen. estudio estudiento
5. ¿***Beber*** (Tú) jugo de tomate o de naranja? debes bebiendo
6. Ellos No ***practicar*** ahora. practican practiendo
7. Uds. ***comprar*** mucho, ¿no? compra comprando
8. Rosita ***Ver*** un programa muy interesante en la televisión. ve viendo
9. Los mariachis ***tocar*** música mexicana. tocan tocando
10. Yo no ***comprender*** la lección. comprenden comprendaro

I. Complete the sentences with the Present Tense of Verb **Estar**.

1. ¿Dónde ________ tú ahora?
2. ¿Cómo ________ usted hoy, Profesor Gallo?
3. Yo ________ muy bien, gracias.
4. Nosotros ________ en la clase de español ahora.
5. Ellos ________ estudiando español en **MCC**.

J. Complete the paragraph with the appropriate form of **ser** or **estar.**

MARIA

Hola, Me llamo María y (Yo) ______________ (1) de Barcelona, España. (Yo) ______________ (2) alta y morena. Mi novio ______________ (3) guapo y simpático. Yo ______________ (4) en Madrid en la universidad. Yo ______________ (5) preocupada porque tengo muchos exámenes.

JOSE

Hola, yo ______________ (6) José López y yo ______________ (7) de Edison, Nueva Jersey, pero ahora (but now) yo ______________ (8) en Boston, estudio aquí en la Universidad. Mi familia ______________ (9) pequeña. Mis padres ______________ (10) muy felices porque los voy a visitar hoy.

K. Complete the paragraph with the appropriate form of **ser** or **estar.**

1. Nosotros A) ***estamos*** B) ***somos*** de Nueva Jersey.

2. Ella A) ***es*** B) ***está*** muy bonita hoy.

3. Yo A) ***soy*** B) ***estoy*** inteligente y guapo.

4. ¿ A) ***Eres*** B) ***Estás*** tú cansado (tired)?

5. Ellos A) ***son*** B) ***están*** en la clase de español.

6. Hoy A) ***es*** B) ***está*** el cuatro de junio.

7. A) ***Son*** B) ***Están*** las cuatro de la tarde.

8. Tú A) ***eres*** B) ***estás*** José.

9. ¿A) ***Son*** B) ***Están*** ustedes estudiantes de español?

10. Ellos A) ***son*** B) ***están*** profesores.

Charlando

José Antonio Acompaña a sus Padres a Comprar un Apartamento en la Costa del Sol para Ir en las Vacaciones

Don Pepe—Queremos un apartamento de dos dormitorios y dos baños, con un comedor grande, una terraza con vista al mar, en un edificio con pistas de tenis, piscina y jardines.

Vendedor—Tenemos un apartamento en la sexta planta en unas torres frente al mar. El salón de estar es muy grande y el comedor también. La terraza es enorme con muchas flores. Los dormitorios son muy grandes con vestidores. La vista es espectacular.

Don Pepe—¿Cuánto cuesta?

Vendedor—Quieren (They want) 400.000 Euros. Es una ganga porque está en una zona muy buena en un edificio muy elegante. Van a venderlo muy rápido.

Don Pepe—¿Y tú, hijo, qué crees?

José Antonio—Papá, creo que es una oportunidad fenomenal.

Don Pepe—Bien, vamos a verlo y si me gusta lo compro.

Adriana Quiere Acompañar a Lupe y Quedarse en su Apartamento en Acapulco

Adriana—¿Cuándo se van para Acapulco?

Lupe—Nos queremos ir el martes, pero mi abuelita no viene porque no se siente bien.

Adriana—Entonces, eso quiere decir que la habitación de la abuelita no va a ser usada.

Lupe—Sí, porque ya invitamos a mi amiga Inés. Ella va a quedarse en la habitación de la abuelita.

Adriana—Ya, pero la habitación de la abuela es muy grande. Yo puedo compartir la habitación con Inés. ¿Te parece?

Lupe—¡Sí, claro! ¡Fenomenal! Se lo voy a decir a mamá.

María Luisa Invita a sus Compañeras de Dormitorio a Pasar unas Vacaciones en su Casa

María Luisa—Niñas, ¿Que piensan hacer en las vacaciones de primavera?

Gloria—No sé. No tengo planes. ¿Por qué me preguntas?

María Luisa—Si quieres, puedes venir a mi casa. Tenemos una casa bastante grande en La Florida, cerca de las playas y sitios de diversión. Juanita y Ana María pueden venir también. Nos vamos a divertir mucho.

Gloria—Me parece una idea genial. ¿Voy a preguntarle a Juanita y a Ana María?

Cultura

Mi Casa es Su Casa

Mi Casa es Su Casa

El concepto de la casa en la cultura hispana es diferente al concepto de casa en otras culturas. Dentro del mundo hispano ese concepto también cambia dependiendo de si es una zona rural o una zona urbana o dependiendo del país del que se trate. En Madrid, por ejemplo, la mayoría de la gente vive en edificios de pisos. Los vecinos viven con mayor privacidad y aunque se saludan cordialmente, no mantienen relaciones estrechas. Los pisos son generalmente bastante grandes; sin embargo la gente sólo recibe a los amigos mas íntimos en sus casas y prefiere encontrarse con ellos en lugares públicos como cafés y restaurantes. En ciudades pequeñas y zonas rurales, la gente es más amable y les gusta que los visiten. Viven en casas mas amplias donde la familia se reúne en un patio para comer una parrillada o en el portal donde charlan y ven pasar a los vecinos. La familia come en el comedor, no en la cocina. Los abuelos también viven con la familia, al igual que alguna tía aún soltera. Los vecinos se conocen muy bien y se visitan frecuentemente.

Las casas se protegen de ladrones y poniendo rejas en las ventanas y las puertas. Las casas están muy bien construidas con ladrillos y cemento para que duren por mucho tiempo. Los incendios son muy poco frecuentes ya que las casas no son de madera, y frecuentemente los pisos, los baños y las cocinas son de losetas (Tiles) de cerámica y los techos de cemento y tejas. Aunque el agua es bastante cara la gente cultiva flores en los jardines. Las huertas sólo se ven en sitios más rurales.

Preguntas

1. ¿Dónde vive la mayoría de la gente en Madrid?
2. ¿Cómo se tratan los vecinos en una casa de pisos en Madrid?
3. ¿Cómo son los pisos en Madrid?
4. ¿Dónde se reúnen con los amigos?
5. ¿Cómo son la gente en ciudades más pequeñas o zonas rurales?
6. ¿Dónde viven usualmente la gente en las ciudades pequeñas?
7. ¿Dónde disfrutan de las parrilladas?
8. ¿Come la familia en la cocina habitualmente?
9. ¿Quiénes comparten la casa?
10. ¿Cómo se tratan los vecinos?
11. ¿Cómo están construidas las casa?
12. ¿Cómo se protegen las casas de los ladrones?
13. ¿Por qué no hay muchos incendios en las ciudades hispanas?
14. ¿Cómo son los techos?
15. ¿Es cara el agua?

Proverbios

Con dinero hasta el perro baila.
Perro que ladra no muerde.

Capítulo Cuatro

Mi Comida Favorita

Monólogos

Escuche, Observe e Imite

Mi Comida Favorita

José Antonio

Mi plato favorito es el cocido madrileño. En la comida, como las verduras, los garbanzos, las patatas y la carne. De postre, me gusta el arroz con leche. A mi padre le gusta beber vino tinto. Yo prefiero mezclar el vino con una gaseosa. A mi madre le gusta comer una fruta de postre. Todos tomamos un café después de la comida.

María Luisa

Mis platos favoritos son: el arroz con pollo con verduras, las papas fritas y la ensalada de aguacate. De postre, me gusta el flan de coco. Para beber siempre tomamos algún refresco. A mi hermanito le gusta beber malta con las comidas. Mi padre prepara un lechón asado en la barbacoa cuando se reúne toda la familia.

Oscar

Mi plato favorito es el churrasco con dos huevos fritos "a caballo" (with fried eggs). A mi hermano Julián le gusta una milanesa. Mamá siempre sirve gnocchi antes de la carne. Todos bebemos el vino que el abuelo hace. Es bastante bueno. La abuela prepara un dulce de leche delicioso. Cuando tenemos fiestas, papá hace una parrillada exquisita.

A + el = al

Preguntas de los Monólogos

5 to 10

Piense, Pregunte y Conteste

1. ¿Cuál es el plato favorito de Antonio? cocido madrileno

   Al Padre le gusta berber ~~vrato~~ vino tinto.

2. ¿A quién le gusta beber vino tinto? Antonio's father

3. ¿Cómo le gusta beber el vino a Antonio? He prefers to mix wine with soda. Antonio le gusta mezclar vino con gasera

   A antonio le gusta mezclar vino con gaseosa

4. ¿Qué toma Antonio después de la comida? coffee

5. ¿El arroz con pollo y con verduras es el plato favorito de quién? LOUISE

   un café — the whole answer besides quien and than put Louise

6. ¿Qué clase de ensalada le gusta a María Luisa? Cafe

7. ¿Qué toma de postre ella? coconot flan

8. ¿Y qué bebe? drink malt

9. ¿Qué prepara en la barbacoa el padre de María Luisa? Prepares Roast

10. ¿Qué bebe el hermano de ella? little brother likes to drink malt with meal

    what is oscars favorite dish

11. ¿Cuál es el plato favorito de Oscar? – Chorrasco with fried eggs

    what kind of wine does oscar drink

12. ¿Qué clase de vino toma Oscar?

    drink that grandpa make

what does oscars gradmother prepare for dessert

13. ¿Qué suele preparar la abuela de Oscar de postre?

what does oscars family prepare when they have parties

14. ¿Qué prepara la familia de Oscar cuando hacen fiestas?

what is your favorite food

15. ¿Cuál es tu comida favorita?

you like to eat salad. what is your favorite

16. ¿Te gusta comer ensalada? ¿Cuál es tu favorita?

do you like barbecues

17. ¿Te gustan las parrilladas?

which is your favorite dessert

18. ¿Cuál es tu postre favorito?

13) dulce de leche

14 delicios barbecue

Vocabulario

De Lecturas

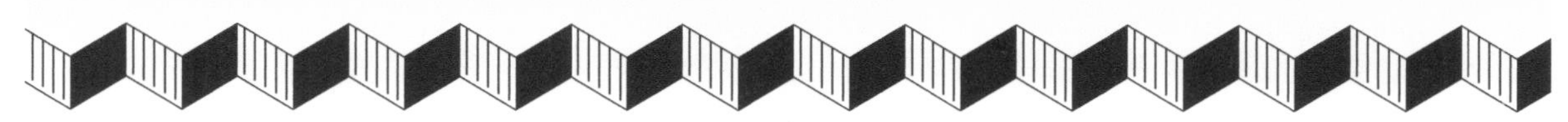

Sustantivos

El /la abuelo(a)	grandfather / grandmother
El aguacate	avocado
El arroz con leche	a dessert
El arroz con pollo	chicken with rice
El arroz	rice
El café	coffee
El caldo	consommé / broth
El chorizo	Spanish sausage
El churrasco	grilled steak
El cocido	stew
El dulce de leche	Spanish dessert
El flan con coco	Spanish dessert
El lechón	pork
El mediodía	noon
El placer	pleasure
El plato	dish
El postre	dessert
El refresco	soda
El vino	wine
La barbacoa	barbecue
La carne	meat
La cena	dinner
La comida	dinner / food
La compañía	company of people
La ensalada	salad
La fruta	fruit
La gaseosa	carbonated drink
La malta	nonalcoholic drink

La milanesa	popular Spanish dish
La necesidad	necessity
La parrillada	grilled meat
Las arepas de maíz	corn tortillas
Las carnes	meat
Las comidas	food
Las fiestas	parties
Las papas	potatoes (Latin America)
Las parrilladas	barbecue
Las patatas	potatoes (Spain)
Las tortillas de maíz	corn tortillas
Las verduras	vegetables
Los cocidos	stew dishes
Los garbanzos	chickpea
Los huevos	eggs
Los platos asados	roasted dishes

Verbos

Almorzar	to have lunch
Beber	to drink
Cenar	to eat dinner
Comer	to eat
Desayunar	to eat breakfast
Gustar	to be pleasing / to like
Hacer	to make / to do
Mezclar	to mix
Poder	to be able
Preferir	to prefer
Preparar	to prepare
Reunirse	to get together
Servir	to serve
Tener	to have
Tomar	to take / to drink
Ver	to see

Vocabulario Práctico

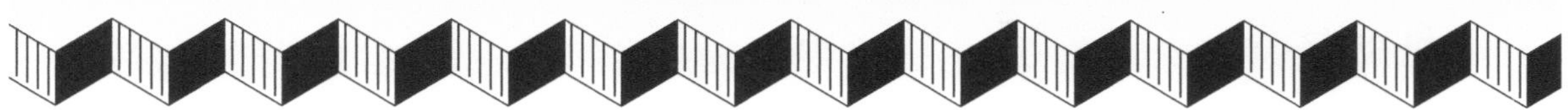

Carnes—Meat

El bistec	steak
El chorizo	Spanish sausage
El cochinillo asado	suckling pig
El cordero	lamb
El jamón	ham
El perro caliente	hot dog
El picadillo	ground meat
El solomillo	sirloin
El tocino	bacon
La carne de puerco/de cerdo	pork
La carne de res	beef
La carne de ternera	veal
La hamburguesa	hamburger
Las chuletas	chops
Las salchichas	sausages

Pescados y Mariscos—Fish and Shellfish

El atún	tuna
El pargo	snapper
La langosta	lobster
La trucha	trout
Las almejas	clams
Las sardinas	sardines
Las vieiras	scallops
Los calamares	squids
Los camarones	shrimp
Los mejillones	mussels
Los ostiones	oysters

Vegetales y Verduras—Vegetables

El aguacate	avocado
El arroz	rice
El maíz	corn
El pepino	cuccumber
El tomate	tomato
La berenjena	eggplant
La cebolla	onion
La espinaca	spinach
La lechuga	lettuce
La patata / papa	potato
El plátano	plantain
La zanahoria	carrot
Los frijoles	beans
Los guisantes	peas

Frutas—Fruits

El melocotón	peach
El limón	lemon
El mango	mango
El plátano	banana
La fresa	strawberry
La guayaba	guava
La manzana	apple
La naranja	orange
La pera	pear
La piña	pineapple
La sandía	watermelon
La toronja	grapefruit
Las uvas	grapes

Condimentos—Condiments

El aceite	oil
El azúcar	sugar
El vinagre	vinegar
La crema	cream

La mantequilla	butter
La mayonesa	mayonnaise
La mostaza	mustard
La pimienta	pepper
La sal	salt

Bebidas y Refrescos—Drinks

El agua	water
El batido	shake
El café	coffee
El chocolate	chocolate
El jugo / zumo	juice
El té	tea
El vino	wine
La cerveza	beer
La leche	milk
La limonada	lemonade

Platos y Comidas—Dishes

A la parrilla	barbecued
A la plancha	on the grill
Aderezo	dressing
Asado	roast
Cocido	baked
El bocadillo	sandwich
El pan	bread
El pastel	pie
El queso	cheese
Frito	fried
Horneado	baked
La empanada	turnover
La ensalada	salad
La sopa	soup
La tortilla (Am)	tortilla
La tortilla (Sp)	omelet
Los huevos	eggs

Cubiertos—Utensils

El cuchillo	knife
El plato	dish
El tenedor	fork
El vaso	glass
La copa	wineglass
La cuchara	spoon
La cucharita	teaspoon
La servilleta	napkin
La taza	cup

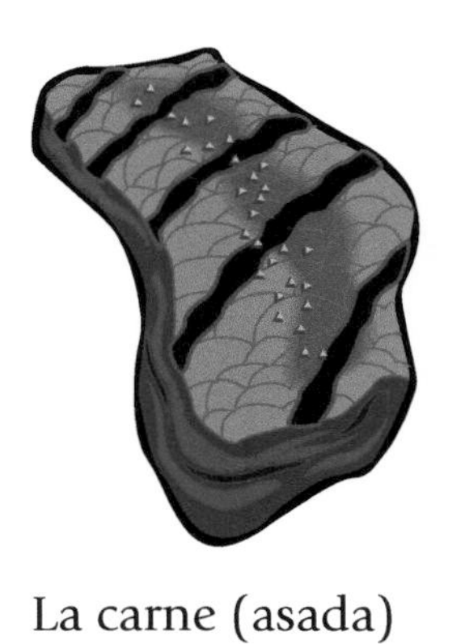

La carne (asada)

Las frutas

La taza (de café)

La ensalada

Los cubiertos: el tenedor, el cuchillo, la cuchara, el plato

Los huevos

La copa de vino

El postre

Las verduras

Adjetivos

Algún	some
Asado	roasted
Bueno	good
Delicioso	delicious
Diferentes	different
Exquisita	exquisite
Favorito	favorite
Frita	fried
Fritos(as)	fried
Fuerte	heavy
Ligera	light
Lleno	full
Madrileño	related to Madrid
Picante	spicy
Satisfecho	satisfied
Tinto	red (red wine)

Gramática

Possessive Adjectives

Possessive adjectives are used in Spanish to express possession or ownership. These adjectives are placed before the modified noun, agreeing in both number and gender with the person(s) or object(s) possessed.

mi, mis	my
tu, tus	your (familiar, singular)
su, sus	your (formal), his, her, its, their
nuestro, -a, -os, -as	our
vuestro, -a, -os, -as	your (familiar, plural)

The possessive adjectives *mi, mis, tu, tus, su,* and *sus* agree only in number with the noun they modify:

Mi casa y mi carro	Mis amigos y mis amigas
Tu casa y tu carro	Tus amigos y tus amigas
Su casa y su carro	Sus casas y sus carros

The remaining possessive forms must also agree in gender with the modified noun:

Nuestro apartamento	Vuestro apartamento
Nuestros apartamentos	Vuestros apartamentos
Nuestra casa	Vuestra casa
Nuestras casas	Vuestras casas

The meaning of *su* or *sus* (your, his, her, their, its) can be determined by their use in a sentence. However, a prepositional phrase may be used to further clarify the possessor:

La(s) casa(s) { de él / de ella / de Ud. / de ellos / de ellas / de Uds. }

El / Los apartamento(s) { de él / de ella / de Ud. / de ellos / de ellas / de Uds. }

Note that the definite articles *el, la, los,* and *las* are now used with the corresponding noun, and the prepositional phrase *de él, de ella, de Ud,* etc. follows the noun.

Stem Changing Verbs in the Present Indicative

There are a number of verbs that change either the vowel ***e*** or ***o*** when the syllable in the stem of the present indicative is stressed. These changes are predicted and follow a pattern. The ***e*** becomes either ***ie*** or ***i*** and the ***o*** changes to ***ue.*** It is better to visualize these changes if we think of a boot. The four forms inside the boot are the stressed forms, and thus suffer the anticipated change. The *nosotros* and *vosotros* forms lie outside of the boot and do not change.

querer e>ie (to want)

Other verbs like ***querer:***

Cerrar	*to close*
Consentir	*to consent*
Comenzar	*to begin*

Defender	*to defend*
Despertar(se)	*to awaken, to wake up*
Divertir(se)	*to amuse, to have a good time*
Empezar	*to begin*
Entender	*to understand*
Mentir	*to lie*
Pensar	*to think*
Perder	*to lose, to miss*
Preferir	*to prefer*
Sentar(se)	*to sit, to sit down*
Sentir	*to feel (sorry)*
Sentirse	*to feel*
*Nevar**	*to snow*

**Nevar* is only used in the third person singular *nieva,* "it snows."

servir e>i (to serve)

Other verbs like ***servir:***

Despedir(se)	*to fire, to say goodbye*
Medir	*to measure*
Pedir	*to order, to ask for*
Reírse	*to laugh*
Repetir	*to repeat*
Sonreír	*to smile*
Vestir(se)	*to dress*

volver o>ue (to return)

Other verbs like ***volver:***

Acordarse de	*to remember*
Acostar(se)	*to place in bed, to go to bed*
Almorzar	*to have lunch*
Contar	*to count, to tell stories*
Devolver	*to return something*
Dormir	*to sleep*
Encontrar	*to find*
Jugar	*to play sports or games*
Mostrar	*to show*
Mover	*to move*
Poder	*to be able (can)*
Soler	*to do something habitually*
Volar	*to fly*
*Llover**	*to rain*

**Llover* is only used in the third person singular *llueve,* "it rains."

Irregular Verbs

"Ir" means "to go." Its conjugation is irregular:

Ir	
voy	vamos
vas	vais
va	van

¿Adónde van Uds?	*Where are you going?*
Vamos a la biblioteca.	*We are going to the library.*
¿Adónde vas?	*Where are you going?*
Voy al cine con Elena.	*I am going to the movies with Elena.*

The preposition *a* means "to". When *a* is followed by the definite article *el* (the) the two words are contracted to form one word *al* (to the). There are no contractions with *los, la,* and *las* (the).

Ellos van a la fiesta de cumpleaños de Miguel.
They are going to Miguel's birthday party.

¿Vas a las montañas?
Are you going to the mountains?

Me gusta ir a los conciertos de música.
I like to go to music concerts.

Stating Future Actions with "*ir a* + Infinitive"

Native speakers frequently state a near future activity using the present tense of the verb *ir* followed by the preposition ***a*** and a verb in the infinitive. This construction conveys the meaning of (I'm going to do something, and so on):

Esta tarde voy a comer en un restaurante cubano.
This afternoon I'm going to eat in a Cuban restaurant.

Mis amigos van a llegar mañana de Chile.
My friends are going to arrive from Chile tomorrow.

Nosotros vamos a preparar una deliciosa parrillada argentina para el aniversario de bodas de nuestros padres.
We are going to prepare a delicious Argentinean barbecue for our parents' wedding anniversary.

Saber and *Conocer*

Both *saber* and *conocer* mean "to know." They are not interchangeable, each one having specific uses. Let's learn to distinguish their usage.

Saber: sé, sabes, sabe, sabemos, sabéis, saben

Saber means:

1. "to know" facts or information

 Yo sé que la casa de José Antonio está en el barrio de Salamanca, Madrid.
 I know that José Antonio's house is in the Salamanca neighborhood, Madrid.

 Nosotros ya sabemos muchas palabras nuevas en español.
 We already know many new Spanish words.

 ¿Sabes el número de teléfono del profesor?
 Do you know the professor's telephone number?

2. "to know how to do things" (using the infinitive of the second verb)

 Los estudiantes saben contestar correctamente las preguntas de la profesora.
 The students know how to answer correctly the professor's questions.

 ¿Saben Uds. bailar salsa o merengue?
 Do you know how to dance salsa or merengue?

Conocer: conozco, conoces, conoce, conocemos, conocéis, conocen

Conocer means "to know" in the sense of being quite familiar or acquainted with people, places, or specific things (art, food, literature, music, etc.). The preposition ***a*** is required whenever one is acquainted with people. This ***a*** is called the *"personal a"* and has no translation in English.

Yo no conozco a los padres de María Luisa.
I don't know María Luisa's parents.

Conozco la música cubana.
I know (I am acquainted with) Cuban music.

¿Conocen Uds. la Ciudad de México?
Are you familiar with Mexico City?

¿Conoces la literatura chilena?
Do you know (are you acquainted with) Chilean literature?

Ejercicios

Ejercicios de Gramática

a + el = al

A. El verbo "IR." Ask your partner if he/she goes to the following places.

MODELO *Roberto, ¿vas a la biblioteca ahora?*
Sí, voy a la biblioteca ahora.
No, no voy a la biblioteca ahora.

1. las tiendas Si voy a las tiendas

2. el supermercado Si voy al el supermercado

3. el banco No, No voy al banco.

4. la casa de tu amigo Si la case de tu amigo

5. al restaurante mexicano Si, voy al restaurante mexicano

6. Nueva York No, no voy a la neuva york

7. la lavandería

8. el parque

9. el aeropuerto

10. la clase de español

11. la fiesta

B. María Luisa is talking about where she and her friends are going this afternoon. Complete the sentences with the appropriate form of **ir**.

MODELO . . . Sara <u>va</u> a la biblioteca.

1. Yo ____________ al banco.
2. José Antonio y yo ____________ a la farmacia.
3. Lupe y Oscar ____________ al cine.
4. ¿Tú ____________ a la fiesta?
5. Oscar ____________ a las tiendas.

C. Complete the following sentences with the proper possessive adjective.

1. Son los vídeos de Pedro. Son ____________ vídeos.
2. Ana y Ada son las primas de nosotros. Son ____________ primas.
3. Carlos, no es tu silla. Yo la tengo. Es ____________ silla. ¡Levántate!
4. Es el reloj de Juanita. Es ____________ reloj nuevo.
5. Es mi auto y también de Roberto. Es ____________ auto.

D. Complete the blank spaces with the correct form of the stem changing verbs (e>ie), e>i) in parentheses.

1. ¿____________ las películas románticas o las de suspenso? (preferir)
2. Pues, Yo ____________ las películas dramáticas. (preferir)
3. ¿Los estudiantes no ____________ a la profesora Jiménez. (entender)
4. En febrero ____________ mucho en en estado de Maine. (nevar)
5. Nosotros no ____________ perder esa oferta tan increible. (querer)
6. ¿Qué tipo de comida ____________ en ese restaurante cubano? (servir)
7. Pues, allí yo siempre ____________ ropa vieja con frijoles negros. (pedir)
8. ¿____________ Uds. volver mañana? (pensar)
9. ¿Por qué no ____________ las palabras nuevas del vocabulario. (repetir)
10. No me gusta ____________ a mis amigos. (mentir)

E. Complete the blank spaces with the correct form of the stem changing verbs (o>ue), (u>ue) in parentheses.

1. José María ____________ llegar tarde a clase. (soler)

2. Cuando tengo sueño ____________ bien. (dormir).

3. ¿Cuántos perros calientes ____________ comer tú? (poder)

4. Tenemos que ____________ a las dos de la tarde. (volver)

5. Muchos estudiantes ____________ en la cafetería, ¿no? (almorzar)

F. Complete the following sentences with the following stem changing verbs.

cerrar jugar preferir repetir recordar almorzar
querer sentir volver entender mentir

1. No me gusta la ensalada, (yo) ____________ comer pizza.

2. ¿ ____________ (tú) bien al fútbol americano?

3. Yo ____________ en la cafetería con mis amigos.

4. Nosotros ____________ las ventanas porque tenemos frío.

5. El profesor no ____________ a los estudiantes. No estudian y ____________ buenas notas (good grades).

6. Yo no ____________, siempre (always) digo la verdad.

7. ¿____________ (tú) el nombre de mi hermana?

8. Nosotros siempre ____________ las palabras del vocabulario en la clase de español.

9. No me ____________ bien, creo que estoy enfermo.

10. Los estudiantes ____________ mañana a las clases en la universidad.

G. Complete the sentences with the correct form of the stem-changing verbs.

1. Ella no quirere **(querer)** jugar a las cartas *(cards)*. Ella prefiere **(preferir)** ver la televisión.

2. Estoy preocupado. (Yo) pienso **(pensar)** demasiado en mis problemas

3. María cuenta **(contar)** unos chistes *(jokes)* muy divertidos.

4. Yo cierro **(cerrar)** las ventanas porque los vecinos se quejan *(are complaining)* de la música.

5. Sara pone un CD de salsa y empieza **(empezar)** a bailar *(to dance)*.

6. Yo salgo de la fiesta y vuelvo **(volver)** con más refrescos.

7. ¿recuerdas **(recordar)** tú el nombre de la chica que está con Alberto?

H. Now using the expression *"IR A + INFINITIVE"*, ask your partner if he/she is going to go to the same places in exercise A.

MODELO . . .

Roberto, ¿vas a ir a la biblioteca esta noche?/No, pero voy a ir a la fiesta.

conocen

1. ______________________.

2. ______________________.

3. ______________________.

4. ______________________.

5. ______________________.

6. ______________________.

7. ______________________.

8. ______________________.

9. ______________________.

10. ______________________.

11. ______________________.

I. Change the following sentences to the future tense. IR A INFINITIVE

1. Comemos en un restaurante argentino.

no voi a

2. No bailo en la clase de español.

3. Roberta y Luís Miguel **preparan** el desayuno en la cocina.

vas a ir vas a ir

4. ¿**Vas** al gimnasio?

conocen

5. **Descanso y miro** la televisión en la sala de estar.

vemos a Conocemos

6. **Vemos** un programa musical en la televisión.

No voy a vender. Sabes

7. **No vendo** el libro *Yo soy así*.

vas

8. ¿**Compartes** las enchiladas con el profesor?

9. **Abren** el libro.

voy a leo en la clase.

10. **Leo** en la clase.

J. Más FUTURO. Rewrite the sentences in the format **"Ir a Infinitive."**

1. Yo / abrir una cuenta *(account)*

 yo voy a abrir una cuenta

2. Oscar y yo / comprar comida

 oscar y yo vamos comprar comida

3. Lupe y María / ver una película de Almodóvar.

 Lupe y maria van ver una pelicula de almodovar

4. Tú / asistir a un partido de baloncesto

 Tu vas a asistir a un partido de baloncesto

5. Sofía / comprar un DVD

 sofia va a comprar un DVD.

K. ¿Saber o conocer? Complete with the correct form of the verb.

voy vamos
vas vais
va van

1. Yo ____________ a mi profesor de español.

2. Él ____________ cocinar muy bien.

3. Yo no ____________ a su esposa *(wife)*.

4. ¿ ____________ Uds. que *(that)* Madrid es la capital de España?

5. ¿ ____________ Uds. La ciudad de Madrid?

Charlando

Antonia invita a un amigo americano a comer en un restaurante madrileño.

Camarero—¿Qué desean los señores de primero?

Antonia—De primero deseo unas gambas al ajillo, por favor.

William—Una sopa de pollo.

Camarero—¿Y de segundo, qué desean?

Antonia—De segundo, una merluza a la vasca con patatas cocidas.

William—Una hamburguesa, por favor.

Camarero—No tenemos hamburguesas, pero si quiere podemos preparar para usted una carne molida frita con salsa de tomate.

William—Sí, muchas gracias.

Camarero—¿Y de beber?

Antonia—Un vino blanco, un Albariño o un Rioja.

William—Para mí, una Coca-Cola.

Camarero—Muy bien, en unos minutos vuelvo.

María Luisa prepara una comida típica para sus compañeras en la universidad.

Tony—¿Qué estás preparando, Marilú?

María Luisa—Preparo algo especial para ustedes. Como aperitivo estoy preparando croquetas de jamón, empanadas de carne, papas rellenas y frituras de bacalao. Estoy cocinando un arroz con pollo con yuca frita y una ensalada de aguacate. De postre, mamá está cocinando un flan de mango.

Tony—Es mucha comida. ¿A cuántas personas esperas?

María Luisa—Unas diez personas más o menos. Es la primera vez que van a comer comida cubana.

Oscar prepara una parrillada para celebrar el cumpleaños de su abuelo.

Marcelo—¿Qué tal, Oscar? ¿Qué compras?

Oscar—Hoy es el cumpleaños de mi abuelo y le estoy preparando una parrillada. Compro la carne, el pan, una torta y un buen vino tinto como le gusta a él.

Marcelo—Quieres mucho al abuelo, ¿no?

Oscar—Pues claro, lo quiero mucho y esta parrillada es una sorpresa. ¿Quieres venir?

Marcelo—Sí, gracias. Voy a llevar un vino muy bueno para esta ocasión.

Cultura

El Buen Comer

El Buen Comer

El buen comer es muy importante en el mundo hispano. El decir que uno está lleno después de comer indica mala educación. Se dice que uno está satisfecho. Esto significa que en la cultura hispana uno come para disfrutarlo y satisfacerse. El comer no es tan solo una necesidad; es también un placer que se acompaña con buen vino y buena compañía. Hay grandes diferencias entre las comidas de las diferentes regiones del mundo hispano. Por ejemplo, mientras en algunos países se come arroz, en otros se come papas o patatas. En España se come pan, mientras que en México se acompaña la comida con tortillas de maíz y en Colombia con arepas de maíz. En España no se come maíz. En la Argentina y el Uruguay comen platos de pasta como gnocchi, espaguetis y macarrón. Las parrilladas son típicas de los países del Cono Sur. La comida en México y Centroamérica es picante, mientras que en otros países hispanos no lo es. En el sur de España prefieren la comida frita, en el centro prefieren los platos asados, mientras que en el norte prefieren hacer cocidos, fabadas y caldos. En España se desayuna con pan y café con leche. Sin embargo en Colombia se desayuna fuerte con

calentado que lleva carne, arroz, chorizo y huevos. En Colombia se almuerza al mediodía, mientras que en México y España se come entre las dos y las tres de la tarde. La comida de la noche o la cena es ligera en España y se come tarde, después de las nueve de la noche. En Colombia cenan temprano como en los Estados Unidos. Así podemos ver que las diferencias en las comidas entre los diferentes países hispanos son muy grandes.

Preguntas

1. ¿Cuál es el objetivo de comer en la cultura hispana?
2. ¿Es picante la comida hispana?
3. ¿Los hispanos comen mucho arroz con frijoles?
4. ¿Es la cena por la noche la comida más importante?
5. ¿Dónde predominan las comidas fritas?
6. ¿Dónde predominan las comidas asadas?
7. ¿Dónde prefieren comer cocidos?
8. ¿Que es un calentado colombiano?
9. ¿Dónde cenan temprano?
10. ¿Qué es una parrillada?

Proverbios

Averigüe el significado de los siguientes proverbios populares:

No tan solo de pan vive el hombre.
Camarón que se duerme se lo lleva la corriente.

La Ropa y las Estaciones

Monólogos

José Antonio

Cuando hace mucho calor, me voy al trabajo en camisa de manga corta. No quiero ponerme ni calcetines. Mi jefe prefiere que me ponga traje y corbata, pero en el verano (turns a blind eye) nos deja vestirnos con ropa ligera. Me gusta el verano en Madrid porque todo el mundo se va de veraneo a la sierra o al mar y la ciudad queda vacía.

María Luisa

En Miami sólo tenemos dos estaciones, la primavera y el verano. En enero y febrero me pongo un suéter para ir al trabajo. Casi nunca llueve de noviembre a mayo. Siempre hace fresco y sol. En el verano hace mucho calor y llueve todos los días. Tengo cinco trajes de baño porque me gusta mucho la playa, las piscinas y nadar. Me gustan las faldas de hilo y las blusas de algodón, las sandalias blancas y llevar el cabello corto.

Oscar

Me pasé toda la semana pasada esquiando en Bariloche. Estábamos de vacaciones de invierno celebrando el 10 de julio. Cayó mucha nieve aunque después salió el sol. Aquí en Buenos Aires hace mucho frío y llueve todos los días. Tengo que ponerme una chaqueta, una bufanda de lana y un sombrero para ir al trabajo. Por la madrugada hace neblina y escarcha. El clima es muy húmedo.

Lupe

Aquí en el DF llueve y hace bastante frío en julio y agosto, sobretodo por las noches. Aunque nunca hace mucho calor por la altura, en abril es cuando más calor hace. Me visto con pantalones muy cómodos porque trabajo con niños muy pequeños. También uso zapatos de tenis porque tengo que correr y jugar con ellos. Me abrigo bien porque por las noches hace bastante frío. Nos pasamos el fin de semana pasado en Acapulco donde hacía mucho calor.

Preguntas Sobre los Monólogos

Piense, Pregunte y Conteste Jose antonio va al Trabajo

1. ¿Cuándo va José Antonio al trabajo en camisa de manga corta?

2. ¿Se pone calcetines? No, No, se pone

3. ¿Qué prefiere el jefe que se ponga José Antonio? el jefe prefiere traje y corata

4. ¿Dónde veranea la gente en Madrid? la gente veranea el la sierra.

5. ¿Cómo queda la ciudad en el verano? La Ciudad quedan vacia

6. ¿Cuándo se pone un suéter María Luisa?

7. ¿Qué tiempo hace en Miami durante el verano?

8. ¿Le gusta la playa a María Luisa?

9. ¿Qué le gusta vestir?

10. ¿Cómo le gusta llevar el cabello?

11. ¿Le gusta esquiar a Oscar?

12. ¿Cómo estaba el tiempo durante las vacaciones del 10 de julio?

13. ¿Llueve mucho en Buenos Aires?

14. ¿Qué se pone Oscar para ir al trabajo?

15. ¿Cómo está el tiempo en las madrugadas?

16. ¿Qué tiempo hace en el DF?

17. ¿Cómo se viste Lupe para ir a trabajar?

18. ¿Por qué se pone zapatos de tenis?

19. ¿Hace frío por las noches en el DF?

20. ¿Y en Acapulco? ¿Cómo está el tiempo?

me gusta llevo

Vocabulario

De Lecturas

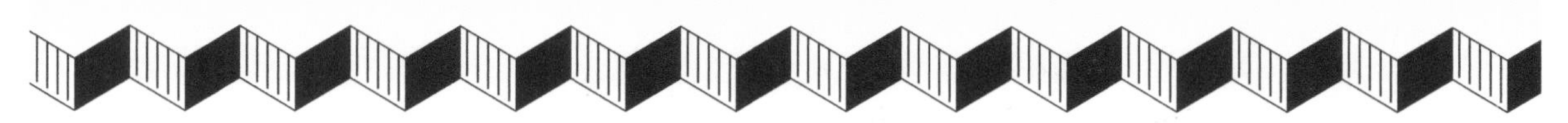

Sustantivos

El aseo	cleanliness
El balón	ball
El bolso de cuero	leather bag
El cabello	hair
El clima	climate
El escote	neckline
El frío	cold
El invierno	winter
El jefe	boss
El mar	ocean/sea
El nivel social	social level
El regalo	gift
El sol	sun
El trabajo	work
El verano	summer
La altura	altitude
La careta	mask
La chaqueta	jacket
La ciudad	city
La escarcha	frost
La estación	season of the year
La fiesta de quince	sweet fifteen party
La gente	people
La madrugada	dawn
La maleta	suitcase
La moda	clothing style
La neblina	mist
La nieve	snow
La playa	beach

La primavera	spring
La ropa	clothes
La semana	week
La sierra	mountain range
La valija	suitcase
Las blusas de algodón	cotton blouses
Las estaciones	seasons of the year
Las faldas de hilo	linen skirts
Las mujeres	women
Las pelotas	balls
Las piscinas	swimming pools
Las raquetas	racquets
Los hombres	men

Vocabulario – Práctico La Ropa

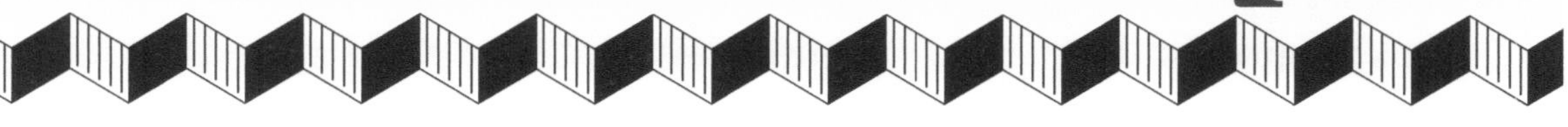

El abrigo	the coat
La blusa	the blouse
El bolso / la cartera	the purse
Las botas	the boots
La bufanda	the scarf
Los calcetines	the socks
El calzado	the footwear
La camisa	the shirt
La camiseta	the t-shirt / undershirt
El chaleco	the vest
La chaqueta	the jacket
El cinturón	the belt
La corbata	the tie
La falda	the skirt
La gabardina	the trench coat
La gorra / el gorro	the cap
Los guantes	the gloves
El impermeable	the raincoat
Las medias	the stockings
Los pantalones cortos	the shorts
Los pantalones vaqueros	the jeans
Los pantalones	the pants
El paraguas	the umbrella
La ropa interior	the underwear
La ropa	the clothes
El saco	the sports jacket
Las sandalias	the sandals
El sombrero	the hat
La sudadera	the sweatshirt

El suéter	the sweater
El traje de baño	the bathing suit
El traje	the suit
El vestido	the dress
Los zapatos de tenis	the tennis shoes
Los zapatos	the shoes
La blusa	the blouse
Los calzoncillos	the underpants
A cuadros	plaid
A rayas	stripes
Algodón	cotton
Los botones	the buttons
La cremallera	the zipper
Lana	wool
Manga corta	short sleeve
Manga larga	long sleeve
Poliéster	polyester
Tacón alto	high heel
Tacón bajo	low heel

Los Colores

Amarillo	yellow
Anaranjado	orange
Azul	blue
Blanco	white
Gris	gray
Marrón	brown
Negro	black
Rojo	red
Rosado	pink
Verde	green

ROPA INTERIOR
ROPA INTERIOR
hombre
mujer
El traje
El vestido
Los pantalones
La corbata
El anillo
La blusa
El reloj
La pulsera
El sombrero
La gorra
La falda
El cinturón
El bolso de cuero
El calzado/Los zapatos
La camisa
La chaqueta
El saco

Verbos

En las Lecturas

Abrigarse	to wrap up in warm clothes
Aumentar	to increase
Bucear	to scuba dive
Caber	to fit
Caer	to fall
Cambiar	to change
Celebrar	to celebrate
Comprar	to buy
Correr	to run
Creer	to believe
Dejar	to allow/to let
Determinar	to determine
Esquiar	to ski
Guardar	to keep
Hacer	to do/to make
Jugar	to play sports
Llevar	to carry/to wear
Llover	to rain
Ofender	to offend
Parecer	to look like/to appear
Pasar	to spend time/to pass
Pedir	to ask for
Pensar	to think
Ponerse	to put on
Preferir	to prefer
Prestar	to lend
Quedar	to stay
Querer	to want
Saber	to know
Salir	to leave/to go out
Trabajar	to work
Usar	to use
Vestirse	to get dressed

Adjetivos

En las Lecturas

Ajustados	tight
Alto	tall
Bajo	short
Blancas	white
Cómodos	comfortable
Corto	short
Difícil	difficult
Húmedo	humid
Ligera	not heavy
Pequeños	small
Sobrios	moderate
Tontos	dumb
Vacía	empty
Veraniego	summerlike
Verde	green

mi casa es de 2
cuartos con 1 bano
yo vivo enedison
con mi mama y padre.

Gramática

Verbal Expressions with *tener* and *hacer*

These two verbs are used in Spanish to convey many English expressions that require the verb *"to be"* followed by an adjective. However, when used idiomatically, *tener* or *hacer* is followed by nouns.

Tener calor	*to be hot*
Tener frío	*to be cold*
Tener hambre	*to be hungry*
Tener sed	*to be thirsty*
Tener sueño	*to be sleepy*
Tener miedo	*to be afraid*
Tener prisa	*to be in a hurry*
Tener cuidado	*to be careful*
Tener (la) culpa	*to be guilty*
Tener razón	*to be right*
Tener suerte	*to be lucky*
Tener años	*to express age*
Tener ganas de + (infinitive)	*to have a strong desire to do something / to feel like "-ing"*
Tener que	*to have to*
Hacer (buen / mal) tiempo	*the weather is (good / bad)*
Hacer sol	*it is sunny*
Hacer calor	*it is hot*
Hacer frío	*it is cold*
Hacer fresco	*it is cool*
Hacer viento	*it is windy*
Hacer un viaje	*to take a trip*
Hacer cola	*to stand on a line*
Hacer las maletas	*to pack suitcases*

Roberto tiene mucha sed porque hace mucho calor.
Roberto is very thirsty because it is very hot.

No me gustan las arañas . . . les tengo mucho miedo.
I don't like spiders . . . I am afraid of them.

Tengo ganas de hacer un viaje a Puerto Rico en el mes de enero porque allí nunca hace frío en el invierno.

I really feel like taking a trip to Puerto Rico in January because it is never cold there in winter.

En el otoño no hace frío, ni calor . . . hace fresco.

In fall it is not cold or hot . . . it is cool.

The Expression *Favor de . . .*

In later chapters we will learn the use and formation of Spanish commands. For now, let's learn the very useful phrase "*favor de* + a verb in the infinitive" that may be used to create commands or requests. This expression may convey affirmative or negative commands.

Favor de no fumar.	*Please no smoking.*
Favor de no correr.	*Please do not run.*
Favor de estudiar la lección.	*Please study the lesson.*
Favor de pagar la cuenta.	*Please pay the bill.*

Irregular Verbs in the First Person Singular

A verb is considered irregular if: (1) the stem changes from the original infinitive spelling; (2) it does not follow the appropriate pattern; or (3) there are changes in both. Many verbs in Spanish have an irregular first person singular. Observe and study the following verbs:

Dar (to give): doy, das, da, damos, dais, dan

Caber (to fit): quepo, cabes, cabe, cabemos, cabéis, caben

Caer (to fall): caigo, caes, cae, caemos, caéis, caen

Conducir (to drive): conduzco, conduces, conduce, conducimos, conducís, conducen

Hacer (to do, to make): hago, haces, hace, hacemos, hacéis, hacen

Poner (to put): pongo, pones, pone, ponemos, ponéis, ponen

Salir (to leave, to go out): salgo, sales, sale, salimos, salís, salen

Traer (to bring): traigo, traes, trae, traemos, traéis, traen

Valer (to be worth): valgo, vales, vale, valemos, valéis, valen

Ver (to see): veo, ves, ve, vemos, veis, ven

Verbs with other irregularities:

Decir (to say, to tell): digo, dices, dice, decimos, decís, dicen
Tener (to have): tengo, tienes, tiene, tenemos, tenéis, tienen
Venir (to come): vengo, vienes, viene, venimos, venís, vienen

* **Haber** is an auxiliary verb, and it is only used to form compound tenses with the main verb in the past participle form.

Haber (to have*): he, has, ha, hemos, habéis, han
Oír (to hear): oigo, oyes, oye, oimos, oís, oyen

Reflexive Constructions

In order to express what people do for themselves, Spanish uses the reflexive pronoun "*-se*" attached to the infinitive of the verb. In this construction the subject creates and at the same time receives the action of the verb. In a conjugated verb form the reflexive pronoun "*-se*" must match the corresponding subject noun or pronoun. Observe the following pairs of sentences.

Llamo a Luis Miguel por teléfono. — I call Luis Miguel on the phone.
Me llamo Luis Miguel. — I call myself Luis Miguel.

Margarita lava los platos. — Margarita washes the dishes.
Margarita **se** lava. — Margarita washes (herself).
Levantamos a los niños temprano. — We get the kids up early.
Nos levantamos temprano. — We get up early.

Let's look at the verb *mirarse*: to look (at oneself)

Yo	**me** miro
Tú	**te** miras
Ud., él, ella	**se** mira
Nosotros(as)	**nos** miramos
Vosotros(as)	**os** miráis
Uds., ellos, ellas	**se** miran

Reflexive pronouns must be placed before conjugated verbs:

Ella se acuesta tarde. — She goes to bed late.
Nos cepillamos los dientes. — We brush our teeth.

They can also be attached to an infinitive:

Abelardo tiene que acostarse temprano. — Abelardo has to go to bed early.
Me gusta levantarme tarde. — I like to get up late.

Or attached to "–ing" endings:

Estamos vistiéndonos.	We are getting dressed.
Estoy bañándome.	I am bathing.

Study the following list of commonly reflexive verbs in Spanish:

Acercarse (ue)	to approach
Acostarse (ue)	to go to bed
Afeitarse	to shave
Bañarse	to bathe
Cepillarse	to brush
Divertirse (ie)	to have fun
Ducharse	to shower
Lavarse	to wash
Levantarse	to get up
Peinarse	to comb one's hair
Sentarse (ie)	to sit down
Despertarse (ie)	to wake up
Sentirse (ie)	to feel
Secarse	to dry off
Maquillarse	to put makeup on
Vestirse (i)	to get dress
Ponerse	to put on
Quitarse	to take off
Dormirse	to fall asleep
Quedarse	to stay, to remain
Irse	to leave

Ejercicios

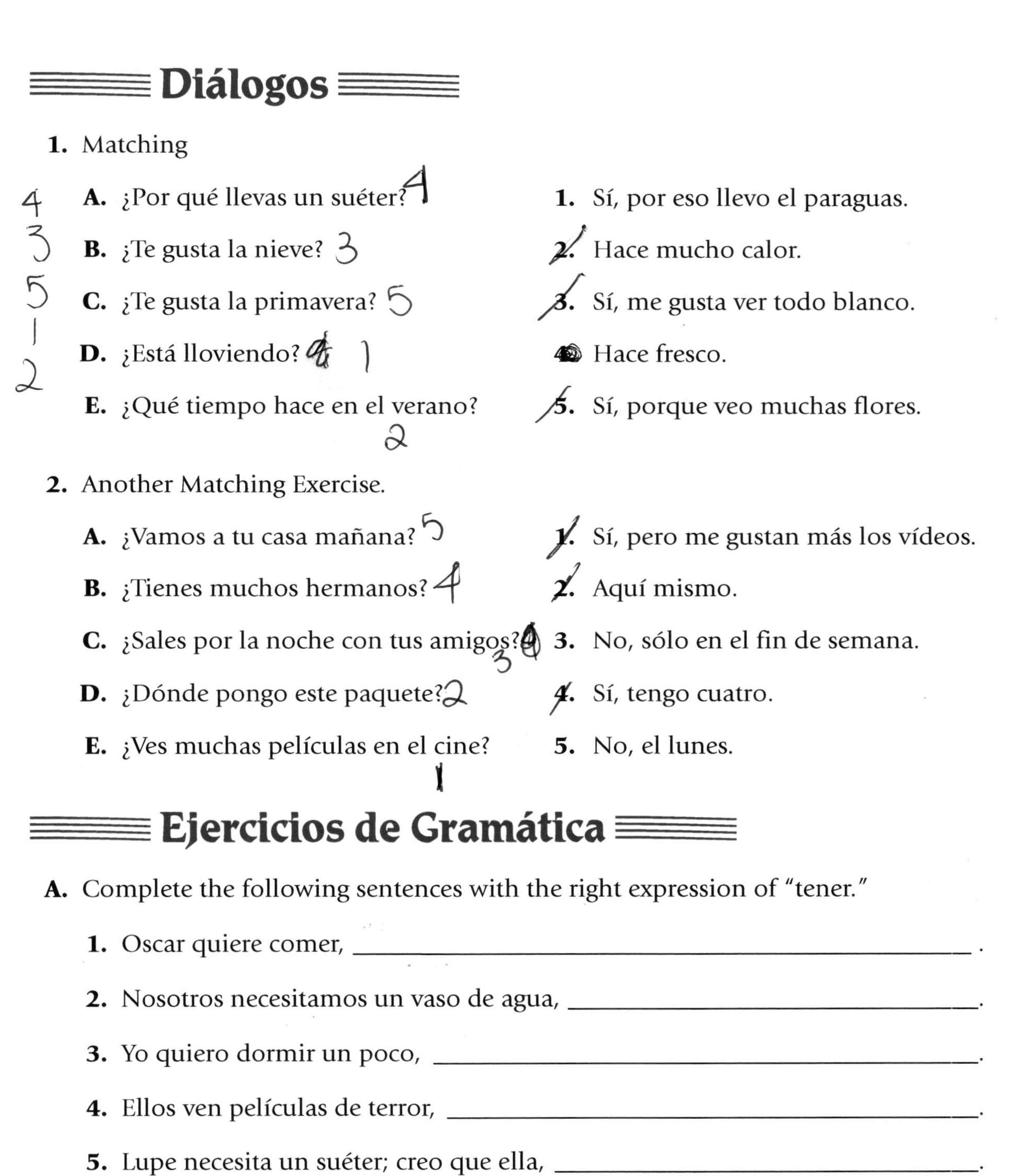

Diálogos

1. Matching

A. ¿Por qué llevas un suéter?
B. ¿Te gusta la nieve?
C. ¿Te gusta la primavera?
D. ¿Está lloviendo?
E. ¿Qué tiempo hace en el verano?

1. Sí, por eso llevo el paraguas.
2. Hace mucho calor.
3. Sí, me gusta ver todo blanco.
4. Hace fresco.
5. Sí, porque veo muchas flores.

2. Another Matching Exercise.

A. ¿Vamos a tu casa mañana?
B. ¿Tienes muchos hermanos?
C. ¿Sales por la noche con tus amigos?
D. ¿Dónde pongo este paquete?
E. ¿Ves muchas películas en el cine?

1. Sí, pero me gustan más los vídeos.
2. Aquí mismo.
3. No, sólo en el fin de semana.
4. Sí, tengo cuatro.
5. No, el lunes.

Ejercicios de Gramática

A. Complete the following sentences with the right expression of "tener."

1. Oscar quiere comer, ______________________________.
2. Nosotros necesitamos un vaso de agua, ______________________________.
3. Yo quiero dormir un poco, ______________________________.
4. Ellos ven películas de terror, ______________________________.
5. Lupe necesita un suéter; creo que ella, ______________________________.

6. El Profesor Saborido (feels like), ______________________ tomar un café.

7. El termómetro marca 100 grados, por eso yo (that's why), ______________.

8. Yo no soy una persona vieja (22 years old), ______________________.

9. Son las 9:25 a.m. Tengo clase a las 9:30 a.m., por eso, ______________.

10. Tú, ______________________ de tu hermanita porque ella es pequeñita.

B. Reflective verbs in the present tense. Complete the blank spaces with the verb in parentheses for the following paragraph. Be careful with stem changing situations also.

Todos los días, el Profesor Gallo ______________ (despertarse) muy temprano. __________ (levantarse), __________ (ducharse), __________ (vestirse) y prepara el café para su esposa. El __________ (irse) para la universidad a las ocho porque tiene clase a las nueve y media. Tiene tanto trabajo que a veces no __________ (acordarse) de almorzar. Por la tarde, cuando llega a su casa, casi siempre __________ (ponerse) contento porque su mujer le prepara unas cenas deliciosas. Siempre __________ (acostarse) temprano porque necesita dormir para levantarse temprano al día siguiente.

C. ¿Qué tiempo hace?

1. Hace ______________________________ (it is sunny)
2. Hace ______________________________ (it is hot)
3. Hace ______________________________ (it is windy)
4. Hace ______________________________ (it is cool)
5. Hace ______________________________ (it is cold)

D. Complete the sentences with the most appropriate conjugation. One in each blank please.

voy, ~~vamos~~ digo tienen venimos ~~oyen~~
decimos salgo pone quepo hago vienen

1. María __pone__ el libro en la mesa.
2. Nosotros __vamos__ a la Universidad de Middlesex todas las mañanas.

3. Yo ___digo___ que no es verdad.

4. Ellos ___tienen___ mucho dinero.

5. Ustedes ___~~vienen~~ ouen___ la explicación del profesor.

6. Yo ___hago___ mi tarea en la casa.

7. Yo ___voy___ a mi trabajo en mi carro nuevo.

8. Yo no ___quepo___ en este pupitre. Es muy pequeño.

9. ¿ Ustedes ___vienen___ a mi casa?

10. Yo___salgo___ por las noches con mis amigos.

E. Conjugate the following irregular verbs.

1. Yo ____________ (oír) música latina.

2. Ellas ____________ (tener) poco dinero.

3. Tú ____________ (venir) a la clase en autobús.

4. Ustedes ____________ (traer) regalos (gifts) para sus amigos.

5. Yo ____________ (poner) mis libros en el carro.

6. Yo ____________ (salir) de la universidad a las cuatro de la tarde.

7. Mi amiga y yo ____________ (ver) mucho la televisión.

8. Yo no ____________ (hacer) errores (mistakes).

9. ¿ ____________ (oír) ustedes las noticias en la radio?

10. ¿Tú ____________ (decir) que sí?

F. Complete the sentences with the forms of the stem-changing verbs.

1. Ella no ____________ **(querer)** jugar a las cartas *(cards)*. Ella ____________ **(preferir)** ver la televisión.

2. Estoy preocupado. (Yo) ____________ **(pensar)** demasiado en mis problemas

3. María ____________ **(contar)** unos chistes *(jokes)* muy divertidos.

4. Yo ____________ **(cerrar)** las ventanas porque los vecinos se quejan *(are complaining)* de la música.

5. Sara pone un CD de salsa y ____________ **(empezar)** a bailar *(to dance)*.

6. Yo salgo de la fiesta y ____________ **(volver)** con más refrescos.

7. ¿ ____________ **(recordar)** tú el nombre de la chica que está con Alberto?

G. Complete the blank spaces with the correct form of the stem changing verbs (e > ie), e > i) in parentheses.

1. ¿ ____________ las películas románticas o las de suspenso? (preferir)
2. Pues, Yo ____________ las películas dramáticas. (preferir)
3. ¿Los estudiantes no ____________ a la profesora Jiménez. (entender)
4. En febrero ____________ mucho en en estado de Maine. (nevar)
5. Nosotros no ____________ perder esa oferta tan increíble. (querer)
6. ¿Qué tipo de comida ____________ en ese restaurante cubano? (servir)
7. Pues, allí yo siempre ____________ ropa vieja con frijoles negros. (pedir)
8. ¿ ____________ Uds. volver mañana? (pensar)
9. ¿Por qué no ____________ las palabras nuevas del vocabulario. (repetir)
10. No me gusta ____________ a mis amigos. (mentir)

H. Complete the blank spaces with the correct form of the stem changing verbs (o > ue), (u > ue) in parentheses.

1. José María ____________ llegar tarde a clase. (soler)
2. Cuando tengo sueño ____________ bien. (dormir).
3. ¿Cuántos perros calientes ____________ comer tú? (poder)
4. Tenemos que ____________ a las dos de la tarde. (volver)
5. Muchos estudiantes ____________ en la cafetería, ¿no? (almorzar)

I. Complete the verb with the corresponding reflexive pronoun.

1. Yo ____________ duermo después de leer en la cama.
2. Luisa y Pepe ____________ quejan del mal servicio.

3. Ana y tú ____________ arrepentís de no haber ido a la fiesta.

4. Antonio y yo ____________ probamos los disfraces.

5. Marichu ____________ atreve a tirarse en paracaídas.

6. Eloisa y yo ____________ bañamos en la piscina del hotel.

7. Tú ____________ duermes en la reunión.

8. Marcelo ____________ quita los zapatos al llegar a la casa.

9. Alberto y Carlos ____________ acuerdan del cumpleaños de la tía.

10. Yo ____________ pruebo unos zapatos nuevos.

J. Organize the different actions one would normally do every morning in chronological order, from waking up to going to school in sentences with the verbs provided.

Example. A las ocho de la mañana me cepillo los dientes.

a. Irse al colegio b. levantarse c. desayunar d. lavarse la boca e. peinarse f. Despertarse g. ponerse desodorante h. vestirse g. afeitarse h. bañarse

1. Despertarse — me despierto
2. levantarse — me levanto
3. lavarse la boca — me lavando la boca
4. desayunar — me desayuno
5. banarse — me bane
6. afeitarse — me
7. ponerse desodorante — me pongo desodorante
8. vestirse - me visto
9. pEinarse — me pieno
10. irse al colegio — me

me levanto por la manana

↑ waking up at any time.

K. Complete the sentences with the correct form of the verbs provided, Llamarse, mirarse, probarse, quitarse, quejarse, arrepentirse, acordarse, parecerse, arrascarse, atreverse, acostarse, dormirse, ducharse, aburrirse.

1. Yo ____________ la ropa en mi habitación.

2. Pepe y yo ____________ de nuestra escuela primaria.

3. Nosotros ____________ con agua caliente en el invierno.

4. Elena ____________ temprano porque tiene sueño.

5. Elvira ____________ en el espejo la cicatriz (scar) que tiene en la cara.

6. Tú ____________ a George Clooney.

7. Yo ____________ Andrés.

8. Cuando me pica(itch) la espalda ____________ con esa regla (ruler).

9. Leonor y María ____________ en los partidos de fútbol.

10. Esteban ____________ de no haber estudiado más para el examen.

Drills

A. Conversation with your students. Formal drill:

"Hola (his/ her name). ¿Qué tiempo hace hoy?"

— ANSWER Hacer sol

"¿Te gusta más el frío o él calor? ¿Qué te pones cuando hace frío?"

— ANSWER Yo prefero Haer sol

Me gusta mas el calor cuando hace mucho

"¿Y cuándo hace mucho calor?" me pongo un vestido, camiseta.

— ANSWER Me gusta pantalones cortos en el calor

"¿Qué tiempo hace en Nueva Jersey durante el verano?"

— ANSWER Hace hace calor y humidad. en el verano

"¿Te gustan los inviernos en tu ciudad?

—ANSWER Si me gusta los inviernos los inviernos

"¿Por qué? No me gusta el frío.

— ANSWER

Charlando

María Luisa y su hermana Diana fueron invitadas a una fiesta de quince.

Diana—¿Qué te vas a poner para ir a la fiesta de Mariela?

María Luisa—No lo sé. Pensé pedirte prestado el vestido verde con escote bajo.

Diana—Sí, pero . . . ¿Crees que quepas en él? Has aumentado tanto últimamente.

María Luisa—Si no quieres prestármelo está bien, pero no tienes que ofenderme con pretextos tontos.

Oscar y su hermano Enrique se van de vacaciones a Punta del Este.

Enrique—¿Te queda espacio en tu valija?

Oscar—¿Qué quieres que te guarde en mi maleta?

Enrique—Necesito que guardes seis calzoncillos, cuatro camisetas, ocho pares de calcetines, tres pantalones y cuatro camisas.

Oscar—¿Y tú, qué llevas en tu maleta?

Enrique—Pues llevo el balón de fútbol, el balón de voleibol, el balón de baloncesto, las pelotas de tenis, la careta para bucear, las raquetas para . . .

Oscar—Bien, de acuerdo, pero tienes que llevar mi raqueta de tenis también.

Lupe y su hermana Adriana van a comprar un regalo a su madre.

Adriana—Mamá ya tiene muchos perfumes. Hay que comprarle algo práctico.

Lupe—¿Y cómo qué?

Adriana—Pues, como un par de zapatos para el diario.

Lupe—¿Estás loca? ¿Sabes lo difícil que es comprar zapatos para otra persona?

Adriana—Pues, ¿qué tal un bolso de cuero?

Lupe—Genial, me parece una idea estupenda.

Lectura

El Buen Vestir

El Buen Vestir

La forma de vestirse es una expresión de la cultura a la que pertenecemos. Por lo tanto, los jóvenes en todos los países hispanos se visten de una forma similar. Se ponen pantalones vaqueros, camisas de tipo polo, y zapatos de cuero o sandalias. Se visten de una forma parecida a la de los jóvenes norteamericanos aunque no igual, ya que el calzado es diferente y por lo general los pantalones son más ajustados.

La moda de los mayores cambia. El buen vestir es sinónimo de saber vivir, y la gente en ciudades como Madrid, Buenos Aires, Santiago, Montevideo y Bogotá se visten formalmente. Los hombres se visten con trajes de colores sobrios. Las mujeres usan pantalones, faldas o vestidos de colores de acuerdo a la estación y con zapatos de tacones. Es frecuente el usar aguas de colonia para después del baño, y las señoras usan perfumes. El aseo personal es algo muy importante en la cultura hispana a cualquier nivel social.

Las diferencias de clima en los diferentes países del mundo hispano determinan la forma de vestir. Mientras que en ciudades como Santiago, Madrid y Buenos Aires hace frío en el invierno, hay sitios como Lima, Medellín y San José donde nunca hace ni mucho frío, ni mucho calor. En ciudades como Veracruz, San Juan o Cartagena la gente se viste con ropa ligera porque el clima es generalmente veraniego.

Preguntas

1. ¿Cómo se visten los jóvenes en los países hispanos?
2. ¿En que se diferencian de los jóvenes americanos?
3. ¿Es importante el vestirse bien en el mundo hispano?
4. ¿Cómo se visten los hombres?
5. ¿Cómo se visten las mujeres?
6. ¿Qué tipo de colonia usan los hombres?
7. ¿Cómo se visten en Cartagena?
8. ¿Es importante el aseo personal en la cultura hispana?
9. ¿Qué clima hace en Medellín?
10. ¿Qué clima hace en Buenos Aires?

Proverbios

Dime con quien andas y te diré quien eres.

Agua que no has de beber, déjala correr.

Capítulo Seis

Las Vacaciones

Monólogos y Diálogos

Oscar Regresó de Vacaciones en México

Acabo de regresar de pasar un mes de vacaciones en México.
Fui a visitar a mi prima Lupe, hija de mi tío Arturo.
Lupe me mostró los sitios más interesantes de la capital de México.
Visitamos el Museo Antropológico, el Parque de Chapultepec,
El Parque de las Tres Culturas, las pirámides en Teotihuacán y
El Valle de Bravo. Lo pasé fenomenal. Una noche fuimos a la Plaza
Garibaldi y vimos cientos de mariachis. Comimos quesadillas, tacos y enchiladas todos los días.
Desayuné huevos rancheros con chocolate caliente casi todos los días.
¡Qué bonito es México!

María Luisa Regresó de Vacaciones en España

Acabo de regresar de pasarme todo el verano con mi primo José Antonio en España. Fuimos a ver a mis tíos que ahora viven en Mallorca. Ellos compraron un piso que tiene vista al mar. Paseamos en el velero de mi tío Arturo. Esquiamos en el mar casi todos los días. Caminamos por el Paseo Marítimo todas las noches. Visitamos la casa de Chopin y George Sand. Recorrimos la isla en moto, y nos bañamos en todas sus playas. Pudimos ir a Mahón, donde se inventó la mayonesa, en el velero del tío Arturo. Tambien nos fuimos de discoteca y la pasé muy bien a pesar de que José Antonio baila muy mal.

José Antonio Regresó de Vacaciones en Nueva York

Llegué muerto de cansancio. Caminé la isla de Manhattan de punta a punta. No descansé ni un minuto. Vi muchas cosas interesantes pero también dejé muchas sin ver por falta de tiempo. Bajé de peso porque no tuve tiempo para comer. Fui al Museo Metropolitano, al Museo de Historia Natural, al Museo de Arte Moderno, al Museo Hispánico con sus pinturas de Sorolla y a muchísimos otros sitios como el Centro Rockefeller, la Catedral de San Patricio y la Bolsa en Wall Street. Anduve a pie por el Parque Central desde el monumento a Martí hasta el lago por la calle 90. De regreso me quedé dormido en el metro y fui a parar a Queens, cerca de un aeropuerto. Nueva York es una ciudad única en el mundo.

Preguntas Sobre los Monólogos

Piense, Pregunte y Conteste

1. ¿A quién fue a visitar Oscar?
2. ¿En dónde está el parque de Chapultepec?
3. ¿Cómo lo pasó Oscar?
4. ¿Qué clase de comida comió Oscar?
5. ¿Le gustó México a Oscar?
6. ¿En dónde estuvo María Luisa en España?
7. ¿Visitó a su familia?
8. ¿Esquió en las montañas?
9. ¿Estuvo en un hotel?
10. ¿En dónde se bañó?
11. ¿Recorrió la isla en carro?
12. ¿Salió por las noches?

13. ¿Cómo baila José Antonio?

14. ¿En dónde se inventó la mayonesa?

15. ¿Vino descansado José Antonio de sus vacaciones?

16. ¿Por qué?

17. ¿Tuvo mucho tiempo para visitar la ciudad?

18. ¿Comió mucho?

19. ¿Qué museos visitó?

20. ¿Qué piensa José Antonio de Nueva York?

Vocabulario

De Lecturas

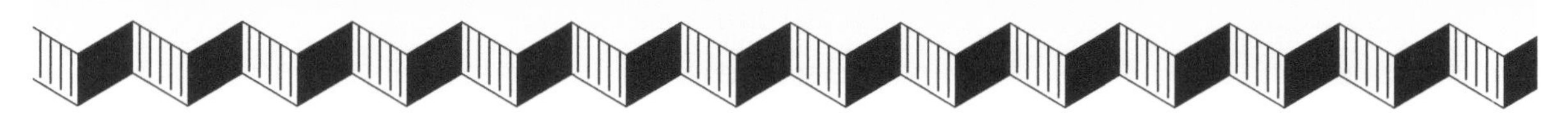

Sustantivos

El abuelo	grandfather
El calor	heat
El lago	lake
El mes	month
El metro	subway
El país	country
El piso	floor/apartment
El salario	wages
El tío	uncle
El velero	sailboat
El verano	summer
La Bolsa	Stock Market
La finca	ranch
La moto	motorbike
La prima	cousin
La rutina diaria	daily routine
La vida nocturna	night life
Las cosas	things
Las hija	daughter
Las pinturas	paintings
Las playas	beaches
Los deportes	sports
Los familiares	relatives
Los huevos rancheros	Mexican breakfast food
Los mariachis	Mexican singers
Los sitios	places
Los trabajadores	workers

Verbos

Acabar de	to finish
Bajar	to go down
Bañarse	to bathe
Caminar	to swim
Compartir	to share
Descansar	to relax
Disfrutar	to enjoy
Esquiar	to ski
Huir	to escape
Inventar	to invent
Pasar	to spend time
Permitir	to allow
Poder	to be able
Preferir	to prefer
Quedarse	to stay
Recibir	to receive
Recorrer	to travel
Regresar	to return
Reunir	to get together
Tener	to have
Tomar	to take

Adjetivos

Caliente	hot
Cientos	hundreds
Muchísimos	a lot
Nocturna	related to night
Única	only
Vecino	neighboring

Otras Expresiones

A pesar de	even though
Andar a pie	to walk
De punta a punta	from end to end
Desde . . . hasta	from . . . until
Falta de tiempo	lack of time
Hacer deportes	to practice sports
Muerto de cansancio	very tired
Quedarse dormido	to fall asleep
Vista al mar	view of the ocean

Vocabulario Práctico

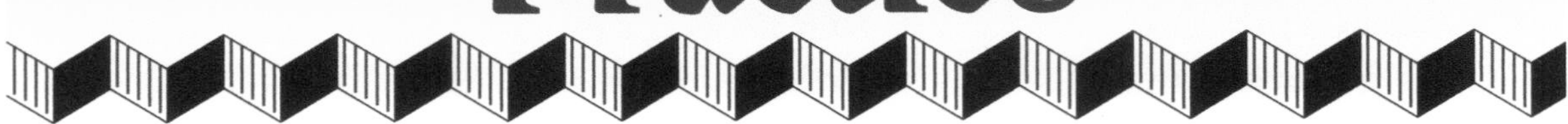

Bucear	to scuba dive
Correr por la playa	to run on the beach
Dar una caminata	to take a hike
Disfrutar . . .	to enjoy . . .
Escribir tarjetas postales	to write postcards
Explorar . . .	to explore . . .
Hacer ejercicios	to exercise
Hacer el camping	to camp out
Hacer el esquí acuático	to water ski
Hacer el surf de vela	to windsurf
Hacer la moto acuática	to jet ski
Hacer un picnic	to have a picnic
Ir de pesca	to go fishing
Montar . . .	to ride
Navegar	to sail
Recorrer	to travel
Remar el bote	to row
Visitar ruinas	to visit ruins
El balneario	beach resort
El hábitat natural	natural habitat
El lago	lake
La selva tropical	rain forest
Las cataratas	waterfalls
Las pirámides	pyramids
Los lugares turísticos	places of interest
Los recuerdos	souvenirs
Sitios arqueológicos	archaeological sites

Gramática

The Past Tense (The Preterit)

Spanish utilizes two tenses to report actions that happened in the past. We use the preterit tense to:

1. Report past actions that are viewed as having a definite beginning and/or end at a specific time.

   Elena salió anoche con sus amigos.
   Elena went out with her friends last night.

   Ellos pasaron la noche en casa de Teresa.
   They spent the night in Teresa's house.

2. Report series of past actions that are viewed as being fully completed.

   Esta mañana me levanté a las siete, me bañé, me vestí y salí de casa a las ocho.
   This morning I got up at seven, bathed, got dressed, and left the house at eight.

Temporal expressions such as: ayer (yesterday), anoche (last night), esta mañana (this morning), el lunes pasado (last Monday), el verano pasado (last summer), and so on, usually describe events in the preterit tense.

Formation of regular verbs in the preterit tense:

-ar	
Yo	-é
Tú	-aste
Ud., él, ella	-ó
Nosotros(as)	-amos
Vosotros(as)	-asteis
Uds., ellos, ellas	-aron

Hablé con mi amiga anoche.
I spoke to my friend last night.

Mi padre no trabajó ayer.
My father did not work yesterday.

¿Estudiaste para el examen?
Did you study for the test?

No llegamos a tiempo.
We did not arrive on time.

Note that the *nosotros(as)* form of regular ***–ar*** verbs is identical to the *nosotros* form in the present. Context will clarify if the form is used describing present or past actions.

Anoche bailamos salsa en la fiesta.
Last night we danced salsa at the party.

Todas las mañanas me levanto a las siete.
Every morning I get up at seven.

The written accent mark in the third person singular (él, ella, Ud.) distinguishes the action between a present tense action and a past event.

Compro	I buy
Compró	He, she, you bought

-er / -ir	
Yo	-í
Tú	-iste
Ud., él, ella	-ió
Nosotros(as)	-imos
Vosotros(as)	-isteis
Uds., ellos, ellas	-ieron

Ella comió chiles rellenos en un restaurante mexicano.
She ate chiles rellenos in a Mexican restaurant.

Los García vivieron en Miami cinco años.
Mr. and Mrs. García lived in Miami for five years.

¿Escribiste una carta a tu amigo Juan?
Did you write a letter to your friend Juan?

The ***nosotros(as)*** form of regular ***–ir*** verbs are also the same in the preterit and the present tenses. Context will clarify their use.

Anteayer escribimos a nuestros tíos en Santiago de Chile.
The day before yesterday we wrote a letter to our uncles in Santiago de Chile.

Todos los días recibimos correos electrónicos de nuestra prima Teresita.
Every day we receive e-mails from our cousin Teresita.

Verbs with Orthographic Changes in the Preterit

Verbs ending in ***–car*** and ***–gar*** show a spelling change in the *yo* form in order to maintain the hard sound of the (g).

*Tocar: to**qu**é, tocaste, tocó, tocamos, tocasteis, tocaron*
*Llegar: lle**gu**é, llegaste, llegó, llegamos, llegasteis, llegaron*

Verbs that end in ***–zar*** also undergo a change in the *yo* form. This is due to the rule that the consonant (z) cannot be followed by the vowels (e) or (i).

Almorzar: almorcé, almorzaste, almorzó, almorzamos, almorzasteis, almorzaron

Verbs such as: *leer, oír, creer,* and *huir* change the regular third person singular and plural forms to "*–yo*" and "*yeron*" to avoid having three consecutive vowels that would make their pronunciation awkward.

Leer: leí, leíste, leyó, leímos, leísteis, leyeron
Oír: oí, oíste, oyó, oímos, oísteis, oyeron

Ver (to see) does not carry accent marks.

Vi, viste, vio, vimos, visteis, vieron

More Irregular Verbs

"**Ser**" and "**ir**" have the same irregular pattern in the preterit:

Ser	Ir
fui	fui
fuiste	fuiste
fue	fue
fuimos	fuimos
fuisteis	fuisteis
fueron	fueron

Ayer fui a visitar a mi amiga Conchita en la Ciudad de Nueva York. Fui en tren. Los dos fuimos a un restaurante argentino. Comimos y bebimos mucho. La comida fue excelente y deliciosa.

Can you guess which forms of **ir** and **ser** in the above paragraph translate as *was* or *went*? Sentence structure and context will clarify the significance.

"**Dar**" also has an irregular preterit. Notice that it uses the regular for of *–er* / *-ir* verbs without the accent marks.

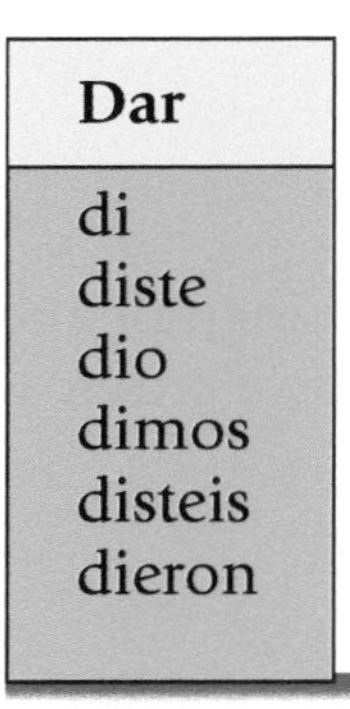

Dar
di
diste
dio
dimos
disteis
dieron

The Irregular Verbs

The following verbs may be grouped showing similar irregularities in the stem of the preterit tense. Notice that the first group (andar = *to stroll,* estar = *to be,* and tener = *to have*) has "**uv**" in the stem.

The second group (poner = *to put,* poder = to be *able/can,* saber = *to know,* caber = *to fit,* and haber = *to have*) shares a common "**u.**"

The next group (venir = *to come,* querer = *to want,* and hacer = *to do/to make*) has the vowel **i.**

The last group (decir = *to say/to tell,* traer = *to bring,* conducir = *to drive,* producir = *to produce,* and traducir = *to translate*) introduces the consonant **j** in the irregular stem.

Also notice that the irregular pattern is a combination of the two regular preterit endings. However, the first and third person singular forms do not carry an accent mark.

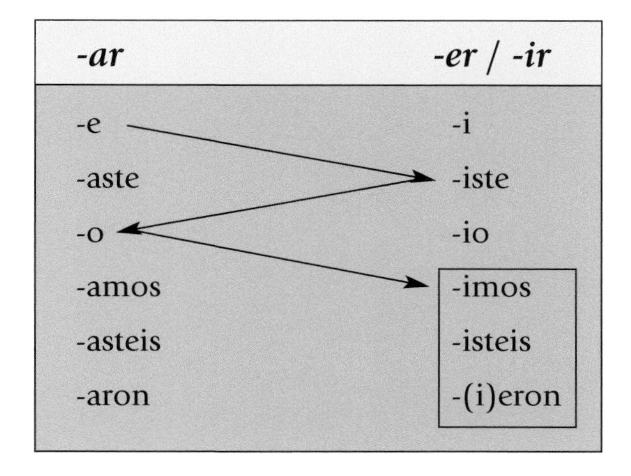

Thus, the irregular pattern for *andar, estar, tener, poner, poder, saber, caber, haber, venir, querer* and *hacer* is:

-e
-iste
-o
-imos
-isteis
-ieron

For *decir, traer, conducir, producir* and *traducir* is:

-e
-iste
-o
-imos
-isteis
-eron

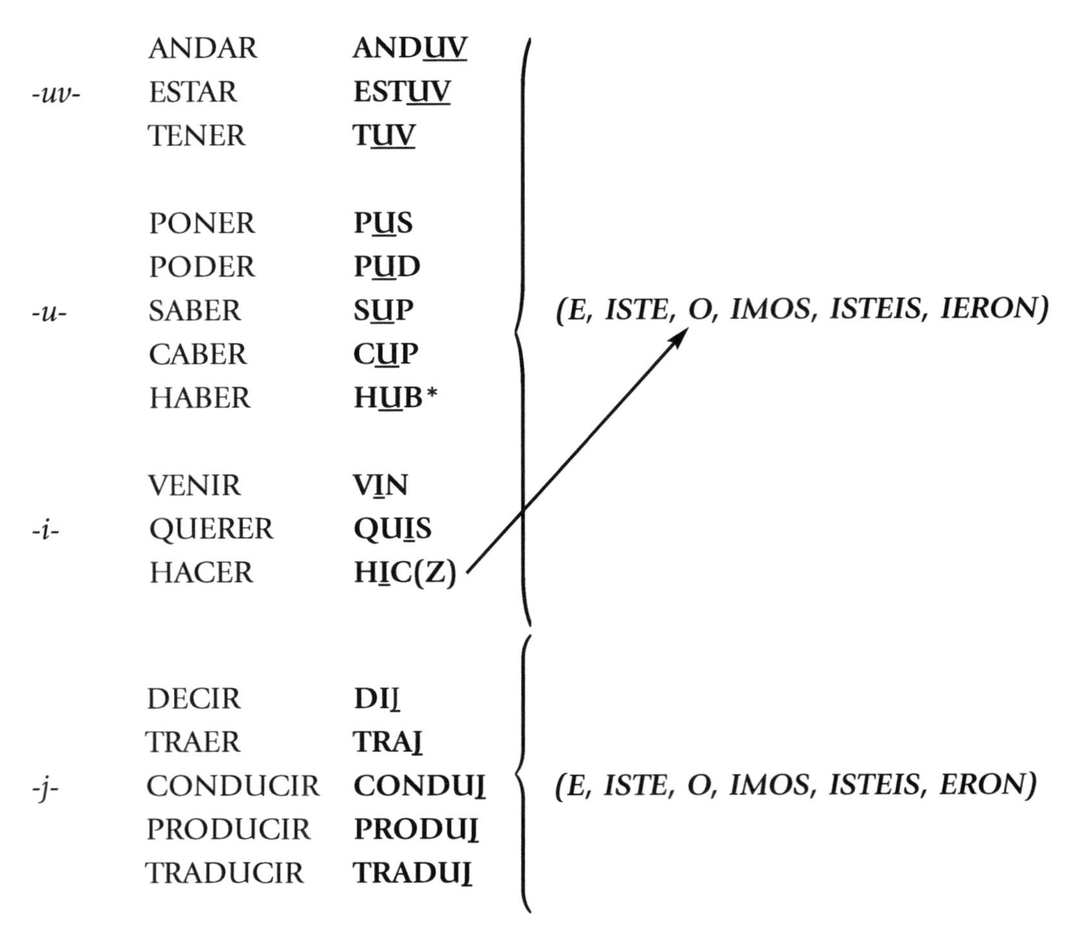

* Used as an auxiliary verb to form compound tenses.

Stem Changing Verbs

Some verbs also show a change in the stem in the preterit tense. These verbs belong only to the *–ir* conjugation family, and previously had also undergone a stem change in the present tense. However, the change only occurs in the third person singular (él, ella, Ud.) and plural (ellos, ellas, Uds.) forms.

The following verbs change the vowel ***e*** to ***i:***

Divertir(se)	Seguir
Mentir	Sentir
Pedir	Servir
Preferir	Sugerir
Repetir	Vestir(se)

Only two verbs change the vowel ***o*** to ***u:***

Dormir(se)
Morir

To help you retain the pattern, remember the "sandal" visual with the two changes.

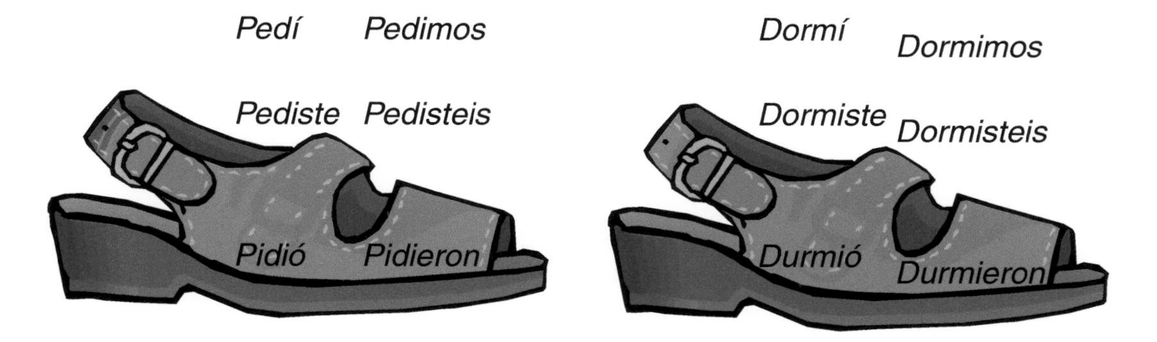

Ejercicios

Diálogos

Matching

A. ¿Te gusta tomar vacaciones?

B. ¿Fuiste de vacaciones últimamente?

C. ¿Cuál es tu lugar preferido para las vacaciones?

D. ¿Hiciste nuevos amigos allí?

E. ¿Compraste muchos recuerdos?

1. No, porque no me gustaron.

2. Sí, amistades fabulosas.

3. Fui a Madrid el verano pasado.

4. Sí, me encanta.

5. El Caribe.

Ejercicios de Gramática

A. Regular preterit. Complete the sentences with the most appropriate conjugation. Use verbs only once.

Bebimos escribió leí comprendimos recibieron
Vivimos bebiste comió leímos escribí vivieron

1. Oscar ____________ una carta a su madre.

2. Nosotros ____________ en Miami.

3. Yo ____________ un buen libro.

4. Ellos ____________ regalos de sus padres.

5. Nosotros ____________ la explicación del profesor.

6. Él ____________ una hamburguesa y papas fritas.

7. José Antonio y yo ____________ el artículo.

8. Yo no ____________ esa frase.

9. ¿ ___________ por un tiempo en Nueva York?

10. Tú ___________ toda la leche.

B. Reflective verbs in the preterit. Complete the blank spaces with the verb in parentheses for the following paragraph.

Esta mañana, ___________ (despertarse) tarde. Por eso (yo) ___________ (levantarse) de la cama rápidamente, ___________ (cepillarse) los dientes y ___________ (ducharse); ni siquiera ___________ (afeitarse) ni ___________ (peinarse). (Yo) ___________ (vestirse) unos pantalones y una camisa y salí de casa. Cuando estaba en el autobús___________ (acordarse) que mis libros estaban en la mesa de la cocina.

C. Verbs with spelling changes in the preterit.

1. Yo ___________ (buscar) una pluma pero no la encontré.
2. Yo ___________ (almorzar) al mediodía con su hermana.
3. Oscar ___________ (jugar) todo el día en la nieve.
4. Ella ___________ (pagar) la cuenta del restaurante.
5. Lupe ___________ (alcanzar / to reach) su sueño.

D. Complete the sentences with the irregular preterit of the verb in parentheses. Then, in groups try to find out the meanings for those sentences.

1. Lupe ___________ (estar) enferma.
2. Nosotros ___________ (hacer) toda la tarea.
3. Yo no ___________ (venir) ayer a clase.
4. José Antonio y Oscar ___________ (poner) los libros encima de la mesa.
5. María Luisa y yo___________ (saber) la verdad ayer.
6. Él ___________ (tener) muchos problemas la semana pasada.
7. Oscar y yo ___________ (andar) por el parque.
8. Yo no ___________ (querer) ir a esa fiesta aburrida.

9. Colombia____________ (producir) muchas toneladas de café el año pasado.

10. Tú no ____________ (poder) dormir en toda la noche.

11. El Profesor Gallo ____________ (traducir) el artículo al inglés.

12. Yo no ____________ (decir) esa mentira.

13. ¿Qué____________ (haber) para comer en la fiesta?

14. El Dr. Blanco y el Profesor Saborido ____________ (poder) llegar a tiempo.

15. Los estudiantes ____________ (decir) que es un exámen difícil.

E. Stem changing verbs in the preterit. Complete the blank spaces with the verb in parentheses.

1. Oscar ____________ (repetir) las palabras del vocabulario.
2. Ella ____________ (seguir) diciendo que hace mucho viento.
3. Lupe ____________ (pedir) otro suéter porque tiene frío.
4. Oscar ____________ (servir) chocolate caliente a sus amigos.
5. Ella ____________ (conseguir) sacar su coche de la nieve.
6. Lupe ____________ (pedir) otro refresco porque hace mucho calor.

F. Irregular verbs in the preterit. Choose the right verb.

1. María Luisa ____________ (vino, anduvo, dijo) a la universidad en bus.
2. El Profesor Saborido ____________ (tradujo, tuvo, hizo) mucho dinero.
3. La estudiante ____________ (puso, vino, quiso) los libros en la mochila.
4. Oscar ____________ (supo, estuvo, dijo) muy enfermo la semana pasada.
5. El Doctor Blanco ____________ (hizo, tradujo, quiso) las frases al inglés.
6. El Profesor Gallo ____________ (estuvo, trajo, condujo) muchos libros hoy.

Drills

A. Conversation with your students. Formal drill:

"Hola (his/her name). ¿Por qué no viniste ayer a la clase?"

— ANSWER

"Ya veo, pero hiciste toda la tarea, ¿verdad?"

— ANSWER

¿Dónde estuviste ayer por la tarde?"

— ANSWER

"¿Y tu libro? ¿En dónde lo pusiste?"

— ANSWER

"¿Tuviste dificultades con la lección de hoy?"

—ANSWER

"¿Tradujiste bien el párrafo al español?"

— ANSWER

Charlando

Antonio invita a una amiga a pasar una semana en el apartamento de su familia.

Antonio—Begoña, mis padres compraron un apartamento en Marbella y me dieron las llaves para que lo estrene estas vacaciones de Semana Santa. Yo fui con ellos y me gustó mucho.

Begoña—Lo siento Antonio pero el profesor de Biología nos dio un proyecto que no pude terminar y voy a pasar las vacaciones trabajando.

Antonio—Yo saqué sobresaliente en Biología. Si tú vienes conmigo te prometo ayudarte con tu proyecto.

Begoña—Es que Ignacio hizo un proyecto parecido al mío y él ya me dijo que me iba a ayudar.

Antonio—¡Ignacio! Ese tipo no es de confiar.

Oscar regresó de sus vacaciones en Viña del Mar.

Mónica—Hola, Oscar, hace tiempo que no te veía.

Oscar—Me fui a Viña del Mar de vacaciones porque un amigo me invitó. Él es chileno y su familia tiene un apartamento en la playa.

Mónica—¿Te gustó Viña? ¿Qué tal la gente por allá?

Oscar—Mis amigos chilenos fueron muy simpáticos y amables. El agua estuvo muy fría pero hizo sol todos los días. Fuimos a diferentes discotecas en Valparaíso. Tuve que salir a bailar todas las noches. También fuimos al Festival de Música.

Mónica—¿Trajiste fotos para verlas?

Oscar—Si, pero las dejé en casa. Mañana las traigo.

María Luisa regresó de pasar un mes en Colombia.
Sus padres le hacen muchas preguntas.

Doña Alicia—Marilú, ¿Qué ciudades visitaste en Colombia?

María Luisa—Estuve en Cartagena, en Medellín, en Pereira, en Cali y por supuesto en Bogotá.

Doña Alicia—¿Qué hiciste en Cartagena?

María Luisa—Fuimos a la playa y a la parte histórica de la ciudad. Fue muy interesante. Cartagena es muy bonita. Hizo mucho calor pero no llovió.

Doña Alicia—¿Y qué más hiciste?

María Luisa—En Pereira me llevaron a un cafetal donde bebimos café y después montamos a caballo. Yo me caí del caballo, pero tuve suerte, no me lastimé. En Bogotá, fui al Museo del Oro, a la Catedral de Sal y escalé un cerro que se llama Montserrat. Me divertí mucho y Colombia me gustó mucho.

Cultura

Las Vacaciones

Las Vacaciones

Mientras que en España la gente prefiere tomar sus vacaciones dentro de España, en Ibero-América les gusta viajar a los Estados Unidos o a algún país vecino. En España la familia pasa el verano en la finca del abuelo, o el piso en la costa que comparten con los familiares más cercanos. Muchos madrileños tienen un apartamento o un chalet en la sierra donde el aire fresco de montaña les permite huir del calor de Madrid. Los más jóvenes disfrutan haciendo deportes en los Pirineos o en Los Picos de Europa. Otros prefieren la vida nocturna en islas como Mallorca, Ibiza o Gran Canaria. Los argentinos van a las playas en el Uruguay. Los paraguayos visitan las playas en Brasil. Muchas familias hispano-americanas visitan los Estados Unidos, principalmente las ciudades de Orlando y Miami en la Florida. En algunos países como en Colombia las vacaciones se toman en noviembre y diciembre, en la Argentina y Chile el verano se extiende de diciembre a marzo. En algunos países como en España los trabajadores reciben un mes de salario adicional en agosto para sus vacaciones. Lo importante en las vacaciones es reunir a la familia y descansar de la rutina diaria.

Preguntas

1. ¿Dónde prefieren tomar sus vacaciones los españoles?
2. ¿Dónde prefieren tomar sus vacaciones los ibero-americanos?
3. ¿Dónde pasan usualmente el verano las familias españolas?
4. ¿Dónde pasan las vacaciones muchos madrileños?
5. ¿Cómo disfrutan sus vacaciones algunos jóvenes atléticos?
6. ¿Qué sitios tienen una vida nocturna activa?
7. ¿A dónde van los argentinos a la playa?
8. ¿A dónde van los paraguayos a la playa?
9. ¿Qué ciudades son populares con los turistas ibero-americanos?
10. ¿Qué reciben los trabajadores en España antes de sus vacaciones en agosto?

Proverbios

Al que madruga, Dios lo ayuda.
No por mucho madrugar amanece más temprano.

Capítulo Siete

La Familia

Monólogos

La Familia

José Antonio

Cuando era un niño pequeño, mis abuelos venían a buscarme para salir a pasear en su coche todas las noches antes de dormirme. Los fines de semana íbamos a tomar helado. A mi abuela le gustaba el helado de vainilla y a mi abuelo le gustaba el helado de chocolate.

María Luisa

Cuando era una niña, mi tía Emilia me llevaba al parque con mis primas Teresita y Paloma. Teresita era muy deportista y siempre traía un lazo para saltar y un balón muy grande. Paloma traía un libro y se pasaba todo el tiempo leyendo.

Lupe

Cuando era estudiante me pasaba todas las tardes estudiando con mis primas en un café que estaba frente al Palacio de Bellas Artes. Amalia siempre pedía un chocolate con churros y Matilde solo tomaba agua mineral porque quería bajar de peso. Era tan agradable que el tiempo pasaba muy rápido y no me daba cuenta. Llegaba tarde a mi casa y mis padres se enojaban mucho.

Oscar

Mis hermanos querían comprarle un regalo a mi madre por su cumpleaños pero no sabían que regalarle. Mi padre quería regalarle un boleto para una ópera en el Teatro Colón. Sin embargo, mamá solo deseaba tener una reunión en casa con toda la familia: mis abuelos, sus hermanos, sus sobrinos, sus cuñadas y hasta los perros de la familia.

Preguntas del Monólogo

Piense, Pregunte y Conteste

1. ¿Con quién salía mucho José Antonio de pequeño?
2. ¿Qué helado le gustaba al abuelo de José Antonio?
3. ¿A quién le gustaba el helado de vainilla?
4. ¿Crees que José Antonio extraña a sus abuelos?
5. ¿Con quién pasaba el tiempo María Luisa de niña?
6. ¿En dónde?
7. ¿A Teresita le gustaba leer?
8. ¿Qué le gustaba hacer a Teresita?
9. ¿Quién traía un libro para leer en el parque?
10. ¿Era Paloma muy deportista?
11. ¿Era estudiosa Lupe?
12. ¿En dónde le gustaba leer?

13. ¿Qué tomaba Amalia siempre en el café?

14. ¿Por qué Matilde tomaba siempre agua mineral?

15. ¿Por qué se enojaban los padres de Lupe?

16. ¿Qué quería hacer Oscar para su madre?

17. ¿Para qué ocasión?

18. ¿Qué quería regalarle a su esposa el papá?

19. ¿Qué quería hacer la mamá?

20. ¿Invitaban a mucha gente?

Vocabulario

De Lecturas

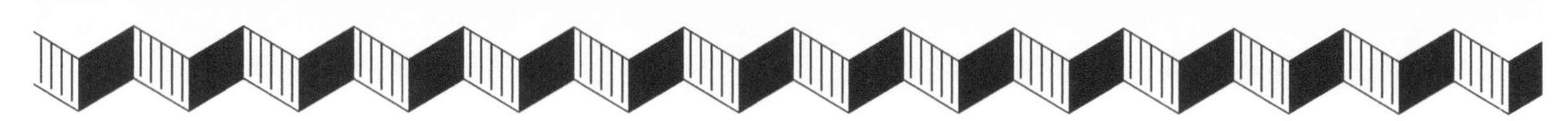

Sustantivos

El apoyo	help
El balón	ball
El boleto	ticket
El cuidado	care
El cumpleaños	birthday
El deportista	sports figure
El divorcio	divorce
El helado	ice cream
El lazo	rope
El papel	the role
El regalo	gift
Las cuñadas	sisters-in-law
Los abuelos	grandparents
Los churros	Spanish breakfast fritter
Los consejos	advice
Los fines de semana	weekends
Los hermanos	brothers
Los matrimonios	married couples
Los nietos	grandchildren
Los sobrinos	nephews
Los tíos	uncle and aunt
Los vecinos	neighbors

Verbos

Ayudarse	to help each other
Buscar	to look for
Compartir	to share
Desear	to desire

Dormirse	to fall asleep
Ejercer	to exercise one's rights
Enojarse	to get upset
Llevar	to carry/to wear
Pedir	to ask for
Regalar	to give gifts
Saltar	to jump
Traer	to bring
Venir	to come

Otras Expresiones

Bajar de peso	to lose weight
Darse cuenta	to realize
El vivir diario	daily activities
Hasta	until
Pasar el tiempo	to spend time
Salir a pasear	to go out
Sin embargo	nevertheless

Vocabulario Práctico

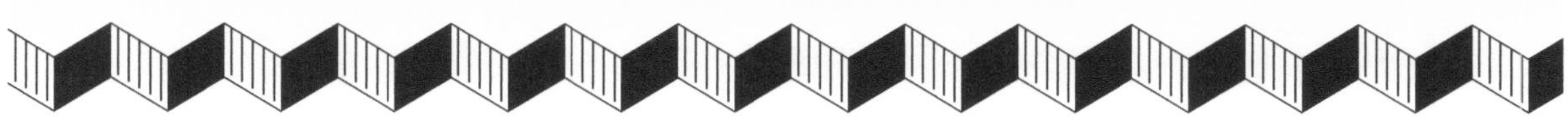

La Familia

Los parientes	relatives
Los abuelos	grandparents
El abuelo	grandfather
La abuela	grandmother
Los padres	parents
El padre	father
El papá	dad
La madre	mother
La mamá	mom
El padrastro	step-father
La madrastra	step-mother
Los hijos	children
El hijo	son
La hija	daughter
Los hermanos	siblings
El hermano	brother
La hermana	sister
El hermanastro	step-brother
La hermanastra	step-sister
El medio hermano	half-brother
La media hermana	half-sister
Los nietos	grandchildren
El nieto	grandson
La nieta	granddaughter
Los primos	cousins
El primo	male cousin
La prima	female cousin

Los sobrinos	nephews and nieces
El sobrino	nephew
La sobrina	niece
Los tíos	uncles and aunts
El tío	uncle
La tía	aunt
Los suegros	in laws
El suegro	father-in-law
La suegra	mother-in-law
El yerno	son-in-law
La nuera	daughter-in-law
El cuñado	brother-in-law
La cuñada	sister-in-law

La Familia

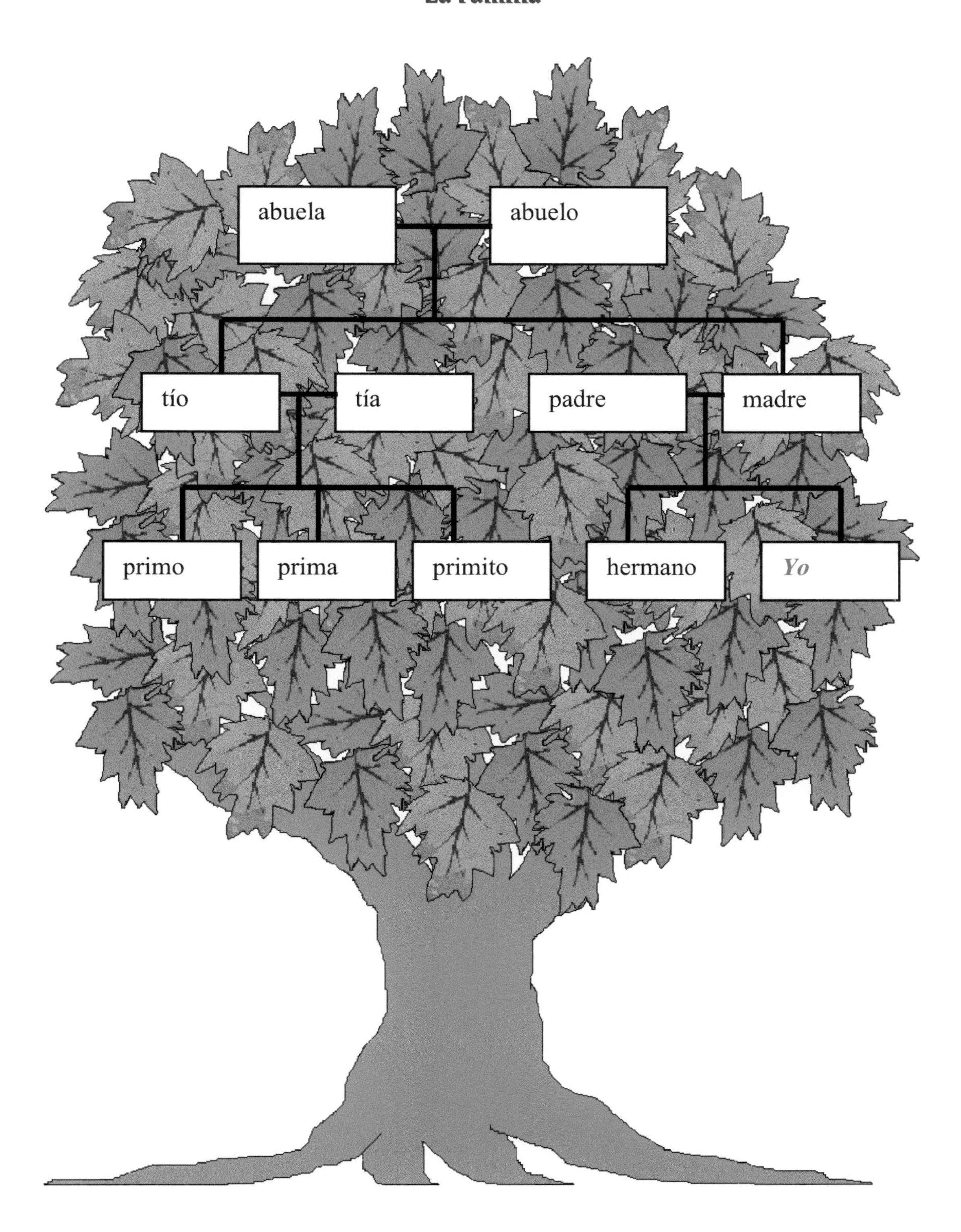
abuela
abuelo
tío
tía
padre
madre
primo
prima
primito
hermano
Yo

Gramática

The Past Tense: The Imperfect

The imperfect is the other simple tense used in Spanish to express actions in the past. It is used to:

1. Describe actions in the past that occurred habitually or continuously over an indefinite period of time, without any reference to its beginning or ending. Time expressions that may be used with the imperfect to emphasize the repetition of the action are:

siempre	a menudo	con frecuencia
generalmente	todos los días	mientras
frecuentemente	muchas veces	
de vez en cuando	los lunes / los martes . . .	

   Cuando yo era niña vivía cerca de mis abuelos.
   When I was a child I used to live near/close to my grandparents.

   Comíamos frecuentemente en casa de mis tíos.
   We often ate at my aunt and uncle's house.

   De vez en cuando visitábamos a los primos en Los Angeles.
   From time to time we would visit our cousins in Los Angeles.

2. Narrate actions or events in progress in the past. The emphasis here is the middle of the action. English uses *was / were* + verb ending in *–ing.*

   Rosita jugaba con sus hermanos.
   Rosita was playing with her brothers.

   Francisco miraba la televisión mientras sus padres hablaban.
   Francisco was watching television while his parents were talking.

Yo leía un libro en la sala.
I was reading a book in the livingroom.

3. Describe situations, emotions, conditions, people, places, weather, and time in the past when no reaction to time is implied.

Mi papá era un hombre muy simpático.
My father was a very nice man.

Nuestra casa estaba en un barrio viejo de Madrid.
Our house was located in an old neighborhood of Madrid.

De niño no me gustaba comer zanahorias.
As a child, I did not like to eat carrots.

Estábamos muy contentos cuando vivíamos en Panamá.
We were very happy when we lived in Panama.

Formation of the Imperfect: Regular Verbs

-ar	
Yo	-aba
Tú	-abas
Ud., él, ella	-aba
Nosotros(as)	-ábamos
Vosotros(as)	-abais
Uds., ellos, ellas	-aban

Ellos jugaban tranquilamente en el parque.
Tú estudiabas las lecciones todas las noches.
A Joaquín le gustaba nadar en el mar.

-er / -ir	
Yo	-ía
Tú	-ías
Ud., él, ella	-ía
Nosotros(as)	-íamos
Vosotros(as)	-íais
Uds., ellos, ellas	-ían

Todos asistíamos a las reuniones familiares.
Frecuentemente comíamos en la casa de nuestros abuelos.
Rosa y Elena leían las lecciones todas las noches.

Formation of the Imperfect: Irregular Verbs

Ser	Ir	Ver
era	iba	veía
eras	ibas	veías
era	iba	veía
éramos	íbamos	veíamos
erais	ibais	veíais
eran	iban	veían

Contrasting the Preterit and the Imperfect

The use of the preterit or the imperfect depends on how the speaker wants the past action to be interpreted. If the action refers to completed actions with definite beginning and endings, use the preterit.

Esta mañana salí de casa temprano.
This morning I left home early.

Llegué a la universidad a las 8:00.
I arrived at the university at 8:00.

Inmediatamente fui a la oficina de mi profesor para discutir un proyecto.

Immediately I went to my professor's office to discuss a project.

However, use the imperfect tense to describe habitual or recurrent past actions. The time that the action started or ended is not significant.

Todas las tardes salía de casa a eso de las cinco y llegaba a casa de mi novia para discutir las actividades del día. Después íbamos al centro comercial y nos reuníamos con otros amigos.

Every afternoon I used to leave my house around five and I would arrive at my girlfriend's house to discuss the daily activities. Afterward we would go to the mall, and there we would get together with other friends.

In order to facilitate the correct use of both past tenses, refer to the following visual aid:

1. Repeated or habitual actions require the use of the imperfect tense.

De niño, todos los veranos mi familia iba de vacaciones a Cancún. Allí pasábamos unas semanas maravillosas en las hermosas playas. Todos nadábamos y tomábamos el sol.

2. Ongoing and descriptive actions are also expressed in the imperfect tense.

Mientras Flora compraba regalos en los mercados al aire libre, a mí me gustaba visitar lugares turísticos.

3. Series of events with definite beginnings and definite ends require the use of the preterit.

Esta mañana me levanté a las seis, me bañé, me vestí y salí de casa a las siete. Llegué a la universidad a las siete y media. Asistí a mi clase de español y después fui a la biblioteca donde estudié para un examen.

This morning I got up at six, I bathed, got dressed, and left the house at seven. I arrived at the university at seven thirty. I attended my Spanish class and afterward I went to the library where I studied for a test.

4. When an action was going on (imperfect), and another action interrupted this ongoing action, use the preterit to emphasize the interruption.

Mientras estudiaba para el examen, mi amiga Marta me llamó al teléfono móvil para decirme que estaba enferma.

While I was studying for the test, my friend Marta called me on my cell phone to tell me that she was sick.

Change of Meaning for Preterit

The following verbs denote different English meanings depending on their use in either the preterit or imperfect tense (conocer, saber, querer, poder). Observe:

	Preterit	Imperfect
Conocer	*to meet*	*to know (to be acquainted with)*
Saber	*to find out*	*to know (facts)*
Querer	*to try*	*to want*
No querer	*to refuse*	*not to want*
Poder	*to manage*	*to be able to*
No poder	*to fail to do*	*not to be able*

Ayer conocimos al padre de Roberto. — Yesterday we met Roberto's father.
Pero conocíamos a su mamá. — But we knew his mother.

Supe la verdad. — I found out the truth.
Ellos ya lo sabían. — They already knew it.

Quisieron salir. — They tried to leave.
Querían comer temprano. — They wanted to eat early.

No quisieron hacerlo. — They refused to do it.
No querían hacerlo. — They did not want to do it.

Pudo terminar temprano. — She managed to finish early.
Podía hablar italiano. — She could speak Italian.

No pude terminarlo. — I failed to finish it.
No podía hacerlo. — I could not do it.

The Imperfect Progressive

The imperfect progressive tense is formed using the imperfect tense of ***estar*** and the gerund of the main verb (the **-ing** ending in English). It is used to express actions that were in progress in the past.

Remember that the gerund is formed by dropping the *–ar* infinitive ending and replacing it with *–ando.* Most *–er* and *–ir* ending verbs take the *–iendo* to form the gerund.

Infinitive	**Tomar**	**Vender**	**Vivir**
-ing	tomando	vendiendo	viviendo

Nosotros estábamos hablando con el profesor.
We were talking with the professor.

Alfonso y Rodrigo estaban jugando en el parque cuando comenzó a llover.
Alfonso and Rodrigo were playing in the park when it started to rain.

The following verbs have irregular gerunds:

Creer	creyendo	(believing)
Leer	leyendo	(reading)
Oír	oyendo	(hearing)
Traer	trayendo	(bringing)
Caer	cayendo	(falling)

Estaba leyendo un ensayo muy interesante.
I was reading a very interesting book.

Estábamos oyendo las noticias.
We were listening to the news.

Ejercicios

Diálogos

Matching

A.	¿Dónde vivías de niño/a?	**1.**	El arroz con camarones.
B.	¿A qué escuela asistías?	**2.**	Sí, era muy guapo/a.
C.	¿Cuál era tu comida favorita?	**3.**	En Staten Island, Nueva York.
D.	¿Tenías novio/a?	**4.**	Salir con mis amigos al cine.
E.	¿Qué te gustaba hacer en tu tiempo libre?	**5.**	P.S. 35, en la calle veinte.

Ejercicios de Gramática

A. Complete the sentences with the imperfect tense of the verb in parentheses.

1. José Antonio y yo ____________ (trabajar) juntos en esa empresa.
2. María Luisa y tú____________ (estudiar) en esta universidad.
3. Ellas ____________ (hablar) todos los días por teléfono.
4. Oscar y Lupe ____________ (escribir) en su diario todas las noches.
5. El profesor no ____________ (entender) lo que pasaba con su estudiante.
6. Nosotros ____________ (querer) ir de vacaciones todos los veranos.
7. Yo no ____________ (almorzar) con Lupe todos los días.
8. Yo ____________ (comprar) mi café en esa tienda todas la mañanas.
9. Mi familia ____________ (reunirse) durante las fiestas.

10. Tú no ____________ (vivir) en los Estados Unidos por ese tiempo, ¿verdad?

11. El Profesor Gallo ____________ (asistir) a la Universidad de Rutgers.

12. El Dr. Blanco ____________ (preparar) sus clases todos los días.

13. Los estudiantes no ____________ (saber) nada de gramática.

14. Ustedes no ____________ (comprender) a sus hijos cuando eran jóvenes.

15. ¿Qué____________ (pasar) con tu carro la semana pasada?

B. Irregular verbs in the imperfect. Complete the blank spaces with the verb in parentheses.

1. Oscar ____________ (ser) muy inteligente.
2. Ella ____________ (ver) todas las películas españolas.
3. Nosotras ____________ (ser) estudiantes de la Universidad de Middlesex.
4. El profesor ____________ (ir) a Chile todos los veranos.
5. María Luisa ____________ (ir) a su trabajo por las tardes.
6. Lupe ____________ (ver) a su hijo jugar en el parque todas las tardes.

C. The imperfect tense. Choose the right verb.

1. María Luisa ____________ (comía, iba, decía) siempre arroz con pollo.
2. El Profesor Saborido ____________ (traducía, bebía, hacía) muchos refrescos.
3. La estudiante ____________ (vivía, trabajaba, hablaba) en el centro comercial.
4. Oscar ____________ (trabajaba, asistía, leía) muchos libros.
5. El Doctor Blanco ____________ (tenía, trabajaba, vivía) en España.
6. El Profesor Gallo ____________ (vivía, asistía, comía) a sus clases de aeróbicos.

D. Imperfecto o presente. Tell what you used to do or used to be as a child and what you now do (or are).

1. (Ser) De niño/a, yo ________ gordito/a, ahora ________ delgado/a.

2. (Comer) Yo ________ mucho, ahora ________ poco.

3. (Ir) ________ a muchas fiestas, ahora no ________.

4. (Tener) ________ muchos amigos/as, ahora no ________.

5. (Jugar/ue) ________ con mis amigos en la calle, ahora ________ con mi computadora.

E. Antes . . . pero ayer . . . Use the Preterit and the Imperfect in the following sentences.

1. (Trabajar) Yo antes ________ mucho, pero ayer no ________ nada.

2. (Estudiar) Yo antes ________ poco, pero ayer ________ mucho.

3. (Ver) Yo antes ________ mucha tele, pero ayer no la ________.

4. (Oír) Yo antes ________ música rap, pero ayer ________ música clásica.

5. (Comer) Yo antes ________ muchas hamburguesas, pero ayer ________ una ensalada de lechuga y tomate.

Drills

A. Conversation with your students. Formal drill:

"Hola (his/ her name). ¿Dónde vivías cuando eras niño/a?"

— ANSWER

"¿A qué escuela asistías?"

— ANSWER

¿Eras rebelde o eras un niño/a bueno/a?"

— ANSWER

"¿Qué te gustaba comer?"

— ANSWER

"¿Adónde ibas de vacaciones durante los veranos?"

—ANSWER

"¿Tenías muchos amigos?"

— ANSWER

"¿Cómo se llamaba tu mejor amigo/a?"

— ANSWER

Charlando

Oscar habla de sus abuelos con sus primos.

Claudio—Oscar, cuéntame como eran mis abuelos. Yo era muy niño cuando ellos murieron.

Oscar—Nuestros abuelos vinieron de la provincia de Lugo, en Galicia. Llegaron después de la guerra civil. Me acuerdo que trabajaban mañana, tarde y noche. El abuelo trabajaba como sastre y la abuela le ayudaba cosiendo en una máquina de coser muy vieja. Así se ganaban la vida. Vivían en un pequeño piso cerca del centro.

Claudio—¿Y por qué vinieron a vivir aquí?

Oscar—Creo que huían de problemas políticos y económicos en España. En aquella época España era muy pobre, aunque ahora es muy próspera.

Claudio—El abuelo tenía dinero. ¿Por qué vivían en ese pequeño piso?

Oscar—No sé, era un hombre modesto. No le gustaba ostentar. Ahorraba todo el dinero para que papá pudiera estudiar. El soñaba con regresar a España. Enviaba mucho dinero a sus hermanas en España para ayudarlas.

María Luisa y su hermana están mirando unas fotos de familia.

Adriana—¿Qué foto es ésta?

María Luisa—Es una foto de cuando te estaban bautizando. Aquí estaban tus padrinos, el tío Alberto y la tía Clara. El cura estaba echándote el agua y cuando te puso los óleos comenzaste a llorar.

Adriana—¿Dónde estaba el tío Luis?

María Luisa—El tío Luis estaba en Vietnam. Él servía como enfermero durante la guerra. Aquí hay una foto de él. Era muy guapo.

Adriana—¿Y quién era esta mujer tan guapa?

Maria Luisa—¿No la conoces? Es la abuela. Se veía tan bien. Aquí estaba cargándote a ti. Tenía un cabello tan largo y tan negro.

Julián y Ernesto están mirando el anuario del colegio de ellos.

Julián—¿Te acuerdas cuando jugábamos fútbol?

Ernesto—Sí, tú siempre tenías el número 13 y yo jugaba con el número 7.

Julián—¿Te acuerdas de esta chica?

Ernesto—Sí, éramos casi novios pero ella se pasaba el tiempo estudiando y yo me pasaba el día divirtiéndome.

Julián—¿Y qué pasó con ella?

Ernesto—Creo que ahora es médico pediatra.

Julián—Tú nunca estudiabas y sin embargo entraste en una buena universidad.

Ernesto—No, Julián, yo jugaba mucho pero yo también estudiaba mucho, por eso sacaba buenas calificaciones.

Cultura

La Familia

La Familia

Una de las instituciones más importantes en la cultura hispana es la familia. La familia hispana es muy unida. Sin embargo el concepto hispano de familia es muy diferente al concepto en otras culturas. La familia está compuesta por el padre, la madre, los abuelos, los tíos, los primos, algunos amigos muy íntimos de la familia, y hasta algunos vecinos. Todos comparten su vivir diario; a veces se ayudan, otras discuten, juegan cartas o dominó, todos dan consejos, celebran fiestas juntos, y en fin forman un pequeño universo. La familia no tiene que ser perfecta, a veces unas tías solteras viven con los padres, al igual que es posible que el padre ni viva ya con el resto de la familia. El divorcio no fue aceptado hasta hace relativamente unos pocos años. Sin embargo siempre han existido las separaciones de matrimonios. Aunque los padres se hayan separado o divorciado, la familia continua existiendo dando apoyo a todos sus miembros. En algunas regiones del mundo hispano, la familia es matriarcal donde la madre ejerce mucha influencia, como por ejemplo en Cataluña. En otras regiones la familia tiende a ser más patriarcal, como en México o Colombia. Las responsabilidades de

cada miembro de la familia cambian de acuerdo al país o a la región donde vivan. Por lo general los abuelos juegan un papel muy importante en la educación de los nietos. Igualmente, el cuidado de los abuelos al final de sus vidas depende de todos los miembros de la familia.

Preguntas

1. ¿Cómo es la familia hispana?
2. ¿Quiénes forman parte de la familia en la cultura hispana?
3. ¿Qué actividades hacen juntos?
4. ¿Son perfectas las familias hispanas?
5. ¿Fue el divorcio siempre aceptado?
6. ¿De dónde es la familia matriarcal?
7. ¿De dónde es la familia patriarcal?
8. ¿Qué hacen los abuelos?
9. ¿Quién cuida de los abuelos cuando están muy ancianos?
10. ¿Es la familia hispana realmente diferente a su familia?

Proverbios

Más vale precaver que tener que lamentar.
Hombre precavido vale por dos.

Capítulo Ocho

El Amor y la Amistad

Monólogos

José Antonio

Voy a comprar un ramo de rosas para mi novia por el Día del Amor y la Amistad. La quiero mucho. Se llama Alicia. Me siento muy feliz con ella. Nos casaremos cuando yo termine mis estudios. Por el momento ella está estudiando también. Para mí, Alicia es la mujer más bella del mundo. Ella terminará la carrera de periodismo en tres años, y yo terminaré ingeniería mecánica dentro de dos años. Antes de casarnos queremos ahorrar algún dinero para comprarnos un pequeño piso en Villalba.

Oscar

Tengo muchos amigos en mi barrio pero este año nos separaremos. Pedro entrará en el ejército. Wilson regresará a Puerto Rico. Miguel ingresará en la marina, y yo iré a una universidad que está muy lejos de aquí. Me gusta mucho jugar al baloncesto con Pedro porque juega muy bien. Miguel juega fútbol mejor que todos, pero mi mejor amigo es Wilson porque con él puedo hablar por horas sobre cualquier asunto. Además es muy simpático y me hace reír mucho.

Lupe

Mi novio Marcos, hace cuatro años que estudia en los Estados Unidos. Lo extraño mucho. Él vendrá a visitarme este verano como lo hace todos los años. Hablamos por teléfono todos los fines de semana. Compramos tarjetas de llamadas y hablamos hasta que el tiempo se acaba. Es una relación muy difícil porque tengo novio y al mismo tiempo no lo tengo. Me gustaría poder salir con otros muchachos pero no puedo. Le quiero mucho. Cuando regrese este verano iremos a Cancún. Me gustaría estar con él pero tengo que terminar mis estudios.

María Luisa

Me reúno frecuentemente con mis amigas para charlar. Somos amigas desde que éramos jóvenes. Nuestros novios también son amigos desde hace mucho tiempo. Ellos también se reúnen de vez en cuando para jugar al béisbol. Muchos de ellos son amigos desde hace muchos años. María José es mi vecina y también una gran amiga. Aquí todos los vecinos nos conocemos bien y nos ayudamos mucho.

Preguntas de los Monólogos

Piense, Pregunte y Conteste

1. ¿Qué le compra José Antonio a su novia por San Valentín?
2. ¿Quién es Alicia?
3. ¿Quieren casarse?
4. ¿Crees que está enamorado José Antonio?
5. ¿Por qué quieren ahorrar dinero?
6. ¿Estarán Oscar y sus amigos juntos este año?
7. ¿Adónde va Wilson?
8. ¿Quién va a la universidad?
9. ¿A qué le gusta jugar mucho a Oscar?
10. ¿Quién es el mejor amigo de Oscar?
11. ¿Lupe y su novio están siempre juntos?
12. ¿Y este verano estarán juntos?

13. ¿Crees que tienen una relación fácil?

14. ¿Cómo se mantienen en contacto?

15. ¿Adónde irán juntos este verano?

16. ¿Qué hace María Luisa frecuentemente?

17. ¿Está casada María Luisa?

18. ¿Qué hacen sus novios cuando se reúnen?

19. ¿Crees que ellos son amigos?

20. ¿Son amigos los vecinos en ese barrio?

Vocabulario

De Lecturas

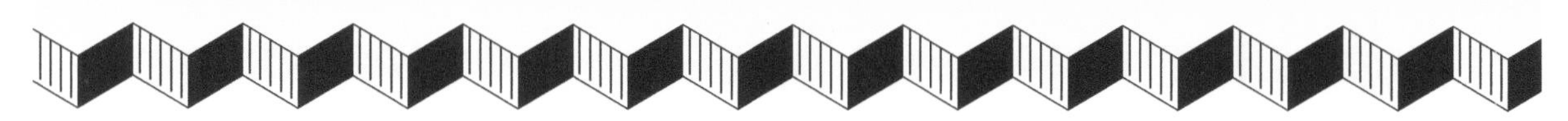

Sustantivos

El abrazo	hug
La amistad	friendship
El asunto	topic
El baloncesto	basketball
El barrio	neighborhood
La carrera	career
Los desconocidos	unknown
El ejército	army
Los empleos	employments
El esposo	husband
La ingeniería mecánica	mechanical engineering
La intimidad	closeness
La juventud	youth
La marina	navy
La mujer	woman/wife
El mundo	world
Los negocios	businesses
El periodismo	jounalism
El piso	apartment/floor
El ramo de rosas	bouquet of roses
El recelo	distrust
Las tarjetas de llamadas	calling cards
La vecina	neighbor
El verano	summer

Verbos

Ahorrar	to save
Ayudar	to help

Caminar	to walk
Casarse	to get married
Charlar	to chat
Compartir	to share
Conceder	to grant
Conservar	to conserve
Emplear	to employ
Entablar	to begin
Esperar	to wait/hope
Extrañar	to miss
Hacer reír	to make someone laugh
Ingresar	to join
Reunirse	to get together
Saludar	to greet
Despedirse	to say goodbye
Sentirse	to feel
Separarse	to part company
Suceder	to happen
Terminar	to end
Vender	to sell
Venir	to come

Adjetivos

Algún	some
Bella	beautiful
Cualquier	any
Difícil	difficult
Feliz	happy
Mayor	older
Pequeño	small
Todos	every

Otras Expresiones

Caminar del brazo	to walk holding each other
Desde hace muchos años	for many years
El Día del Amor y la Amistad	Saint Valentine's Day
Hace cuatro años	four years ago
Hasta con . . .	even with
Hasta que el tiempo se acaba	until there is no more time
Jugar al tute	to play a Spanish card game
Jugar canasta	to play canasta
Jugar cubilete	to play a Spanish dice game
Mal visto	not well received
Por lo tanto	therefore

Gramática

Direct Object Pronouns

The direct object of the verb is the noun that follows the verb and receives the action of such verb. Just as in English, it is easy to distinguish the direct object in a sentence by asking *what* / *qué* or *whom* / *a quién(es)* with the verb.

Luisita quiere estudiar italiano en la universidad.
¿Qué quiere estudiar Luisita? → *italiano* (direct object)

Teresa va a llamar a su hermana. *
¿A quién va a llamar Teresa? → *a su hermana* (direct object)

Notice that a direct object of the verb can be a lifeless object (italiano) or a person (a su hermana).

In order to avoid using the same object noun without repeating it, we often replace it with a direct object pronoun.

Luisita **lo** quiere estudiar en la universidad.
Luisita wants to study ***it*** *at the university.*

Teresa **la** va a llamar.
Teresa is going to call ***her.***

* When the direct object refers to a specific known person, the vowel ***a*** precedes the noun. This is referred to as "*the personal a.*" *The personal a* has no direct translation onto English!

In Spanish, direct object pronouns are the same as reflexive object pronouns with the exception of the third person singular (**lo** / **la**) and the third person plural (**los** / **las**).

Singular		Plural	
me	*me*	nos	*us*
te	*you (fam.)*	os	*you (fam.)*
lo	*him, it, you (form.)*	los	*them, you (form.)*
la	*her, it, you (form.)*	las	*them, you (form.)*

Direct object pronouns are placed in front of any conjugated verb.

¿Dónde están los libros? ¿Los libros? No ***los*** veo.

¿Ves a la profesora? ¿A la profesora? No ***la*** veo.

However, in sentences with back-to-back verbs (one conjugated and the other in the infinitive), the object pronoun may be placed immediately before the conjugated verb, or it may also be attached to the verb in the infinitive.

Teresa va a llamar a su hermana. *Teresa is going to call her sister.*
Teresa ***la*** va a llamar. *Teresa is going to call her.*
Teresa va a llamar***la.***

In progressive constructions (*estar* + *-ando* / *-iendo*), the object pronoun may also precede the conjugated form of *estar,* or it can also be attached to the gerund (*-ando* / *-iendo*). In this case an accent mark must be placed over the vowel preceding the gerund ending.

Estamos leyendo una novela. *We are reading a novel.*
La estamos leyendo. *We are reading it.*
Estamos leyéndo**la.**

Indirect Object Pronouns

The indirect object of the verb is the person / persons *for whom* or *to whom* the action is executed. The forms of the indirect object pronouns are identical to the direct object pronouns with the exception of the third person singular (***le***), and the third person plural (***les***).

¿Quién ***te*** compró el regalo?

Who bought *you* the present?

Singular		Plural	
me	*to / for me*	nos	*to / for us*
te	*to / for you (fam.)*	os	*to / for you (fam.)*
le*	*to / for him, her, it, you (form.)*	les*	*to / for them, you (form.)*

Mi novia **me** compró el regalo.
My girlfriend bought me the present.

Who bought the present *for you*?
My girlfriend bought the present for me.

The position of indirect object pronouns is the same as direct object pronouns. Place them before conjugated verbs:

Le compro la comida. *I buy (you, him, her) food.*
I buy food for (you, him, her).

*Notice that third person singular and plural pronouns do not express gender.

In sentences with back-to-back verbs (one conjugated and the other in the infinitive), the object pronoun may be placed immediately before the conjugated verb, or it may also be attached to the verb in the infinitive.

Te queríamos invitar a la fiesta. *We wanted to invite you to the party.*
Queríamos invitar**te** a la fiesta.

In progressive constructions (*estar* + *-ando* / *-iendo*), the object pronoun may also precede the conjugated form of *estar,* or it can also be attached to the gerund (*-ando* / *-iendo*). Similarly, an accent mark must be placed over the vowel preceding the gerund ending if the indirect object pronoun is attached.

Te estoy diciendo la verdad. *I am telling you the truth.*
Estoy diciéndo***te*** la verdad.

In order to clarify or emphasize the indirect receiver, it is extremely common in Spanish to use a prepositional phrase in conjunction with the indirect object pronoun. Although this would be considered incorrect and redundant in the English language, this construction is grammatically correct in Spanish. The prepositional phrase may be excluded but not the pronoun.

Le compré un regalo *a mi mamá.* *I bought her a present (to my mother).*
Le compré un regalo.

Teresa ***le*** dio un beso *a él.*	*Teresa gave him a kiss.*
Teresa ***le*** dio un beso.	
¿***Me*** vas a decir la verdad *a mí*?	*Are you going to tell me the truth?*
¿***Me*** vas a decir la verdad?	

Use the following prepositional pronouns in combination with their corresponding indirect object pronouns.

me	a mí	nos	a nosotros(as)
te	a ti	os	a vosotros(as)
le	a (él, ella, Ud.)	les	a (ellos, ellas, Uds.)

Double Object Pronouns

If the indirect and direct object pronouns appear in the same sentence, the indirect is placed before the direct. The two pronouns are placed before any conjugated verb or are attached to verbs in the infinitive *-ar*, *-er* or *-ir*, or to the gerund forms "*-ando*" or "*-iendo.*"

Conjugated verb:	¿Las cartas?	¿Te las doy?
	The letters?	*Should I give them to you?*
Infinitive:	¿La tarea?	¿Vas a entregármela?
	The homework?	*Are you going to give it to me?*
Gerund:	¿La cuenta?	Ya estoy preparándotela.
	The check?	*I am already preparing it for you.*

Notice that when the double object pronouns are attached to an infinitive, an accent mark must be placed on the third syllable from the end. If they are attached to a gerund, the accent mark is placed on the fourth syllable.

Also observe that in the second and third example above, the object pronouns may also be placed in front of the conjugated helping verb:

¿La tarea?	¿Me la vas a entregar?
¿La cuenta?	¿Ya te la estoy preparando.

If the indirect object pronouns *le* or *les* appear in front of the direct object pronouns *lo, la los* or *las,* one must change the *le* or *les* to *se.* This is done to avoid the same consecutive phonetic sound.

Le		lo
		la
	→ Se	
Les		los
		las

Vanesa, Verónica y Sofía le compraron un regalo de cumpleaños a su tío Juan
Vanesa, Verónica y Sofía se lo compraron.

Vanesa, Verónica y Sofía bought a birthday present for their uncle Juan.
Vanesa, Verónica y Sofía bought it for him.

The Future Tense

You have already learned a useful expression (***ir*** + a + verb in the infinitive) to create a future activity:

Esta tarde vamos a comer en un restaurante argentino.
This afternoon we are going to eat in an Argentinean restaurant.

Mañana van a salir para Santiago de Chile.
Tomorrow they are going to leave for Santiago de Chile.

There is another way to express future actions in Spanish that corresponds to the common *will* + *verb* in English. It is formed by adding the pattern (**-é, -ás, -á, -emos, -éis, -án**) to the infinitive (*-ar, -er* and *–ir*) of the verb. Note that with the exception of **–emos** all other forms carry an accent mark.

	hablar	**comer**	**escribir**
yo	hablaré	comeré	escribiré
tú	hablarás	comerás	escribirás
él, ella, Ud.	hablará	comerá	escribirá
nosotros(as)	hablaremos	comeremos	escribiremos
vosotros(as)	hablaréis	comeréis	escribiréis
ellos, ellas, Uds.	hablarán	comerán	escribirán

Ellos nos visitarán la semana que viene.
They will visit us next week.

Estudiaré lenguas extranjeras en la universidad.
I will study world languages at the university.

Some useful adverbial expressions of futurity:

mañana
mañana (por la mañana, por la tarde, por la noche)
(la semana, el mes, el año, el verano, el otoño, el invierno, la primavera) que viene
de hoy en cinco días

Los visitaremos el verano que viene.
We will visit them next summer.

Llegarán mañana por la noche.
They will arrive tomorrow night.

Te llamaré en tres días.
I will call you in three days.

Irregular Future Construction

A. Drop the ***ec*** / ***ce*** combinations in the stem for:

decir diré, dirás, dirá, diremos, diréis, dirán
hacer haré, harás, hará, haremos, haréis, harán

B. Drop the vowel ***e*** for:

caber cabré, cabrás, cabrá, cabremos, cabréis, cabrán *(to fit)*
poder podré, podrás, podrá, podremos, podréis, podrán

querer querré, querrás, querrá, querremos, querréis, querrán
saber sabré, sabrás, sabrá, sabremos, sabréis, sabrán

C. Drop either the vowel ***e*** or ***i*** and replace it with a ***d*** for:

poner pondré, pondrás, pondrá, pondremos, pondréis, pondrán
salir saldré, saldrás, saldrá, saldremos, saldréis, saldrán
tener tendré, tendrás, tendrá, tendremos, tendréis, tendrán
venir vendré, vendrás, vendrá, vendremos, vendréis, vendrán
***valer** valdrá, valdrán *(to be worth)* *Most common forms.

The future of **hay** (there is/are) is **habrá** (there will be).

Remember that sometimes the simple present can also be used to indicate a not-distant future action:

Te veo mañana.	*I will see you tomorrow.*
Regreso en cinco minutos.	*I'll be back in five minutes.*

Conjecture or Probability

Spanish also uses the future tense to express probability or conjecture in present time. This construction may take several English expressions: *I wonder, it is probably, it must be,* and so on.

¿Quién será?	*I wonder who it may be.*
Estarán trabajando.	*They are probably working.*
¿Qué hora será?	*I wonder what time it is.*
Serán las tres.	*It must be three o'clock.*

The Conditional Tense

The conditional tense just as in English is used in Spanish to communicate what would or would not take place under certain situations.

Iría con vosotros, pero no puedo porque tengo que trabajar.

I would go with you, but I can't because I have to work.

To form the conditional, add the pattern (**-ía, -ías, -ía, -íamos, -íais, -ían**) to the infinitive form of the verb. Note that the *–ía* pattern is exactly the same used to create the imperfect tense of **-er** and **-ir** verbs. However, in the conditional, the infinitive ending is not dropped.

	hablar	**comer**	**escribir**
yo	hablaría	comería	escribiría
tú	hablarías	comerías	escribirías
él, ella, Ud.	hablaría	comería	escribiría
nosotros(as)	hablaríamos	comeríamos	escribiríamos
vosotros(as)	hablaríais	comeríais	escribiríais
ellos, ellas, Uds.	hablarían	comerían	escribirían

Compraríamos la casa, pero no tenemos suficiente dinero.
We would buy the house, but we don't have enough money,

Jugaría al tenis, pero está lloviendo.
I would play tennis, but it is raining.

Irregular Conditional Construction

The same verbs that had an irregular future will also have the same irregular formation in the conditional.

A. Drop the ***ec*** / ***ce*** combinations in the stem for:

decir diría, dirías, diría, diríamos, diríais, dirían
hacer haría, harías, haría, haríamos, haríais, harían

B. Drop the vowel ***e*** for:

caber cabría, cabrías, cabría, cabríamos, cabríais, cabrían
poder podría, podrías, podría, podríamos, podríais, podrían
querer querría, querrías, querría, querríamos, querríais, querrían
saber sabría, sabrías, sabría, sabríamos, sabríais, sabrían

C. Drop either the vowel ***e*** or ***i*** and replace it with a ***d*** for:

poner pondría, pondrías, pondría, pondríamos, pondríais, pondrían
salir saldría, saldrías, saldría, saldríamos, saldríais, saldrían
tener tendría, tendrías, tendría, tendríamos, tendríais, tendrían
venir vendría, vendrías, vendría, vendríamos, vendríais, vendrían
valer valdría, valdrían

The conditional of **hay** (there is / are) is **habría** (there would be).

Conjecture or Probability

Spanish also uses the conditional tense to express probability or conjecture in past time. This construction may take several English expressions: *I wonder, it was probably, it could have been,* and so on.

¿Quién sería? *I wonder who it was.*
Estarían trabajando. *They were probably working.*
¿Qué hora sería? *I wonder what time it was.*
Serían las tres. *It must have been three o'clock.*

Ejercicios

Diálogos

Matching

A. ¿Crees en el amor a primera vista?

B. ¿Cómo se llama tu novio/a?

C. ¿Crees que te casarás con él/ella?

D. ¿Por qué existe tanto divorcio?

E. ¿Quieres tener hijos?

1. Sí, por lo menos cuatro.

2. Puede ser.

3. Sí, creo en Cupido.

4. No tengo.

5. Porque la gente no se entiende.

Ejercicios de Gramática

A. Los pronombres: Conversacion con tu novio/a sobre el Día de San Valentín. Answer in the affirmative his/her questions, using two pronouns together to avoid repetition.

1. ¿Vas a comprarme bombones?

2. ¿Vas a darme una tarjeta romántica?

3. ¿Le enseñaste mi regalo a tus amigos/as?

4. ¿Cuándo vas a comprarme el anillo de compromiso?

5. ¿Quién te dijo que yo no te compré nada?

B. Conditional tense. Complete the blank spaces with the verb in parentheses in the conditional. Be careful with the irregularities.

1. Mis padres ___________ (comprar) una casa grande, pero no tienen dinero.

2. Los estudiantes ___________ (hacer) la tarea, pero no comprenden.

3. Nosotros ___________ (estudiar) en la Universidad de Princeton, pero es muy cara.

4. Yo ___________ (ir) a Chile todos los veranos, pero no tengo dinero.

5. María Luisa ___________ (ir) a su trabajo en carro, pero no lo tiene.

6. El profesor ___________ (comer) paella, pero no sabe cocinarla.

C. The future tense. Choose the right verb.

1. María Luisa ___________ (comerá, irá, estudiará) toda la lección.

2. El Profesor Gallo ___________ (comprará, beberá, hará) un libro nuevo.

3. La estudiante ___________ (verá, hablará, asistirá) con su hermana.

4. Yo ___________ (saldré, leeré, miraré) al restaurante con Lupe.

5. El Doctor Blanco ___________ (beberá, trabajará, pondrá) café por las mañanas.

6. Los estudiantes___________ (asistirán, podrán, querrán) a sus clases.

D. Escribe en el futuro los siguientes verbos 1-5 y en el condicional 6-10.

1. yo/querer ___________

2. yo/hablar ___________

3. Nosotros/hacer ___________

4. Ellas/dormir ___________

5. Tú/salir ___________

6. nosotros/decir ___________

7. ustedes/poder ___________

8. Tú/escribir ___________

9. Ella/saber ___________

10. Ellos/leer ___________

E. Future tense. Rewrite in the future tense.

1. Yo **voy a hacer** la tarea. ________________
2. Ellos **van a decir** la verdad. ________________
3. Nosotros **vamos a trabajar** mucho. ________________
4. Tú **vas a ir** de vacaciones en enero. ________________
5. Usted **va a salir** de la clase. ________________
6. Ella **va a poder** venir. ________________
7. Nosotros **vamos a saber** qué pasó. ________________
8. Yo **voy a ser** un doctor. ________________
9. Tú **vas a estudiar** mucho. ________________
10. Ustedes **van a venir** mañana. ________________

F. Everyone will give gifts for Valentine's Day. Complete the sentences with the appropriate **indirect object pronoun**.

1. (a Mamá) Angélica ________________ regalará flores.
2. (a ti) Yo ________________ regalaré chocolates.
3. (a mí) Papá ________________ regalará una corbata.
4. (a nosotros) Mamá ______________ regalará unas camisas.
5. (a Angélica y a Beatriz) Tú ________________ regalarás una cesta de fruta.

G. Answer the questions making sure that you change when necessary the underlined **Indirect Object Pronoun** in your answer. (Use the words inside the parentheses as the subject in your answer.)

1. ¿Quién te llamó? (Mi abuela)

____

2. ¿Quiénes nos invitaron a la fiesta? (Josefina y Ricardo)

____

3. ¿Va Ud. a comprarles un regalo de boda *(wedding gift)* a Tomás y a María José?

____

4. ¿Os van a preparar una comida especial? (*Sí*)

____

5. Sra. Martínez, ¿Qué le compró su esposo para su aniversario? *(Alberto)*

____

H. Vamos a hacer una fiesta de San Valentín en casa. Answer the questions your mate is asking you using the **Future Tense** and the appropriate **Direct Object Pronoun**.

1. ¿Vas a comprar las flores? (Sí, mañana)

____s

2. ¿Vas a invitar a tus padres? (Sí, esta tarde)

____

3. ¿Vas a comprar las decoraciones? (Sí, pasado mañana)

____

4. ¿Vas a traer el champán? (Sí, mañana por la mañana)

____

5. ¿Vas a hacer la comida? (Sí, esta noche)

____

I. Traducción. Complete with **Direct** and **Indirect** object pronouns.

1. María wrote it (f) for you (usted form).

   María __________ __________ escribió.

2. María wrote them (f) for us.

   María __________ __________ escribió.

3. María wrote it (m) for you (tú).

   María __________ __________ escribió.

4. María wrote it (m) for me.

María ____________ ____________ escribió.

5. María wrote them (m) for him.

   María ____________ ____________ escribió.

J. You have invited some friends over to see your new house on Valentine's day. Answer their questions using **two pronouns together** to avoid repetition.

1. ¿Vas a enseñarles la casa a José Antonio y a Julián?

   ____

2. ¿Vas a servirnos vino y tapas?

   ____

3. ¿Les enseñaste la piscina a nuestros amigos?

   ____

4. ¿Le enseñaste tu habitación a Beatriz?

   ____

5. ¿Le compraste los muebles a "Muebles Pepe"?

   ____

Drills

A. Conversation with your students. Formal drill:

"Hola (his/her name). ¿Tienes muchos/as amigos/as?"

— ANSWER

"¿Cómo se llama tu novio/a?"

— ANSWER

¿Cuándo te casarás con él/ella?"

— ANSWER

"¿Dónde vivirán?"

— ANSWER

"¿Cuántos hijos tendrán?

—ANSWER

"Tienes muchos planes para tu futuro. ¿Qué harías con un millón de dólares?

— ANSWER

Charlando

Lupe Marcos hablan todos los domingos por teléfono.
Él estudia en los Estados Unidos y ella en la UNAM, en la Ciudad de México.

Lupe—Hola, amor. ¿Cómo estás?

Marcos—Extrañándote mucho. ¿Me quieres todavía?

Lupe—No sé. Estás tan lejos . . . te querría pero estás tan lejos. A veces me canso de esperarte.

Marcos—Quererme no, te pregunto. ¿Me amas? ¿Sí o no?

Lupe—¿Amarte? Tal vez un día . . . cuando pueda verte, tocarte, olerte y escucharte.

Marcos—Eso es imposible ahora. Tengo que estudiar aquí en los Estados Unidos. Yo sí te amo con toda mi alma. Te extraño. Te pienso. Te adoro.

Lupe—Yo te tengo cariño, mucho afecto, estima, aprecio. Me gustas mucho pero quererte o amarte, no lo sé. Eres mi mejor amigo. Un día en el futuro estaremos juntos y podremos ver qué es lo que de verdad siento.

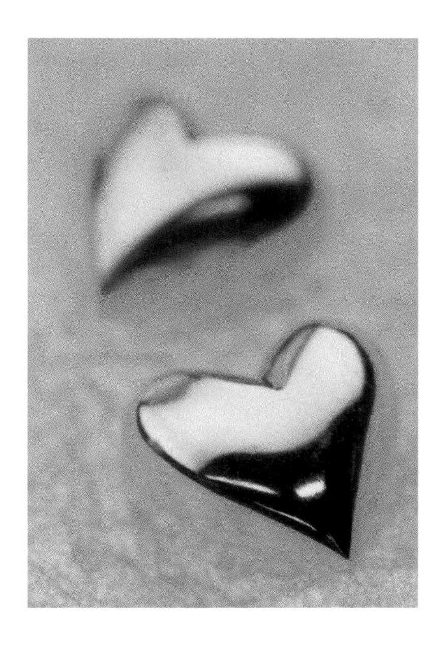

Marcos—Se acaba el tiempo en la tarjeta. Adiós, amor. Te llamaré la semana que viene.

Lupe—Cuídate. Te esperaré. Regresa pronto. Un beso . . . adiós.

Julián invita a su madre a un concierto por el Día de las Madres.

Oscar—Mamá. ¿Vendrás al concierto de David Bisbal conmigo mañana?

Doña Ana—¿Yo? ¿Por qué? Pensé que irías con una de tus amigas.

Oscar—No, Mamá. Te llevaré a ti porque mañana es el Día de las Madres.

Doña Ana—¿Me llevarás a mí? No lo puedo creer. ¿Y que haremos con tu padre?

Oscar—No te preocupes, mamá. papá irá a un partido de fútbol con Manolo Juega el River Plate. Comeremos temprano. Abrirás tus regalos y después cada uno se irá por su lado. Yo te llevaré al concierto de David Bisbal y papá se irá al partido de fútbol. ¿Crees que le gustará el plan?

Doña Ana—Claro, hijo. Estoy muy contenta aunque daría cualquier cosa por que tu padre viniera con nosotros.

Oscar—Bueno, mamá. Eso sería imposible.

Pedro, Oscar y Wilson se reunirán para recibir a Miguel que regresará del entrenamiento militar.

Pedro—Mañana llegará Miguel del campamento. Deberíamos ir a buscarlo. Llegará un poco temprano. Tal vez yo podría ir solo, y después lo traeré a mi casa. Ustedes vendrán un poco más tarde y saldremos a tomarnos unas copas y comeremos en el Café del Mediodía.

Oscar—Yo vendré a tu casa y saldré a tomarme una copa con ustedes pero no podré comer porque comeré con mi familia y después saldré con ellos.

Wilson—Yo no podré venir a tu casa porque tengo algo que hacer pero más tarde me encontraré con ustedes en El Café del Mediodía. ¿De acuerdo?

Cultura

Las Amistades en el Mundo Hispano

El concepto de la amistad en el mundo hispano es diferente al concepto de la amistad en otras culturas. La amistad es muy importante en la cultura hispana. Los amigos son también amigos de la familia. Visitan nuestras casas y entablan una relación con nuestros padres y hasta con nuestros abuelos. Mientras que en otras culturas los amigos son para actividades específicas, como para practicar un deporte, en el mundo hispano las amistades son como una extensión de la familia. Por lo tanto se comparte con ellos los eventos importantes y también el vivir diario. Las amistades se conservan a través del tiempo y la distancia. Cuando un hombre y una mujer se casan, cada uno conserva sus amigos de juventud. Se espera mucho de un amigo por lo que a veces se piden y se conceden muchos favores, y se espera una gran tolerancia mutua. Existe un recelo con respecto a los desconocidos por lo que existe una tendencia a hacer negocios con amigos o personas recomendadas por los amigos. Lo mismo sucede con los empleos, ya que existe una preferencia por emplear solamente a personas conocidas o recomendadas por los amigos. Aunque existe una gran intimidad con los amigos, también existe un gran respeto y una gran discreción. La casa y la familia son muy respetadas por lo que no es usual el organizar reuniones para venderles productos a las amistades. Eso

está muy mal visto. En muchos países hispanos, las amigas caminan del brazo unas de otras, y entre los amigos el tradicional abrazo nunca falta al saludarse o al despedirse.

Preguntas

1. ¿Cómo es el concepto de la amistad en la cultura hispana?
2. ¿Qué relación mantienen los amigos con la familia?
3. ¿Qué actividades hacen los amigos juntos?
4. ¿Duran mucho usualmente las amistades?
5. ¿Qué pasa cuando un hombre y una mujer se casan con respecto a sus amigos?
6. ¿Qué se espera de un amigo?
7. ¿Por qué prefieren hacer negocios con los conocidos?
8. ¿A quiénes dan empleos?
9. ¿Cómo caminan las amigas por la calle?
10. ¿Cómo se saludan los hombres que son amigos?

Proverbios

Al amigo lo escojo yo, al pariente no.
El que a buen árbol se arrima, buena sombra le cobija.

Poesía

Poesía de Manuel Acuña,
(1849–1873) posiblemente el más famoso escritor
mexicano del período romántico. Estas son sólo
tres estrofas de diez.

Nocturno a Rosario

¡Pues bien! Yo necesito
decirte que te adoro,
decirte que te quiero
con todo el corazón;
que es mucho lo que sufro,
que es mucho lo que añoro,
que ya no puedo tanto,
y al grito en que te imploro
te imploro y te hablo en nombre
de mi última ilusión.

II

Yo quiero que tú sepas
Que ya hace muchos días
Estoy enfermo y pálido
De tanto no dormir;
Que ya se han muerto todas
Las esperanzas mías,
Que son mis noches negras,
Tan negras y sombrías,
Que ya no sé ni dónde
Se alza el porvenir.

....

I

Comprendo que tus besos
Jamás han de ser míos,
Comprendo que en tus ojos
No me he de ver jamás,
Y te amo y en mis locos
Y ardientes desvaríos
Bendigo tus desdenes,
Adoro tus desvíos,
Y en vez de amarte menos,
Te quiero mucho más.

Capítulo Nueve

Los Deportes

Monólogos

José Antonio

Me gusta jugar al baloncesto. Es muy popular aquí en España ahora. Mi primo Diego juega mejor que yo porque él es más alto. Yo juego al fútbol mejor que él porque soy más rápido. Tengo muy buenos reflejos y a veces juego como portero, pero yo prefiero jugar como delantero. La última vez que jugamos en el colegio metí tres goles. Diego reacciona rápidamente cuando el entrenador está presente, pero cuando el entrenador no nos está observando él no presta atención. Yo creo que mi primo Diego es el tipo más perezoso del mundo.

Julián (El novio de María Luisa)

Lo mío es el béisbol. Me gusta jugar en primera base porque es el sitio más movido en el cuadrilátero. Rubén juega béisbol tan bien como yo. Él es el mejor lanzador que he conocido aunque no es tan fuerte como yo. Pertenecemos a una liga juvenil. En nuestro último partido, en el último tiempo Rubén lanzó la pelota sorpresivamente con gran precisión. Por eso ganamos rompiendo el empate seis a cinco. Para ser un buen lanzador hay que practicar mucho y saber calentar el brazo.

María Luisa

Mi sueño es ser una nadadora olímpica aunque sé que es un sueño dificilísimo de alcanzar. Tenemos una piscinita en casa y yo nado todas las tardes cuando regreso del colegio. También practico en la Venetian Pool que es una piscina pública que está a siete cuadras de mi casa en Coral Gables, porque es más grande y más bonita que la piscina que tenemos en la casa. Mi amiga Loli y yo estamos siguiendo un curso de clavados en la piscina de la Universidad de Miami. Tienen varios trampolines pero el más alto me da mucho miedo porque es altísimo.

Beatriz (una amiga colombiana de Lupe)

Mi abuelo tiene una finca a 30 kilómetros de Bogotá. Mi hermana Pilar y yo vamos a la finca del abuelo a montar a caballo todos los fines de semana. Mi caballo es menos brioso que el de Pilar pero es más obediente que Saltarín, el caballo de ella. Son caballos de paso muy costosos que el abuelo compró en una subasta. El abuelo también tiene caballos de paso nadadores. A mi mamá le gusta montar los caballos de paso nadadores porque son muy fáciles de cabalgar. Pilar ha ganado ocho premios de equitación con Saltarín.

Preguntas de los Monólogos

Piense, Pregunte y Conteste

1. ¿Qué deporte le gusta a José Antonio?
2. ¿Por qué juega mejor Diego?
3. ¿A qué deporte le gusta jugar a José Antonio?
4. ¿Juega Diego bien al fútbol?
5. ¿Cree José Antonio que Diego es un gran deportista?
6. ¿Qué deporte le gusta a Julián?
7. ¿Quién juega mejor, Julián o Rubén?
8. ¿A qué liga pertenecen?
9. ¿Ganaron o perdieron el último partido?
10. ¿Qué necesitas para ser un buen lanzador?
11. ¿Cuál es el sueño de María Luisa?
12. ¿Crees que le gusta nadar a ella?

13. ¿Por qué?

14. ¿Dónde vive ella?

15. ¿Qué curso siguió con su prima?

16. ¿Dónde vive el abuelo de Beatriz?

17. ¿Cómo se llama el caballo de la hermana de Beatriz?

18. ¿Es un caballo ganador el de la hermana de Beatriz?

19. ¿Por qué lo sabes?

20. ¿Qué tipo de caballos le gustan a mi mamá?

Vocabulario

De Lectura

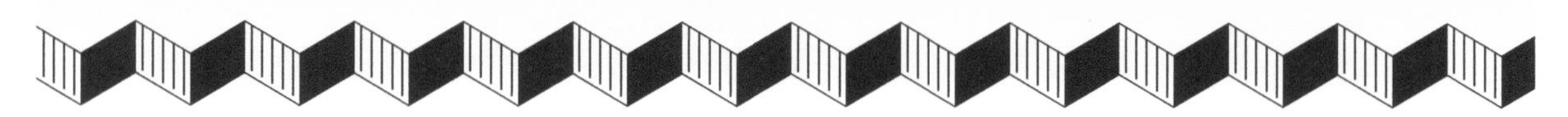

Sustantivos

El abuelo	grandfather
El atletismo	gymnastic
El baloncesto	basketball
El brazo	arm
Los caballos de paso	Paso horse
Los campeonatos	championships
Los ciclistas	cyclists
Los clavados	diving
El colegio	school
Las corridas de toros	bullfights
Las cuadras	city blocks
El cuadrilátero	baseball diamond / home run
La danza	dance
El delantero	forward (in soccer)
Los deportes	sports
Empate	tie
Equipos	team
La equitación	horse racing
La finca	ranch
Culturismo	bodybuilding
Los goles	goals
Los hipódromos	racetracks
Los jinetes	jockeys
El lanzador	pitcher
La mano	hand
Las medallas	medals
El montañismo	mountain climbing
Los nadadores	swimmers
Los países	countries

El partido	game
La pelota	ball
La piscinita	small swimming pool
El portero	goalie
Los premios	awards
El primo	cousins
Los reflejos	reflexes
El senderismo	hiking
La subasta	auction
El sueño	dream
El tipo	person (slang)
Los torneos	championships
Trampolines	diving boards
Vela	sailing

Verbos

Alcanzar	to reach
Cabalgar	to horseback ride
Calentar	to warm up
Creer	to believe
Destacar	to distinguish
Ganar	to win
Lanzar	to throw
Nacer	to be born
Montar	to ride
Parecer	to appear
Pertenecer	to belong
Reaccionar	to react
Regresar	to return
Romper	to break

Adjetivos

Altísimo	very high
Brioso	vigorous
Costosos	costly
Dificilísimo	very hard
Fáciles	easy
Fuerte	strong
Juvenil	related to youth
Mayor(es)	older
Mejor(es)	better
Numerosas	numerous
Perezoso	lazy
Rápido	fast
Último	last

Otras Expresiones

Al igual	equally
Aunque	although
Campeonatos mundiales	world championship
Dar miedo	to create fear
Las Grandes Ligas	Baseball Major League
Llegar a ser	to become
Meter goles	to score goals
Prestar atención	to pay attention
Seguir un curso	to take a course
Sitio más movido	busy place
Sobretodo	specially
Sorpresivamente	surprisingly

Gramática

Comparisons of Inequality

English uses *more than / less than* to express unequal comparisons. In most cases Spanish uses **más + (adjective / adverb / noun) + que** or **menos + adjective / adverb / noun + que** to convey the same condition:

Teresa es más simpática que Elena.
Teresa is nicer than Elena.

Los aviones son más rápidos que los trenes.
Planes are faster than trains.

Miguel tiene más dinero que Jacinto.
Miguel has more money than Jacinto.

Joselito es menos atlético que Julio.
Joselito is less athletic than Julio.

Tu apartamento tiene menos cuartos que el mío.
Your apartment has less rooms than mine.

The preposition **de** replaces **que** when making comparisons with numbers except in negative statements:

Tengo menos de quince dólares en mi cuenta de ahorros.
I have less than fifteen dollars in my savings account.

Necesito más de treinta minutos.
I need more than thirty minutes.

The following adjectives have irregular forms in the comparative and, consequently, are not formed with **más** or **menos.**

bueno	**mejor(es)**	*better*
malo	**peor(es)**	*worse*
viejo*	**mayor(es)**	*older*
joven*	**menor(es)**	*younger*

Marta es mayor que Leonardo pero es menor que Sarita.
Marta is older than Leonardo but she is younger than Sarita.

En inglés recibo mejores notas que en ciencias.
I get better grades in English than in Science.

*The irregular forms of *viejo* or *joven* are in general used in describing people. Use **más viejo(a) que** or **menos viejo(a) que** when describing places or things.

Mi casa es más vieja que tu casa.
My house is older than your house.

Mejor and **peor** are also used as the comparative forms of the adverbs **bien** and **mal:**

Me siento peor que ayer.
I feel worse than yesterday.

Pero mañana me sentiré mejor.
But tomorrow I will feel better.

Superlative Forms

Superlatives are used to indicate the maximum or the minimum levels of value such as the greatest or the worst. Spanish uses the definite article **(el / la / los / las) + más** or **menos + (adjective / adverb) + de.**

Rosa es la más alta de la familia.
Rosa is the tallest in the family.

Ellos son los menos agresivos del grupo.
They are the least aggressive in the group.

When a noun is included in the superlative, the article is placed in front of the noun.

Casa Gallo es el restaurante cubano más auténtico de Miami.
Casa Gallo is the most authentic Cuban restaurant in Miami.

El desayuno es la comida más importante del día.
Breakfast is the most important meal in the day.

El golf es el deporte más aburrido.
Golf is the most boring sport.

The adjectives **bueno, malo, joven,** and **viejo** also have irregular forms in the superlative.

bueno	**el / la mejor**	**los / las mejores**	*the best*
malo	**el / la peor**	**los / las peores**	*the worst*
viejo*	**el / la mayor**	**los/ las mayores**	*the oldest*
joven*	**el / la menor**	**los/ las menores**	*the youngest*

Mi abuela es la mayor de la familia.
My grandmother is the oldest in the family.

Casa Gallo prepara la mejor comida cubana de Miami.
Casa Gallo prepares the best Cuban food in Miami.

*Same as in the comparison, the irregular forms of **viejo** or **joven** are in general used in describing people. Use **el / la más viejo(a) de** or **los / las menos viejos(as) de** when describing places or things.

El Viejo San Juan tiene las casas más viejas de Puerto Rico.
Old San Juan has the oldest houses in Puerto Rico.

Comparisons of Equality

To express comparisons of equality *as . . . as* with adjectives and adverbs, Spanish uses **tan . . . como.**

Lola es tan simpática como Julia.
Lola is as nice as Julia.

Mi tío Pepe es tan gracioso como mi tía Francisca.
My uncle Pepe is as funny as my aunt Francisca.

Los trenes no son tan rápidos como los aviones.
Trains are not as fast as planes.

Inés baila tan bien como Blanquita.
Inés dances as well as Blanquita.

For comparisons of equality of nouns *as much . . . as / as many . . . as,* use **tanto / tanta / tantos / tantas . . . como.**

Los González tienen tanto dinero como los García.
Mr. and Mrs. González have as much money as Mr. and Mrs. García.

En ese restaurante venden tantos tacos como enchiladas.
In that restaurant they sell as many tacos as enchiladas.

It is also possible to make a comparison of equality with verbs by using this structure: **verb + tanto como.**

Rosita come tanto como su hermano.
Rosita eats as much as her brother.

Estos estudiantes estudian tanto como esos estudiantes.
These students study as much as those students.

The Absolute Superlative

The suffix **–ísimo(s) / -ísima(s)** may be added to adjectives to imply "extremely." If the adjective ends in a consonant, add the correct form of **-ísimo** to the singular form of the adjective.

popular *popularísimo, popularísimos, popularísima, popularísimas*
difícil *dificilísimo, dificilísimos, dificilísima, dificilísimas*

However, if the adjective ends in a vowel, drop the vowel before adding the proper **–ísimo** ending.

alto *altísimo, altísimos, altísima, altísimas*

Jose es altísimo.	*Jose y Guillermo son altísimos.*
María es altísima.	*Berta y Lupe son altísimas.*
rico	*riquísimo, riquísimos, riquísima, riquísimas*
Tomás es riquísimo.	*Tomás y Dorotea son riquísimos.*
Lourdes es riquísima.	*Lourdes y Dora son riquísimas.*

Augmentatives and Diminutives

Spanish uses the endings **–ón** / **-ones** / **-ona** / **-onas** to refer to a larger size of a given noun. Augmentatives also may imply a derogatory connotation. Observe the following:

muchacho	**muchachón**	*big boy*
muchachones	**muchachones**	*big boys*

The diminutive ending **–ito** refers to a smaller scale of a specified noun. It is also used to express a complimentary quality of a noun. Observe:

perra	**perrita**	*sweet little female dog*
mesa	**mesita**	*small table*
abuelo	**abuelito**	*delightful grandfather*

If the noun ends in **–n** / **-r** or **–e**, use the ending **–cito.**

león	**leoncito**	*cute little lion*
tren	**trencito**	*little train*
café	**cafecito**	*small cup of coffee*

The Ending "-mente"

The suffix "-mente" corresponds to the English "-ly" ending. To form this adverbial form, add "-mente" to the feminine form of an adjective.

Difícil	difícilmente	General	generalmente
Popular	popularmente	Fácil	fácilmente
Cierto	ciertamante	Básico	basicamente
Triste	tristemente	Normal	normalmente
Valiente	valientemente	Real	realmente
		Necesario	necesariamente

Manolo es un muchacho muy cortés.
Cortésmente, él saludó al profesor.

Manolo is a very courteous boy.
Courteously, he greeted the professor.

Mandatos Formales

Formal Commands

Commands are used to tell people what to do or not to do. Spanish uses two distinct forms: informal or familiar commands (tú / vosotros), and formal commands (Ud. / Uds.) In this chapter we will learn to form and use formal commands.

Regular affirmative and negative Ud. and Uds. commands:

These commands are formed by adding the opposite third person singular and plural endings used to form the present indicative tense. In other words, *-ar* verbs will use the "*–e*" and *–en*" endings, while the *–er* and *–ir* verbs will apply the "*–a*" and "*–an*" endings. Remember that the use of any subject pronoun is not required in Spanish; however, if one chooses to include it, its position will be behind the verb.

Infinitive	comprar	comer	escribir
Command	(no) compre Ud. (no) compren Uds.	(no) coma Ud. (no) coman Uds.	(no) escriba Ud. (no) escriban Uds.

Sr. Campos, hable más alto. — *Mr. Campos, speak louder.*
Srta. Franco, comparta la comida. — *Miss Franco, share the food.*
Dr. Iglesias, no discuta más. — *Dr. Iglesias, don't argue any more.*

Sr. Díaz y Sra. Díaz, no asistan a la reunión.
Mr. and Mrs. Díaz, do not attend the reunion.

If a verb had an irregularity in the stem of the "yo" form of the present indicative, that irregularity will continue in the formal affirmative and/or negative commands.

decir	**diga**	**digan**	**no diga**	**no digan**
hacer	**haga**	**hagan**	**no haga**	**no hagan**
poner	**ponga**	**pongan**	**no ponga**	**no pongan**
salir	**salga**	**salgan**	**no salga**	**no salgan**
tener	**tenga**	**tengan**	**no tenga**	**no tengan**
venir	**venga**	**vengan**	**no venga**	**no vengan**
conducir	**conduzca**	**conduzcan**	**no conduzca**	**no conduzcan**
traer	**traiga**	**traigan**	**no traiga**	**no traigan**
ver	**vea**	**vean**	**no vea**	**no vean**

Boot verbs will show the same orthographic changes in formal affirmative as well as in negative commands:

almorzar	o>ue	**almuerce**	**almuercen**	**no almuerce**	**no almuercen**
jugar	u>ue	**juegue**	**jueguen**	**no juegue**	**no jueguen**
cerrar	e>ie	**cierre**	**cierren**	**no cierre**	**no cierren**
volver	o>ue	**vuelva**	**vuelvan**	**no vuelva**	**no vuelvan**
mentir	e>ie	**mienta**	**mientan**	**no mienta**	**no mientan**
pedir	e>i	**pida**	**pidan**	**no pida**	**no pidan**

An easy way to remember how to form regular formal commands, follow these steps:

1) Go to the "**yo**" form of the present indicative

2) Drop the "*–o*" ending

3) Switch the command endings:

-**ar** verbs	> *-e*	*-en*
-**er** / -**ir** verbs	> *-a*	*-an*

Irregular formal commands:

The following verbs have irregular formal commands. They must be learned individually:

Ser	**sea**	**sean**	**no sea**	**no sean**
Ir	**vaya**	**vayan**	**no vaya**	**no vayan**
Dar	**dé**	**den**	**no dé**	**no den**
Saber	**sepa**	**sepan**	**no sepa**	**no sepan**

Profesor Freyre, no sea tan exigente.	*Profesor Freyre, don't be so demanding.*
Doña Luisa, vaya a la ceremonia.	*Doña Luisa, go to the ceremony.*
Señores, den más dinero.	*Gentlemen, give more money.*

Position of object pronouns with commands:

Object pronouns are attached to affirmative commands, but they precede negative commands. In affirmative commands, an accent mark is required on the third syllable from the end with single object pronouns; an accent mark is required on the fourth syllable with double object pronouns. (In monosyllabic commands, there is no need for accent marks.)

Búsquelo Ud.	*Look for it.*
Cómprenlos Uds.	*Buy them.*
Dígamelo.	*Say it to me.*
Hágalo.	*Do it.*
Delo	*Give it.*

No le diga eso.	*Don't tell him that.*
No lo hagan.	*Don't do it.*
No se lo repita.	*Don't repeat it to him.*
No me lo dé	*Don't give it to me.*

Ejercicios

Diálogos

Matching

A. ¿A qué deporte te gusta jugar más?

B. ¿Te gusta más el fútbol o el baloncesto?

C. ¿Practicaste el tenis últimamente?

D. ¿Cuál es tu deportista favorito?

E. ¿Qué opinas del golf? ¿Es aburrido?

1. Me gusta Rafa Nadal mucho.

2. No lo creo. Pero no lo practico.

3. Me gusta el fútbol más.

4. No, tengo mi raqueta rota.

5. Al fútbol.

Ejercicios de Gramática

A. Comparaciones de desigualdad. Compare con ". . . más que . . . " o ". . . menos que . . .". Usted elige la que desee. Acuérdese: use "tener" para comparar nombres y "ser/estar" para adjetivos.

1. Oscar / dinero / María Luisa.

____

2. Julián / inteligente / Lupe.

____

3. El Profesor Gallo / libros / el Dr. Blanco.

____

4. Mi hermano / guapo / tu hermano.

____

5. Mi novio(a) / bueno(a) / tu novio(a).

____

B. Comparaciones de igualdad. Compare con "tan/tanto(a) / tantos (as)" en las siguientes frases.

1. Mis padres son ____________ buenos como tus padres.
2. El estudiante tiene ____________ paciencia como el profesor.
3. Nosotras somos ____________ inteligentes como ellas.
4. Tu hermana tiene un coche ____________ bueno como el de Oscar.
5. María Luisa tiene ____________ dinero como Julián.
6. El Profesor Saborido tiene ____________ libros como el Profesor Gallo.

C. Escriba dos frases comparando con ". . . más que . . .", dos con ". . . menos que . . ." y dos con ". . . "tan . . . como."

1. ____.
2. ____.
3. ____.
4. ____.
5. ____.
6. ____.

D. Escriba los adverbios a partir de los siguientes adjetivos.

1. Fácil ____________
2. Rápido ____________
3. Necesario ____________
4. General ____________
5. Básico ____________
6. Lógico ____________
7. Exacto ____________
8. Tranquilo ____________
9. Inteligente ____________
10. Estúpido ____________

E. You are going to play sports. Give **formal commands** as indicated.

1. Traer el balón de fútbol / usted

   ____

2. Comprar una pelota de baloncesto / ustedes

   ____

3. No olvidar el casco de béisbol / usted

   ____

4. Ponerse el uniforme del equipo / ustedes

   ____

5. Entrenar para el partido / usted

   ____

F. **Un juego importante de fútbol.** Beatriz is nervous about tomorrow's soccer game. Complete the sentences with **formal commands** that Beatriz is giving to the coach.

1. No ________________ (olvidar) los uniformes.
2. ________________ (traer) los balones nuevos.
3. ________________ (comprar) refrescos para el equipo.
4. ________________ (poner) botas extras en la bolsa.
5. ________________ (decirme) lo que tengo que hacer.

Drills

A. Conversation with your students. Formal drill:

"¿Te gusta practicar deportes?"

— ANSWER

"¿Cuál es el que más te gusta ver en la tele?"

— ANSWER

"¿Y el que más te gusta practicar?"

— ANSWER

"¿Estás en algún equipo (team) en la universidad?"

— ANSWER

"¿Qué te gusta más, el béisbol o el fútbol americano?"

—ANSWER

"¿Cuál es tu deportista favorito?"

— ANSWER

Charlando

Julián y Rubén planean un partido de béisbol con unos amigos.

Julián—Este domingo nos vamos a reunir con nuestros compañeros en el parque de la calle 78 para jugar un partido de béisbol.

Rubén—Tenemos que invitar a Carlos, a Pepe, a Fernando y a los hermanos Ochoa. Tú eres el mejor lanzador de todos, pero yo corro tan rápido como Pepe.

Julián—Sí, es verdad. Carlos al bate es mejor que Fernando. Él siempre mete un par de cuadriláteros en todos los partidos.

Rubén—Yo voy a llevar un par de bates y varias pelotas. Cada cual llevará su guante.

Julián—Yo llevaré unas empanadas y algo de beber.

Rubén—¿Llamarás a los chicos de ingeniería con la hora exacta?

Julián—Si, los llamaré y les diré que nos reuniremos a las cuatro de la tarde.

José Antonio y su primo Diego planean ir a un partido de fútbol en el Santiago Bernabeu en Madrid.

Diego—¿Tienes ya los boletos para el partido del sábado?

José Antonio—Pues claro. Juega el Real Madrid con el Deportivo La Coruña. Menuda paliza que le pegarán los madridistas a los gallegos.

Diego—No lo creas, porque el Deportivo está jugando mejor que el Real Madrid.

José Antonio—Mira, te iba a dejar llevar mi bandera y mi camiseta del Real, pero por lo que veo no eres muy leal. Además, si le fueras al Barca, lo comprendería, pero al Deportivo, si es el peor equipo de La Liga.

Diego—El peor es el Sporting de Santander. Esos son tan malos como el Betis.

José Antonio—Nuestros jugadores son los mejores del mundo y nuestro equipo es el más rico del mundo.

Diego—Sí, ganan mucho dinero. Todos son estrellas pero no juegan tan bien.

Beatriz y su amiga Pilar van a un partido demostración de tenistas famosas.

Beatriz—Te tengo un regalo de cumpleaños fenomenal. Vamos a ir a ver a Arantxa Sánchez Vicario, a Conchita Martínez, a Mary Jo Fernández y a Gabriela Sabatini. ¿Qué te parece?

Pilar—No lo puedo creer. Lo único que nos faltaría sería a Venus, Serena y Anna Kournikova.

Beatriz—Venus y Serena no vendrán pero Anna Kournikova vendrá con su novio, Enrique Iglesias. Será un espectáculo fantástico.

Pilar—Todas juegan muy bien y son campeonas de tenis. Arantxa juega tan bien como Conchita aunque tienen estilos diferentes.

Beatriz—Te imaginas que maravilla será el ver a las mejores jugadoras de tenis del mundo.

Cultura

Los Deportes en el Mundo Hispano

Los Deportes en el Mundo Hispano

Los deportes, la danza, el atletismo, la gimnasia y las corridas de toros son una parte muy importante de la cultura hispana. Sin embargo, aunque todas estas actividades son muy populares en todos los pueblos hispanos, por lo general son menos organizadas que en otros países. Son por lo general actividades espontáneas del pueblo. Los niños en el Caribe parece que nacen con un bate y una pelota en la mano, y llegan a ser grandes jugadores de béisbol. Un gran número de jugadores en Las Grandes Ligas vienen del Caribe hispano. El fútbol es uno de los deportes más populares en España y en Ibero-América. El Real Madrid es uno de los mejores equipos de fútbol en el mundo, al igual que el River Plate en Argentina. Equipos hispanos han ganado numerosos campeonatos mundiales. Algunos países como Cuba y España han ganado numerosas medallas en las Olimpiadas. Jugadores mexicanos, chilenos, argentinos y españoles se han destacado en torneos de tenis. Hay famosos jinetes en casi todos los países latino-americanos y también grandes hipódromos. Los ciclistas colombianos y españoles se destacan en rutas montañosas. El esquí se practica en países como Argentina, Chile y España. Montañismo, senderismo, baloncesto, balón mano, golf, culturismo, natación, vela, atletismo y muchos otros deportes se practican en toda Hispano-América.

Las corridas de toros todavía tienen algunos adeptos, sobretodo entre las personas mayores en España, Colombia, México y el Perú.

Preguntas

1. ¿Cómo se organizan los deportes en los pueblos hispanos?
2. ¿Qué deporte practican mayormente en El Caribe?
3. ¿Quiénes juegan en las Grandes Ligas?
4. ¿Qué deporte es el más popular en España?
5. ¿Qué equipos de fútbol son famosos en todo el mundo?
6. ¿Qué países han ganado muchas medallas en las olimpiadas?
7. ¿Qué ciclistas son famosos?
8. ¿Dónde se practica el esquí?
9. ¿Qué deportes también se practican en Ibero-América?
10. ¿Dónde tienen corridas de toros?

Proverbios

Mente sana en cuerpo sano.
Quien mucho abarca poco aprieta.

Capítulo Diez

Guía del Ocio

Monólogos

Julián

Nueva York es la ciudad que nunca duerme. En esta ciudad hay tanto que ver que nunca termino de verlo todo. Tampoco hay tiempo de ver nada aquí. Esa es la triste realidad. Cuando mis primos vienen de Puerto Rico me dicen, "Julián, llévame al Museo Metropolitano o sácanos a pasear". Lamentablemente, casi siempre tengo que contestarles que este no es un buen momento porque tengo mucho que trabajar y estudiar.

José Antonio

Madrid es la ciudad más divertida e interesante del mundo. En esto, todo el mundo está de acuerdo, por eso es que vienen tantos turistas a ver este museo, ese palacio o aquel monumento. Los turistas americanos siempre me dicen cuando paso por La Plaza Mayor, "¿Quieres tomarnos una foto, por favor?" Madrid está llena de restaurantes excelentes, bares, discotecas, cafés, teatros, conciertos, charlas, galerías de arte, parques de diversiones, salas de fiesta y muchas otras cosas que hacer.

Lupe

Ven a México y verás lo maravilloso que es esto. No creas que soy patriotera. He viajado mucho y esta tierra es maravillosa. Hay tanto que hacer y ver en este país. Tenemos las mejores playas. Debes venir estas vacaciones. Trae a tus amigos. Visita

Acapulco o vete a Isla Mujeres. Tienes que ver las pirámides en Teotihuacán. Pasea por los Jardines de Chapultepec o escucha a los mariachis en La Plaza Garibaldi. Prueba unas quesadillas o unos huevos rancheros en uno de los numerosos restaurantes en el DF. Visita el Museo de Antropología o la Plaza de las Tres Culturas. La ciudad de México está llena de sitios interesantes. No te la pierdas.

Beatriz

Hay tanto que hacer en Colombia que si nos visitas, te encantará. Tienes que verlo por ti mismo. Abraza esta tierra llena de esmeraldas, orquídeas y café, llena de volcanes y playas maravillosas. Bogotá es una ciudad muy culta donde la gente frecuenta obras de teatro, galerías de arte, museos y conciertos. También tiene una plaza de toros y el Campin, el estadio de fútbol. Cuando vengas disfruta de todo lo que esta zona te puede dar. No te arrepentirás.

Preguntas de los Monólogos

Piense, Pregunte y Conteste

1. ¿Es Julián una persona ocupada?
2. ¿Qué le dicen a Julián sus primos cuando lo visitan?
3. ¿Qué les contesta Julián?
4. ¿Es usted una persona ocupada también?
5. ¿Por qué?
6. ¿Le gusta Madrid a José Antonio?
7. ¿Qué visitan los turistas en Madrid?
8. ¿Qué le dicen los turistas americanos a José Antonio?
9. ¿Piensa usted que Madrid es una ciudad interesante?
10. ¿Por qué?
11. ¿Piensas que Lupe es patriotera?
12. ¿Por qué piensa Lupe que México es maravilloso?

13. ¿Qué puedes comer en los restaurantes del DF?

14. ¿Qué sitios interesantes tiene el DF?

15. ¿Qué te gustaría visitar de México?

16. ¿Qué puedes encontrar en Colombia?

17. ¿Dónde está Colombia?

18. ¿Qué te gustaría hacer en Colombia?

19. ¿Cuál de los cuatro lugares (places), te gustaría visitar?

20. ¿Por qué razón o razones?

Vocabulario

De Lecturas

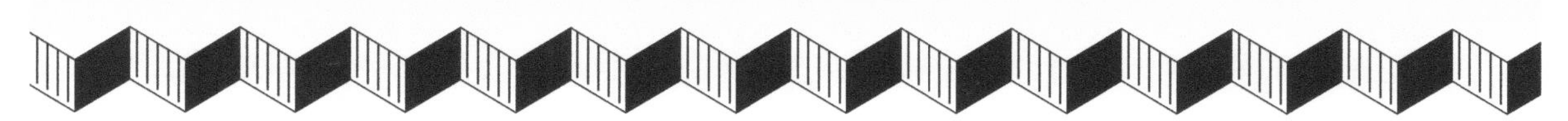

Sustantivos

La alegría	happiness
Los alrededores	surroundings
El entretenimiento	entertainment
Las esmeraldas	emeralds
La espontaneidad	spontaneity
La horchata	beverage made from barley and almond
Las orquídeas	orchids
Los parques de diversiones	amusement parks
La patriotera	exaggeratedly patriotic
Los pintores	artists
La plaza de toros	bull ring
La realidad	truth
Las salas de fiesta	ballrooms
La tierra	land
La variedad	variety

Verbos

Abrazar	to hug
Arrepentirse	to repent
Caracterizar	to characterize
Deber	should
Disfrutar	to enjoy
Dormir	to sleep
Encantar	to love
Encontrar	to find
Existir	to exist
Frecuentar	to frequent
Ofrecer	to offer

Pasear	to stroll
Patinar	to skate
Perder	to miss
Probar	to taste
Regalar	to give (as a gift)
Reunirse	to get together
Sobresalir	to excel
Viajar	to travel

Adjetivos

Concurridos	well attended
Divertida	enjoyable
Interesados	interested
Llena de	full of
Maravillosa	wonderful
Menos	less
Numerosos	numerous
Tantos	so many
Triste	sad

Otras Expresiones

Estar de acuerdo	to be in agreement
Lamentablemente	unfortunately
Sacar a pasear	to take someone for a walk
Tanto que hacer	so much to do
Tomar fresco	to get fresh air

Gramática

Familiar Commands

Commands are used to tell people what to do or not to do. Spanish uses two distinct forms: informal or familiar commands (**tú** / **vosotros**) and formal commands (**Ud.** / **Uds.**). In this chapter we will only learn to form and use familiar singular commands.

Regular Affirmative Tú Commands

These commands have the same form as the third person singular form of the present indicative (**él** / **ella** / **Ud.**) but instead are now used with the personal pronoun **tú.** Remember that the use of any subject pronoun is not required in Spanish; however, if one chooses to include it, its position will be behind the verb.

Infinitive	comprar	comer	escribir
Command	**compra (tú)**	**come (tú)**	**escribe (tú)**

Miguelito, estudia la lección.
Miguelito, study the lesson.

Rosita, come más frutas.
Rosita, eat more fruits.

Boot verbs will show the same orthographic changes in familiar affirmative commands:

almorzar	**o > ue**	**almuerza**
jugar	**u > ue**	**juega**
cerrar	**e > ie**	**cierra**
pedir	**e > i**	**pide**

Irregular Affirmative Commands

decir	**di**
hacer	**haz**

ir	**ve**
poner	**pon**
salir	**sal**
ser	**sé**
tener	**ten**
venir	**ven**

Negative Tú Commands

These commands have a totally different construction from the affirmative forms. To form regular negative commands, follow the following steps:

1. Go to the **yo** form of the present indicative.
2. Drop the *–o* ending.
3. Switch the command endings:

   -**ar** verbs > *-es*
   -**er** / -**ir** verbs > *-as*

hablar	**no hables**
comer	**no comas**
escribir	**no escribas**
decir	**no digas**
hacer	**no hagas**
poner	**no pongas**
salir	**no salgas**
tener	**no tengas**
venir	**no vengas**
ver	**no veas**

Consuelo, no mires tanto la televisión.
Consuelo, don't watch so much TV.

Caridad, no comas tantos dulces.
Caridad, don't eat so many sweets.

No digas mentiras.
Don't tell lies.

Observe the following orthographic changes in verbs ending in *-car, -gar,* and *-zar.*

tocar	**c > qu**	**no toques**
llegar	**g > gu**	**no llegues**
lanzar	**z > c**	**no lances**

Boot verbs will show the same orthographic changes in familiar negative commands:

almorzar	**o > ue**	**no almuerces**
jugar	**u > ue**	**no juegues**
cerrar	**e > ie**	**no cierres**
pedir	**e > i**	**no pidas**

Irregular Negative Commands

dar	**no des**
estar	**no estés**
ir	**no vayas**
saber	**no sepas**
ser	**no seas**

Position of Object Pronouns with Commands

Object pronouns are attached to affirmative commands. However, place them in front of negative commands. In affirmative commands, an accent mark is required on the third syllable from the end with single object pronouns; an accent mark is required on the fourth syllable with double object pronouns. (In monosyllabic commands, there is no need for accent marks.)

Búscalo	*Look for it.*
Cómpralos	*Buy them.*
Dilo	*Tell it.*
Hazlo	*Do it.*

No le digas eso.	*Don't tell him that.*
No lo hagas.	*Don't do it.*
No se lo repitas.	*Don't repeat it to him.*

The Past Participle

The past participle endings are formed by dropping the infinitive endings and adding *-ado* for all *-ar* ending verbs, and *-ido* for most *-er*/*-ir* verbs.

hablar	**hablado**	*spoken*
comer	**comido**	*eaten*
vivir	**vivido**	*lived*

The following verbs have an irregular past participle.

abrir	**abierto**	*opened*
cubrir	**cubierto**	*covered*

describir	**descrito**	*described*
descubrir	**descubierto**	*discovered*
escribir	**escrito**	*written*
romper	**roto**	*broken*
ver	**visto**	*seen*
morir	**muerto**	*died/dead*
poner	**puesto**	*put*
volver	**vuelto**	*returned (as returning to a place)*
devolver	**devuelto**	*returned (as returning something)*
decir	**dicho**	*said/told*
hacer	**hecho**	*done/made*

The past participle has two main uses. 1. As an adjective - It is commonly used with the verb **estar,** to represent the result of an action or a condition. **Sentirse** *(to feel)* may also be used to show a state of being. It may also be used without a verb.

Since the masculine singular form of the past participle used as an adjective ends in *-o,* there are three other endings to agree with feminine and plural forms.

-ado	*-ados*	*-ada*	*-adas*
-ido	*-idos*	*-ida*	*-idas*

Anoche no dormí bien y por eso estoy muy cansado.
I did not sleep well last night and thus I am very tired.

Pero Teresita durmió nueve horas y por consiguiente no se siente tan cansada.
But Teresita slept nine hours and as a result she does not feel that tired.

¿Cansados? ¿Por qué? ¿No se acostaron temprano?
Tired? Why? Din't you go to bed early?

*****

2. A more common use of the past participle is to form compound tenses. The present perfect tense requires the use of the auxiliary verb **haber** *(to have)* conjugated in the present indicative, followed by the past participle of the main verb. This compound tense expresses a past action that bears a continuance onto the present. Even though **haber** and **tener** are both translated as *(to have),* these two verbs are not interchangeable.

He llegado tan tarde que ahora no tengo tiempo para llamarle.
I have arrived so late that now I don't have time to call her.

The Present Perfect

The present perfect tense is a compound tense requiring the use of the auxiliary verb **haber** *(to have)* conjugated in the present indicative, followed by the past participle of the main verb. The present perfect expresses a past action that bears a continuance onto the present.

Haber	
Yo	he
Tú	has
Ud., él, ella	ha
Nosotros(as)	hemos
Vosotros(as)	habéis
Uds., ellos, ellas	han

Pobre Rosita, ella ha comprado un coche que consume mucha gasolina.
Poor Rosita, she has bought a car that uses a lot of gas.

¿Has aprendido el vocabulario nuevo?
Have you learned the new vocabulary?

No hemos recibido las notas del último examen.
We have not received the grades from the last test.

It is common to use the adverbs **ya** *(already)* or **todavía** *(not yet)* in present perfect constructions.

Es bastante tarde. Ya has comido?
It is quite late. Have you eaten yet?

Ya les hemos escrito.
We have already written to them.

Hace una semana que llegó y todavía no la he visto.
She arrived a week ago and I have not seen her yet.

Es la una de la tarde. Todavía no han llamado.
It is one in the afternoon. They have not called yet.

Note that object pronouns and the negative *"no"* always precede the conjugated forms of *"haber"*. The past participle is always invariable.

The Pluperfect

This compound tense is used to show a past action that took place prior to another past action. In this case, the imperfect tense of the helping verb **haber** agrees in form with the expressed subject, and the past participle of the main verb remains constant (*–ado* for all *–ar* ending verbs, *–ido* for most *–er* / *–ir* verbs).

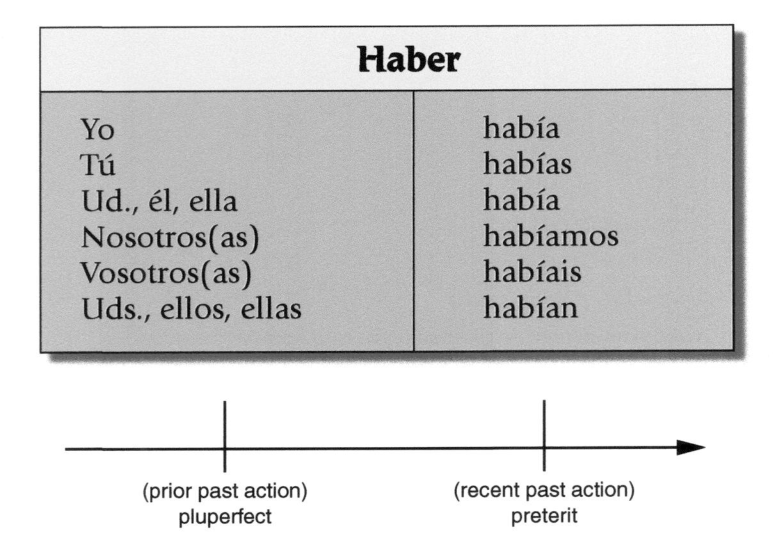

Haber	
Yo	había
Tú	habías
Ud., él, ella	había
Nosotros(as)	habíamos
Vosotros(as)	habíais
Uds., ellos, ellas	habían

Roberto ya había salido cuando nosotros llegamos.
Roberto had already left when we arrived.

Los niños ya se habían acostado cuando sus padres volvieron de la fiesta.
The children had already gone to bed when their parents returned from the party.

Ejercicios

Diálogos

Matching

A.	¿Te gustó la película?	**1.**	Sí, léelo.
B.	¿Te gustó ese libro?	**2.**	Sí, óyelo.
C.	¿Es bueno este disco compacto?	**3.**	Sí, pruébala.
D.	¿Estás contento con ese coche?	**4.**	Sí, vete a verla.
E.	¿Está buena la sopa?	**5.**	Sí, compra uno.

Ejercicios de Gramática

A. Familiar Commands.

Una conversación de tu familia con tu novio/a sobre el Día de San Valentín. Answer in the affirmative, his/her questions, use double object pronoun to avoid repetition.

1. ¿Le compraste un coche nuevo?

____

2. ¿Le diste una tarjeta romántica?

____

3. ¿Le enseñaste mi regalo a tus amigos/as?

____

4. ¿Cuándo vas a comprarle el anillo de compromiso?

____

5. ¿Quién les dijo que yo no les compré nada?

____

B. Familiar Commands for "Tú"

1. Comer ____________
2. Hablar ____________
3. Hacer ____________
4. Dormir ____________
5. Salir ____________
6. Decir ____________
7. Leer ____________
8. Escribir ____________
9. Poner ____________
10. Beber ____________

C. Past Participles as adjectives

Complete the blank spaces using the verb in parentheses as an adjective. Make sure that the past participle agrees with the subject.

1. No puedo usar la computadora porque está ____________. (romper)
2. Las ventanas están ____________ porque hace mucho calor. (abrir)
3. En enero hace mucho frío y normalmente las ventanas están ____________. (cerrar)
4. ¿Cuántos ____________ hay? (morir)
5. ¿Las cartas? Ya están ____________. (escribir)
6. ¡Qué bonitas están! Ustedes están muy bien ____________. (vestir)
7. No podemos ir al concierto. Me han dicho que todas las entradas ya están ____________. (vender)
8. Me siento bastante ____________ porque anoche no pude dormir. (cansar)

D. The Present Perfect Tense.

Choose the right verb and then conjugate it in the Present Perfect.

1. María Luisa ____________ (comer, ir, estudiar) toda la lección.
2. El Profesor Gallo ____________ (comprar, beber, hacer) un libro nuevo.
3. La estudiante ____________ (ver, hablar, asistir) con su hermana.
4. Yo ____________ (salir, leer, mirar) al teatro con Lupe.

5. El Profesor Saborido y el Doctor Blanco no ____________ (tomar, trabajar, poner) esta mañana.

6. Los estudiantes____________ (asistir, poder, querer) a todas sus clases.

E. The Present Perfect Tense of irregular Past Participles.

1. Es tarde y José María no ____________ todavía. (volver)

2. Ramón y Lucho, ¿por qué no ____________ la tarea? (hacer)

3. María del Carmen, ¿dónde ____________ la guitarra? (poner)

4. ¿Quiénes ____________ esa estupidez? (decir)

5. No comprendo por qué mi novia no me ____________. (escribir)

6. Dicen que la nueva película de Antonio Banderas es fantástica. Pero desafortunadamente todavía no la ____________. (ver)

7. Leí recientemente que unos astrónomos gallegos ____________ un planeta nuevo. (descubrir)

8. ¿Quién ____________ esta ventana? (romper)

9. Oí recientemente que ____________ un nuevo restaurante cubano en Edison. (abrir)

10. Lupita, todavía no me ____________ el libro que te presté el semestre pasado. (devolver)

F. Pluperfect Tense.

Complete the blank spaces with the verb in parenthese in the pluperfect. Careful with the irregular past participles.

1. Mi hermana ____________ (cenar) ya cuando sus amigas llegaron.

2. Los estudiantes ____________ (hacer) la tarea cuando yo les llamé.

3. Nosotros ____________ (terminar) los estudios en la universidad e esa época.

4. Yo ____________ (ir) al teatro cuando ellos llamaron.

5. María ____________ (ver) ya la película tres veces.

6. El profesor ____________ (comer) toda la paella cuando nosotros llegamos.

G. ¡Ya lo habían hecho! They had already done it! Follow the model. Use the preterit with the first verb and the pluperfect with the second. Keep the same subjects as in the model sentence.

MODELO (yo) entrar/(ellos) llegar
Cuando yo entré ellos ya habían llegado.

1. salir/comer

____

2. lo hacer/lo terminar

____

3. la ver/la ver

____

4. venir/volver

____

5. lo repetir/lo decir

____

H. Use the **Past Participle** as an adjective for the following verbs.

1. Estos libros están ____________ (escribir) a mano.

2. La mujer está ____________ (morir).

3. Estos juguetes (toys) están ____________ (hacer) en China.

4. El pescado ____________ (cocinar) sin grasas es más saludable.

5. El pastel está ____________ (cubrir) de chocolate.

6. La persona ____________ (amar) es más feliz.

7. Esas computadoras están ____________ (romper).

8. Ya te puedes llevar los libros ____________ (leer).

9. Las plumas ____________ (comprar) en esa librería no escriben bien.

10. Las notas ____________ (tomar) por José no las entiendo.

Drills

A. Conversation with your students. Formal drill:

"¿Qué te gusta hacer en tu tiempo libre?"

— ANSWER

"¿Eres una persona muy ocupada?"

— ANSWER

"¿Tienes familiares o amigos que te visitan?"

— ANSWER

"¿Adónde los llevas cuando vienen a Nueva Jersey?"

— ANSWER

"¿Visitaste alguna ciudad últimamente?"

—ANSWER

"¿Qué es lo que te gustó más?"

—ANSWER

"¿Y lo que te gustó menos?"

— ANSWER

Charlando

Lupe invita a unos amigos americanos al Ballet Folclórico en el Palacio de Bellas Artes en el DF.

Lupe—Esta noche voy a Bellas Artes. Stacey, ven conmigo, te invito.

Stacey—Me encantaría ir pero . . . ¿Que haremos con Craig?

Craig—Pues no cuenten conmigo porque yo no iré a ningún ballet.

Stacey—Bien, no vengas pero invítanos a cenar en Sanborn's, casi al frente del Palacio de Bellas Artes. Visita el Museo de Antropología y después tomas un taxi y le dices al chofer que quieres ir al Sanborn's que está frente a Bellas Artes.

Craig—Repite lo que tengo que decir.

Stacey—Dile :Por favor, llévame al restaurante Sanborn's que está en la Avenida Alameda.

Craig—Bien, de acuerdo. Allá nos veremos después del ballet.

José Antonio va a una fiesta en el Hotel Ritz con sus padres.

Don Antonio—El presidente de la empresa invitó a los ejecutivos con sus familias. Tenéis que vestiros elegantemente. Esta será la fiesta más importante de la empresa.

Doña Ana—José Antonio, ponte el traje nuevo. Usa la corbata roja que la abuela te regaló. Olvida ponerte esos zapatos viejos y esos calcetines de colores. Sé sobrio, sencillo y elegante.

Don Antonio—Si quieres, usa mi colonia. Es importante oler bien.

José Antonio—Bien, de acuerdo. No me gustan estas fiestas pero iré con vosotros para complaceros.

Beatriz se encuentra con un viejo amigo en una discoteca.

Carlos Andrés—Beatriz, baila conmigo. ¿Quieres?

Beatriz—Ahora no. Tengo mucha sed.

Carlos Andrés—Toma esto. Te va a gustar. Es una sangría especial.

Beatriz—Espera un momento. Voy a llamar a mis padres para que me recojan.

Carlos Andrés—Quédate un rato más. Háblame de ti. Hace tanto tiempo que no hablamos. Yo te llevo después.

Beatriz—Llévame ahora, por favor. Tengo que levantarme muy temprano. Mañana nos vamos a la finca.

Carlos Andrés—De acuerdo, pero con una condición, llámame para salir juntos la semana que viene.

Beatriz—Gracias, Carlos, y disculpa mi apuro. Te llamaré para salir contigo.

Cultura

Entretenimientos y Diversiones

Entretenimientos y Diversiones

A los hispanos les gusta disfrutar la vida intensamente. La alegría es una de las cualidades que más caracterizan a los pueblos hispanos, al igual que la espontaneidad. Los países hispanos sobresalen por la variedad, la calidad, y la espontaneidad de sus fiestas. Los carnavales en el mes de febrero son un buen ejemplo. Las ciudades y los pueblos ofrecen una gran variedad de actividades. Los cines son muy concurridos y existen clubes de personas muy interesadas en la cinematografía. Sin embargo no se ve tanta televisión como en los Estados Unidos, y la selección de programas es menos variada. Existen asociaciones que ofrecen charlas sobre todo tipo de temas. Hay muchos museos y galerías de arte ya que el arte es muy importante en el mundo hispano. Ha habido grandes pintores hispanos como Picasso, Miró, Dalí, Rivera, Orozco, Xiqueiro, Botero, Goya, Veláquez, Sorolla y muchísimos más. Los músicos hispanos nos han regalado una gran variedad de composiciones tanto de música culta como popular. El ballet y la ópera son apreciados en muchas ciudades hispanas como en el Teatro Colón en Buenos Aires, El Teatro de la Opera en Madrid o el Teatro de Bellas Artes en la Ciudad de México. La plaza o el parque es en muchos casos el centro de muchos pueblos hispanos, donde la gente se reúne a tomar fresco, charlar, oír música, patinar, o a tomarse un helado o una horchata en una noche de verano. Todo tipo de diversión y entretenimiento se encuentran en los países hispanos.

Preguntas

1. ¿Qué actitud tienen los hispanos sobre la vida?
2. ¿Qué fiestas populares son famosas?
3. ¿Cómo es la televisión?
4. ¿Qué tipo de asociaciones existen?
5. ¿Conoces algunos artistas famosos hispanos?
6. ¿Dónde hay famosos teatros de opera?
7. ¿Dónde se reúne la gente a tomar fresco?
8. ¿Qué entretenimientos encontramos en una ciudad hispana?
9. ¿Son la gente aficionada al cine?
10. ¿Qué beben en una noche de verano?

Proverbios

No dejes para mañana lo que puedas hacer hoy.
Más vale tarde que nunca.

Maps

Provinces of Spain

1. La Coruña
2. Lugo
3. Ovieda
4. Santander
5. Vizcaya
6. Guipúzcoa
7. Pontevedra
8. Orense
9. León
10. Palencia
11. Burgos
12. Alava
13. Navarra
14. Zamora
15. Valladolid
16. Segovia
17. Soria
18. Logroño
19. Zaragoza
20. Huesca
21. Lérida
22. Barcelona
23. Gerona
24. Salamanca
25. Ávila
26. Madrid
27. Guadalajara
28. Teruel
29. Tarragona
30. Cáceres
31. Toledo
32. Cuenca
33. Castellón
34. Badajoz
35. Ciudad Real
36. Albacete
37. Valencia
38. Huelva
39. Córdoba
40. Jaén
41. Murcia
42. Alicante
43. Cádiz
44. Sevilla
45. Málaga
46. Granada
47. Almeria
48. Baleares
49. Santa Cruz de Tenerife
50. Las Palmas

South America
Atlantic Ocean
South Pacific Ocean
South Atlantic Ocean
Barranquilla
Maracaibo
Caracas
Venezuela
San Cristóbal
Ciudad Guayana
Georgetown
Paramaribo
Guyana
French Guiana (France)
Suriname
Cayenne
Medellín
Isla de Malpelo (Colombia)
Bogotá
Cali
Colombia
Boa Vista
Mitú
Macapá
Negro
Quito
Ecuador
Guayaquil
Amazon
Fonte Boa
Manaus
Santarém
Belém
São Luís
Iquitos
Fortaleza
Teresina
Piura
Natal
Recife
Trujillo
Rio Branco
Pôrto Velho
Brazil
Huánuco
Pôrto Nacional
Peru
Lima
Aracaju
Salvador
Cuzco
Bolivia
Ica
Trinidad
Cuiabá
Brasília
Arequipa
La Paz
Cochabamba
Santa Cruz
Goiânia
Arica
Sucre
Belo Horizonte
Victória
Paraguay
Rio de Janeiro
São Paulo
Tropic of Capricorn
Antofagasta
Asunción
Curitiba
Chile
San Miguel de Tucumán
Resistencia
Florianópolis
Isla San Felix (Chile)
Isla San Ambrosio (Chile)
Pôrto Alegre
Córdoba
Salto
Rosario
Uruguay
Valparaíso
Mendoza
Santiago
Juan Fernández Islands (Chile)
Buenos Aires
Montevideo
Argentina
Concepción
Mar del Plata
Bahia Blanca
Puerto Montt
San Carlos de Bariloche
Comodoro Rivadavia
0 500 kilometers
0 nautical miles 500
Stanley
Falkland Islands
(administered by th U.K., claimed by Argentina)
Strait of Magellan
Punta Arenas
Ushuaia
South Georgia (Falkland Islands)
80°
60°
40°
20°
0°

Caribbean Basin
Gulf of Mexico
Atlantic Ocean
Caribbean Sea
Florida (U.S.A.)
The Bahamas
Cuba
Cayman Islands (U.K.)
Jamaica
Haiti
Dominican Republic
Puerto Rico (U.S.)
Turks & Caicos Islands (U.K.)
Honduras
Nicaragua
Costa Rica
Panama
Colombia
Venezuela
Tropic of Cancer
Netherland Antilles
Guadeloupe (Fr.)
Dominica
Martinique (F.R.)
St. Lucia
Barbados
Grenada
Trinidad and Tobago
Havana
Kingston
Port-au-Prince
Santo Domingo
San Juan
Caracas

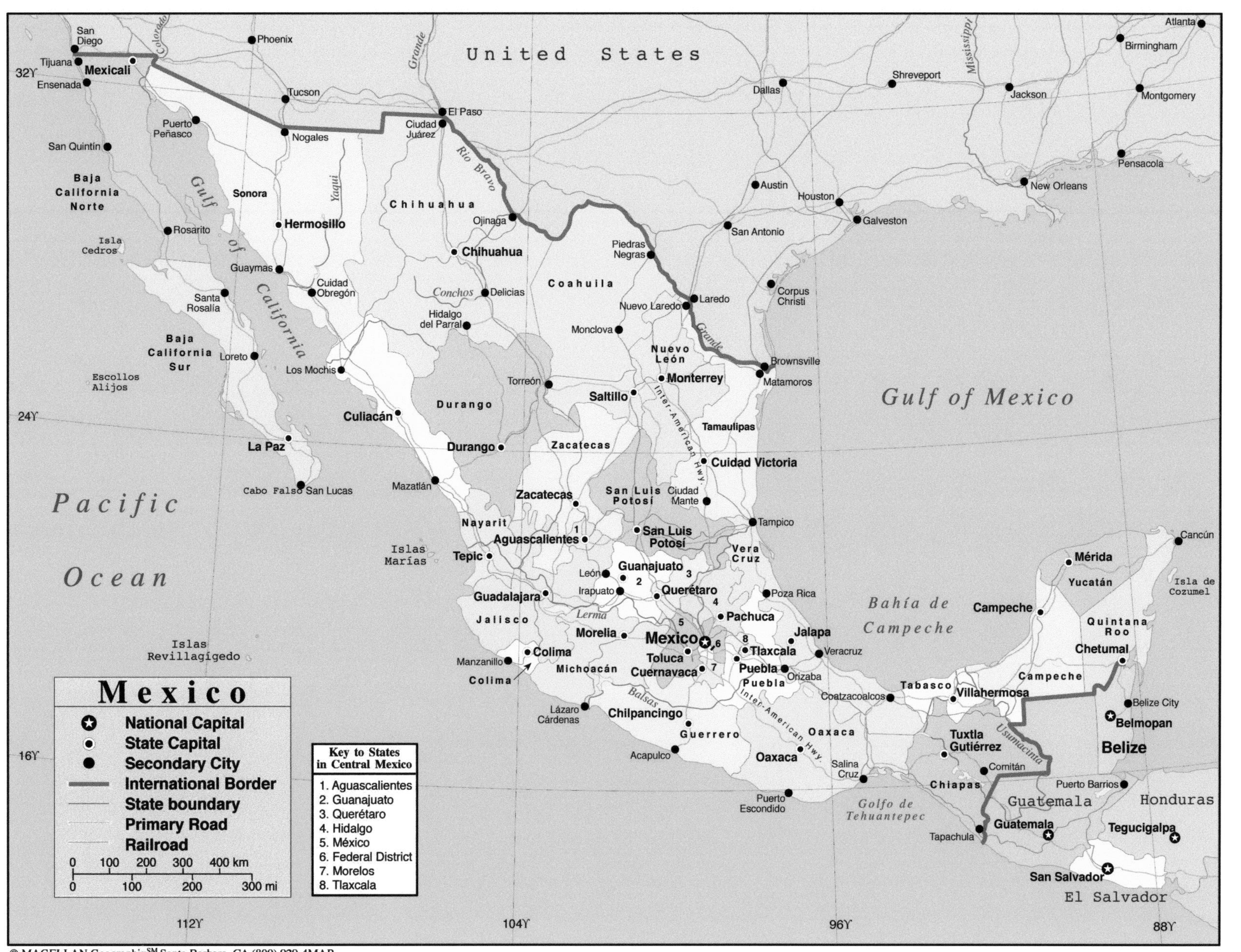
Mexico
National Capital
State Capital
Secondary City
International Border
State boundary
Primary Road
Railroad
0 100 200 300 400 km
0 100 200 300 mi
Key to States in Central Mexico
1. Aguascalientes
2. Guanajuato
3. Querétaro
4. Hidalgo
5. México
6. Federal District
7. Morelos
8. Tlaxcala
United States
Gulf of Mexico
Pacific Ocean
Gulf of California
Bahía de Campeche
Golfo de Tehuantepec
San Diego
Tijuana
Mexicali
Ensenada
San Quintín
Phoenix
Tucson
Nogales
Puerto Peñasco
El Paso
Ciudad Juárez
Baja California Norte
Baja California Sur
Sonora
Hermosillo
Chihuahua
Ojinaga
Coahuila
Isla Cedros
Rosarito
Guaymas
Cuidad Obregón
Santa Rosalía
Loreto
Los Mochis
Escollos Alijos
La Paz
Cabo Falso
San Lucas
Culiacán
Durango
Torreón
Conchos
Delicias
Hidalgo del Parral
Monclova
Piedras Negras
Nuevo Laredo
Laredo
Nuevo León
Monterrey
Saltillo
Brownsville
Matamoros
Tamaulipas
Cuidad Victoria
Zacatecas
Mazatlán
San Luis Potosí
Ciudad Mante
Tampico
Nayarit
Aguascalientes
Tepic
Islas Marías
Islas Revillagigedo
Guadalajara
Jalisco
León
Guanajuato
Irapuato
Querétaro
Lerma
Pachuca
Vera Cruz
Poza Rica
Morelia
Mexico
Toluca
Cuernavaca
Tlaxcala
Puebla
Orizaba
Jalapa
Veracruz
Colima
Manzanillo
Michoacán
Lázaro Cárdenas
Balsas
Chilpancingo
Guerrero
Acapulco
Oaxaca
Inter-American Hwy.
Puerto Escondido
Salina Cruz
Coatzacoalcos
Tabasco
Villahermosa
Campeche
Mérida
Yucatán
Cancún
Isla de Cozumel
Quintana Roo
Chetumal
Usumacinta
Tuxtla Gutiérrez
Comitán
Chiapas
Tapachula
Belize City
Belmopan
Belize
Puerto Barrios
Guatemala
Honduras
Tegucigalpa
San Salvador
El Salvador
Río Bravo
Grande
Colorado
Yaqui
Mississippi
Dallas
Shreveport
Jackson
Birmingham
Atlanta
Montgomery
Pensacola
New Orleans
Austin
Houston
Galveston
San Antonio
Corpus Christi
32°
24°
16°
112°
104°
96°
88°

Central America
Gulf of Mexico
Mexico
Villahermosa
Tuxtla Gutiérrez
Chetumal
Belize City
Belmopan
Flores
Belize
Islas de la Bahia
Guatemala
Puerto Barrios
San Pedro Sula
Guatemala
Honduras
Tegucigalpa
Santa Ana
San Salvador
San Miguel
El Salvador
Nicaragua
Matagalpa
Rio Grande de Matagalpa
León
Managua
Granada
Lago de Nicaragua
Bluefields
Puerto Lempira
Puerto Cabezas
Cayos Miskitos
Swan Islands (Honduras)
George Town
Cayman Islands (U.K.)
Montego Bay
Jamaica
Kingston
Caribbean Sea
Isla de Providencia (Colombia)
Isla de San Andréas (Colombia)
Islas del Maíz
Pacific Ocean
Costa Rica
Puntarenas
San José
Puerto Limón
Bocas de Toro
Golfito
David
Panama
Panama Canal
Colón
Panamá
La Palma
Isla de San José
Isla del Rey
Chitré
Isla de Coiba
Turbo
Colombia
90Y
85Y
80Y
15Y
10Y
0 100 200 kilometers
0 100 200 nautical miles

C000225815

Ripley's
Believe It or Not!®

Vice President, Licensing & Publishing
Amanda Joiner

Editorial Manager
Carrie Bolin

Editor Jordie R. Orlando
Junior Editor Briana Posner
Designer Shawn Biner
Proofreader Rachel Paul
Factchecker Yvette Chin
Reprographics Bob Prohaska
Cover Design Chris Conway, Luis Fuentes

Special thanks to the writers and editors of IFLScience.com and Ripleys.com

Published by Ripley Publishing 2020
under license with IFL Science

10 9 8 7 6 5 4 3 2 1

ISBN: 978-1-52912-569-6

First published in Great Britain in 2020 by Century

Century
20 Vauxhall Bridge Road
London SW1V 2SA

www.penguin.co.uk

Century is part of the Penguin Random House group of companies whose addresses can be found at global.penguinrandomhouse.com

A CIP catalogue record for this book is available from the British Library.

For more information regarding permission, contact:
VP Licensing & Publishing

Ripley Entertainment Inc.
7576 Kingspointe Parkway, Suite 188
Orlando, Florida 32819
Email: publishing@ripleys.com
www.ripleys.com/books

Manufactured in China in January 2020.

PUBLISHER'S NOTE
While every effort has been made to verify the accuracy of the entries in this book, the Publisher cannot be held responsible for any errors contained in the work. They would be glad to receive any information from readers.

a Jim Pattison Company

WEIRD TRUE FACTS

Science frequently teeters on the edge of the unbelievable, often leaving people—even scientists—thinking, "What the. . . ?" For instance, did you know that pink isn't a real color? Or that hip-hop music makes cheese taste better?

The editors of Ripley's Believe It or Not! and IFL Science have joined forces to bring you the strangest, most unbelievable science stories they can find. From historical oddities to cutting-edge technology, and strange animals to cosmic conundrums, there is no shortage of weird, true facts that will leave you scratching your head and thinking. . .

WTF

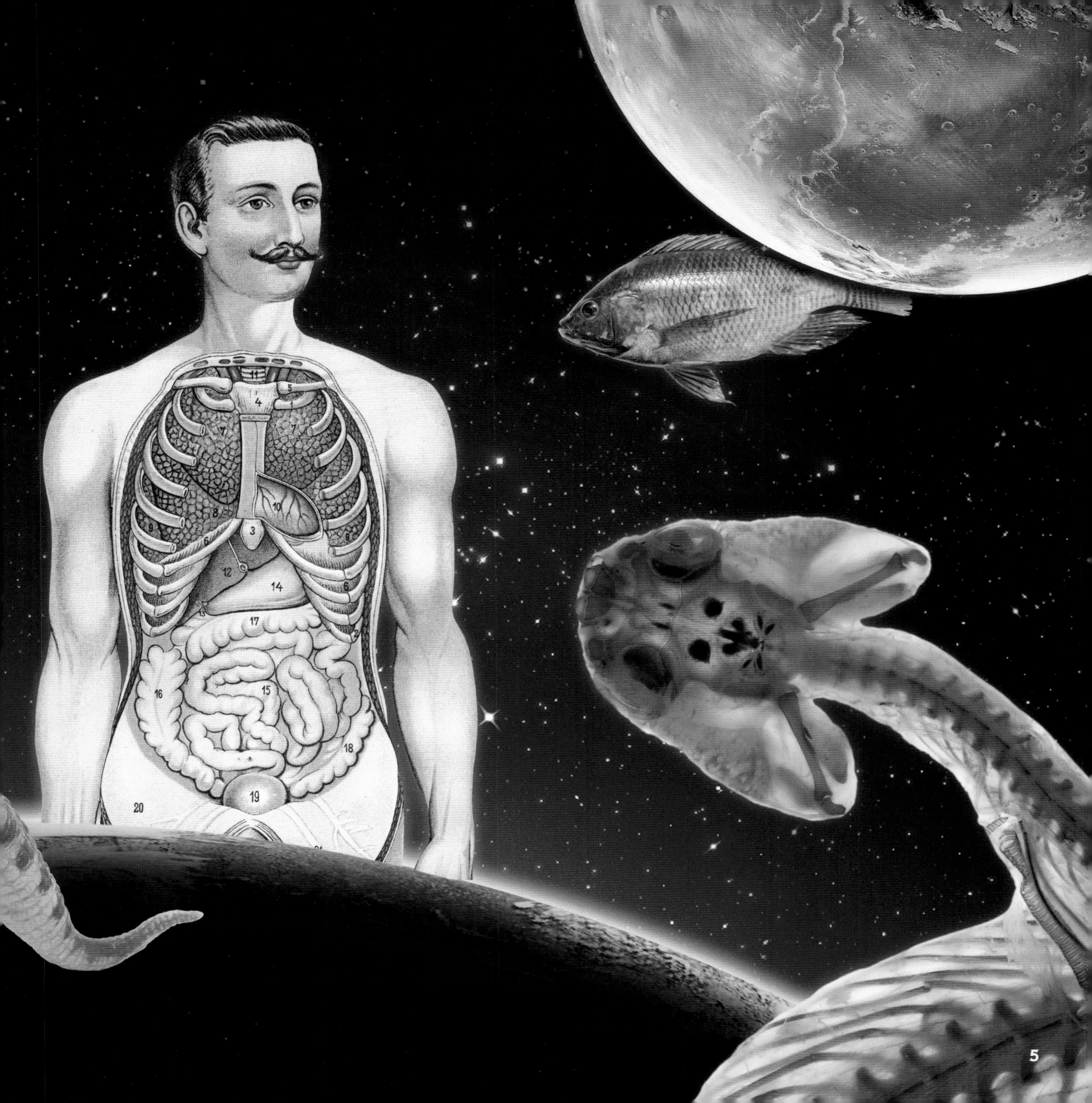

PINK ISN'T REAL

Take a close look at a rainbow and search for the color pink. Did you find it? No? That's because there is no pink wavelength of light.

When you see pink, your brain is actually piecing together red and white wavelengths. Our perception of color is not as simple as a linear spectrum; it also involves tints (added light values) and shades (added dark values). By adding tints to red, we lighten the color, as well as shift it toward the blue end of the spectrum and endow it with a different quality. We call this quality "pink."

If you want to get metaphysical about it, all "colors" are just abstractions based on interpretations of the body and mind that can't exist outside of the visual system. Don't think about it too hard; it can get pretty existential.

INDESTRUCTIBLE SPORES

Molds are present in every human environment, but the pristine vacuum of space must be perfectly clean, right? Wrong!

Mold has been found on the International Space Station (ISS). Since the ISS is technically a human environment, mold growth inside the spacecraft is a common annoyance. Astronauts spend many hours each week making sure the mold stays controlled enough so as not to become a health problem.

Mold can survive many extreme environments, but researchers have found that spores of *Aspergillus* and *Penicillium* can withstand exposure to X-rays 200 times higher than the dose that would kill a human.

Exceedingly resilient, these spores are now thought to be capable of living on the *outside* of the ISS and other spacecrafts. Molds also have the prospect to produce compounds not found in space, which could be beneficial on future space missions!

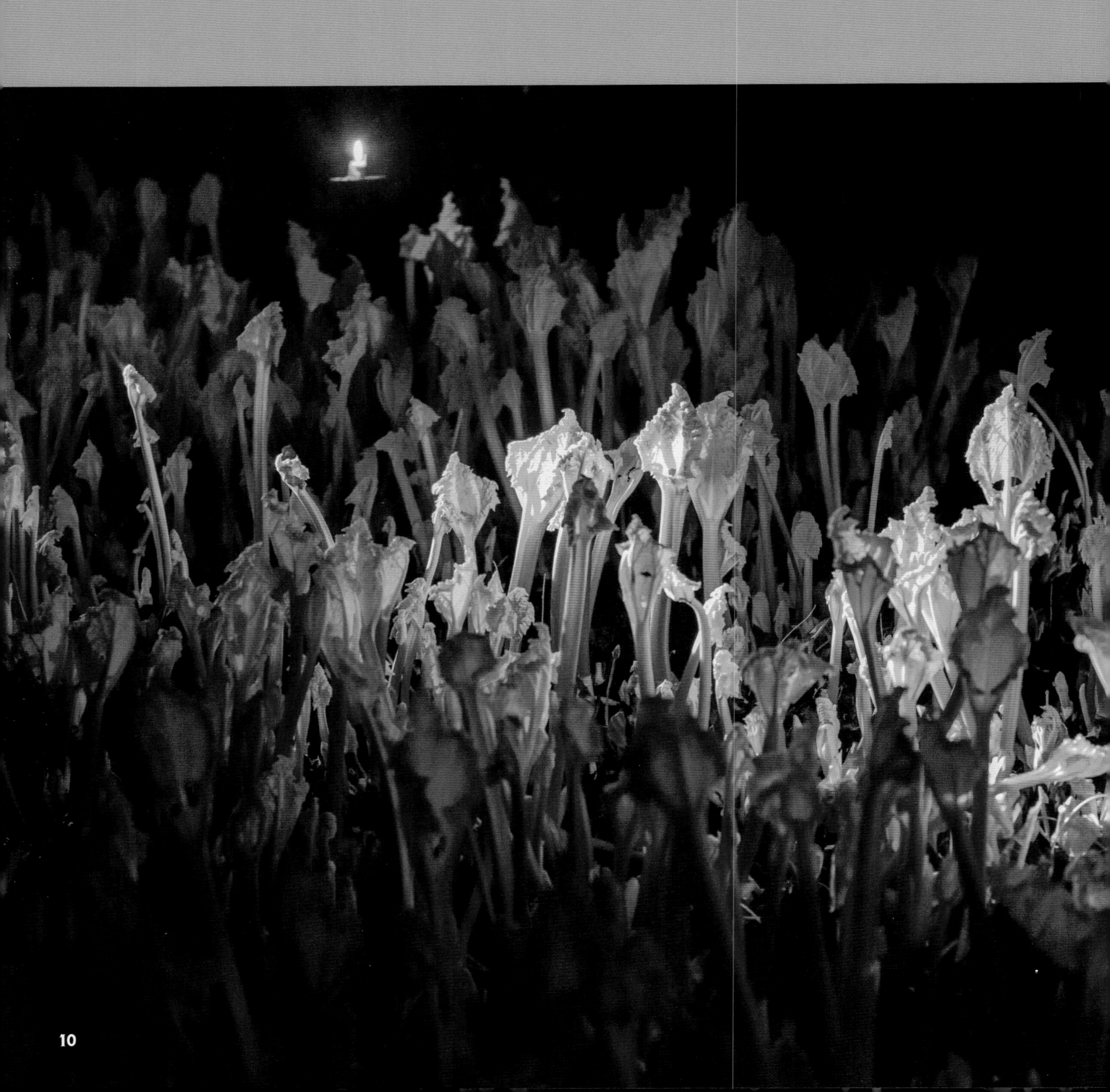

SINGING IN THE DARK

In 19th-century England, rhubarb was in such high demand that it exceeded the demand for opium. To keep up with the growing need for this vegetable, farmers developed a rather aggressive form of agriculture—forced growing.

The rhubarb is first left to grow in a field for two years, harvesting sunlight into their roots, and then they are placed in a forcing shed. This shed is heated and deprives them of all sunlight, which prevents the rhubarb from growing leaf blades. Without the need to grow leafage, the stalks can absorb all the nutrients, causing up to one inch of growth per day.

Though it sounds brutal, rhubarb grown in these conditions actually sing during the growing process! No, they don't sing along to folk songs. The rapid budding creates rhythmic cracking and popping noises.

Rhubarb is still farmed this way in places today, grown and harvested in candlelight. Believe it or not, forced-grown rhubarb is actually sweeter than free-range rhubarb!

CHEMISTRY

TIP FOR A TIPPLE

For those of you who are of legal drinking age, we know how to enhance your nip of whiskey—just add water!

Whiskey enthusiasts and connoisseurs may have told you that adding a few drops of water to your glass heightens the smell and taste, but scientists now have an explanation. The molecules in this liquid contain hydrophobic and hydrophilic parts, meaning half are repelled by water, while the other half are attracted to it.

The more water added to the whiskey, the more intense the flavor. During bottling, the average alcohol content of whiskey is about 45 percent, but some connoisseurs have been known to dilute their beverage to just 20 percent alcohol content!

GRAPE BALLS OF FIRE!

"Caution: Flammable" is what your package of grapes from the market should read. If you place a grape that has been cut slightly—but not all the way through—into the microwave, you'd better take a step back. A single zapped grape will shoot off a burst of plasma—the same stuff that makes up our sun!

Researchers have discovered the reason why these handheld snacks turn into miniature suns in the microwave—their size! Electromagnetic hotspots must be formed for plasma creation, but it takes two hotspots in contact to make plasma sparks. When the hotspots in each half of the grape reach the correct temperature, the sparks ionize sodium and potassium to produce plasma.

Some experiments have resulted in exploding microwaves, so don't try this at home!

ENVIRONMENT

UNDERWATER WATER

From land, the Angelita Cenote in Mexico's Yucatan Peninsula looks like an ordinary swimming hole. It's not until you dive almost 100 ft (30.5 m) that a second, hidden world appears.

A cenote is a deep sinkhole formed from the collapse of limestone bedrock that exposes groundwater underneath. Over time, cenotes can become filled with fresh rainwater. An underwater river is formed when the fresh top water meets the exposed salty groundwater.

The point where the two waters meet and cause a fog-like effect is called halocline. The different density levels of the two waters cause them to separate into layers. The result is a breathtaking convergence of two habitats that can make divers appear as though they are flying above an otherworldly river.

NO PAIN, NO PAIN

There are people who live among us born with what appears to be a superpower—the inability to feel pain.

One such person is Jo Cameron of Scotland. For the first 65 years of her life, she did not realize she was different, despite the countless bruises, burns, and broken bones she has experienced. She only became aware of her condition when she sought treatment for two notoriously painful ailments. To her doctors' surprise, however, she didn't report much discomfort and had no need for any painkillers. It was also noticed that her injuries tended to heal unusually quickly.

But the inability to feel pain is not always a good thing; people with similar conditions often find themselves injured without realizing it—sometimes very seriously. Dr. Ingo Kurth of the Institute of Human Genetics in Aachen, Germany, explains, "Pain is incredibly important to the process of learning how to modulate your physical activity without doing damage to your bodies, and in determining how much risk you take."

Geneticists took a close look at Cameron's DNA and found notable mutations on genes associated with pain sensation, mood, and memory. This unusual gene tweak also helps her feel shiningly optimistic and worry-free. By studying Cameron and people like her, scientists and doctors hope to find information that could help people who suffer from conditions like chronic pain, anxiety, and PTSD.

***Believe It* or *Not!* . . .** The brain processes pain but cannot feel pain itself!

STUCK ON YOU(TUBE)

One of the latest reports from Hootsuite, a social media management platform, and digital marketing agency We Are Social has revealed that the world spends nearly 7 hours online each day.

The Philippines clocks up the most time online each day, at 10 hours and 2 minutes. Japan came in last, at 3 hours and 45 minutes. The United States and United Kingdom are closer to the global average (6 hours and 42 minutes). So what are people spending all that time on? The top five most visited sites were Google, YouTube, Facebook, Baidu, and Wikipedia. Good for you for opening a book.

RADIUM GIRLS

Glow-in-the-dark dial watches made popular in the 1940s clutter antique shops and family jewelry boxes. But these timepieces are more dangerous than they seem. The glowing effect was achieved by the use of radium-based paint applied by Radium Girls.

In the 1940s, working women would hand-paint watches by wetting and shaping the brush tips in their mouths and lips between dipping the brush into the paint. At the time, radium was considered a health and beauty product, and was believed to be safe and even beneficial to the body.

Over time, radium emits radon in the form of an odorless and colorless gas, which causes rapid decay and can lead to cancer. The health of Radium Girls quickly declined, and the most common problem was rapid tooth loss, accompanied by unhealable gum ulcers. The jawbones of some young women eventually crumbled away, and many died young from intense internal bleeding.

The Radium Girls took their illnesses to court, challenging that their employers were responsible for not protecting them against harmful side effects. Ultimately, they won their case, and awareness of workplace safety paved the way for the Occupational Safety and Health Administration (OSHA) to be established in the 1970s.

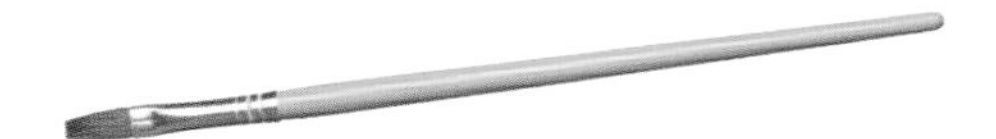

CHEMISTRY

FIZZY FEELINGS

Every time you pop open a can of soda and enjoy the fizzing sensation, you can thank your taste buds! You may believe the sensation you're experiencing is simply the feeling of bursting bubbles, but you're actually tasting the carbonation.

The same cells on your tongue used to sense sour stimuli are responsible for detecting the fizzy carbon dioxide. In a research study conducted using a pressurized chamber that removed the fizziness of the soda, people said there was no difference in taste whatsoever, meaning the flavor of the soda pop doesn't come from the bubbles—you're actually tasting the carbon dioxide!

***Believe It* or *Not!* . . .** **Adult cats don't meow to each other—just to humans!**

A-MEOW-ZING MOVEMENTS

It is often said that cats always land on their feet, but there's actually scientific reasoning behind this phenomenon. No, it's not that cats have nine lives—which we still have no evidence of. It's due to something known as the "righting reflex!"

Including their tails, felines have between 48–53 vertebrae, while humans have only 33. Their flexible backbones, combined with their highly tuned sense of balance, allow them to twist midair and orient their bodies.

When cats jump or fall from a high place, they utilize an inner-ear balance system called the vestibular apparatus to determine up from down. Once cats rotate their upper body to have their paws face down, their lower body follows suit, allowing them to land safely on all of their toe beans.

Believe it or not, kittens as young as seven weeks can master this skill!

THE LIFE AND TIMES OF PHINEAS GAGE

In September 1848, 25-year-old Phineas Gage survived being blasted through the skull with a 3.5-ft-long (1-m), 1.25-in-thick (3.175-cm) iron rod and cemented himself in the annals of medical history as one of the first cases to show a link between personality change and brain trauma.

Gage was a foreman working for a railroad company in Vermont, blasting rocks to clear space for tracks to be laid. Holes would be drilled into rocks and then filled with gunpowder and topped with sand, which was then packed tight with a tamping iron. On this fateful day, Gage went to pack the powder without realizing the sand hadn't been added; the iron ignited the powder and sent the rod through Gage's face and out the top of his skull.

Astonishingly, he survived. It's reported he didn't lose consciousness, spat out "about half a teacupful" of his brain matter, and told the attending physician, "Here is business enough for you." Months later he made a seemingly full recovery, but the once model worker and mild-mannered man had become disrespectful and hotheaded.

It is often said that his personality change was permanent, but doctors he visited years later made no record of his outward behavior. After years of moving around (farming in New Hampshire, making appearances as a medical oddity at P. T. Barnum's American Museum in New York City, and working on a stagecoach in Chile), Gage began suffering seizures and died at the age of 37—12 years after his brain injury. His skull and the offending tamping iron can be seen today at the Warren Anatomical Museum near Boston.

WHY YOU CAN'T STAND YOUR OWN VOICE

Why is it that the voice you hear played back on a speaker doesn't sound like the voice you've heard coming out of your mouth for all these years?

We hear sounds by vibrations being picked up by our eardrum. We perceive external sounds, like a beeping car or a radio, through sound waves passing through the air into our ear canals, into our inner ear, and on to our cochlea. When our voice is played back to us via a speaker, we are hearing air-conducted vibrations.

A lot of what we hear when we speak is perceived in the same way as external noise, but we also pick up on vibrations that have come through our jawbone and skull. This is known as inertial bone conduction, which tends to "bring out" the lower-frequency vibrations, making your voice sound deeper and less squeaky than it actually is. In all likelihood, the fact you don't like the sound of it is simply because you are not used to it.

Unfortunately, the depressing reality is that the awful noise you hear when you play back a recording of your voice is actually how your voice sounds to the 7.6 billion other humans on Earth. Sorry about that, folks.

BETWEEN TWO CONTINENTS

Have you ever wanted to be in two places at once? How about two separate continents? Believe it or not, it's possible within Iceland's Thingvellir National Park. And while this version of being in two places at once won't make you any more productive, it does make for an unbeatable experience and photo op.

The Silfra Crack is a narrow, water-filled chasm that happens to be part of the Mid-Atlantic Ridge, where the North American and the Eurasian tectonic plates are diverging. Most of the Mid-Atlantic Ridge is, as the name suggests, in the middle of the Atlantic Ocean floor. But Iceland is one of the few places, and the largest, where portions of it are above the water.

The volcanic activity of the ridge has created multiple fissures across the country. Over time, glaciers have melted, been filtered through miles of porous volcanic rock, and filled in the Silfra Crack, creating an underwater wonderland where one can float between the continental plates. The water is considered some of the clearest and calmest in the world; divers compare swimming in it to floating in space.

Believe It or Not! **. . . *Apollo* astronauts trained in Iceland because it resembled the Moon's geological make-up!**

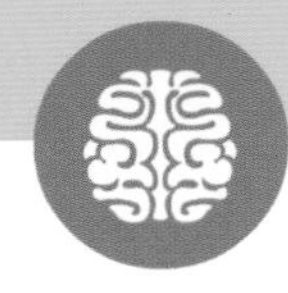

KNOCKING ON DEATH'S DOOR

Trying to find out what happens to our minds when we die is one of life's biggest conundrums. Researchers can't predict when someone will suddenly die, and they can't ethically bring someone to the edge of death in a controlled experiment. That's why the phenomenon of Near Death Experiences (NDEs) is one of the most fascinating elements of the natural—or supernatural—world.

NDEs are rare and unusual moments that occur when someone is perilously close to the brink of death. They are typically recounted after recovery and are described as an out-of-body experience with a bright tunnel of light.

A study published in the journal *Mindfulness* in December 2018 documented 12 Buddhist monks who are highly proficient in the art of self-meditation and put themselves into a near-death state. During these NDE meditation sessions, the monks reported several phases their mind experienced. These included losing the sense of their bodies, losing the concept of time, visualizing otherworldly beings, and feeling a sense of emptiness.

Though these monks reported the ability to control their mind during these NDEs, we highly recommend you don't try this at home.

ROYAL BLUE

In 1810, King George III slipped into pure madness and was soon forced to retire from public life completely. He may be best known in the history books for being the king who lost America, but did you know he had blue urine? Could his mental illness and streams of blue be related? It could all come down to a genetic blood disorder called porphyria.

In the last decade of his life, King George III had lost a majority of his sight and was in constant pain. His once worldly and rich vocabulary quickly diminished as he began constantly repeating himself and writing long, confusing letters. It is also rumored he would walk around completely nude. On top of it all, the blue urine…

A 1969 study suggested King George III suffered from porphyria, a disorder caused by an over-accumulation of porphyrin, which helps hemoglobin, the protein that moves oxygen throughout the body. In some cases, porphyrin is excreted in the urine, giving it a purple or blue hue.

Acute porphyria can also seriously affect the nervous system. Symptoms include hallucinations, delirium, insomnia, anxiety, and even paranoia. Moreover, the king's doctors might have worsened this condition and its symptoms by treating George with doses of arsenic, basically poisoning him.

LOOKING FOR LIFE

In the 1960s, Dr. Frank Drake came up with an equation that tries to assess the likelihood of life starting on a planet. The equation includes factors like the fraction of formed stars that have planets and the average number of those planets in the habitable zone. Even when incredibly conservative estimates are used, the Drake equation suggests the universe is teeming with life—so where is it?

This is a problem that has long plagued astrophysicists, and there's no clear answer. It is known as the Fermi Paradox, and there are a number of possible solutions—some more unnerving than others.

It's possible that space is just too big or we haven't looked hard enough. Another solution suggests there is a Great Filter in the universe, at which intelligent life stops, perhaps through self-destruction or for other reasons. It could be that we are the first species to pass this filter, or that we are yet to reach it—and all other intelligent civilizations before us have been destroyed. Eek.

There is another answer to the Fermi Paradox: perhaps we are alone in this universe. As the late Sir Arthur C. Clarke once famously said, "Two possibilities exist: either we are alone in the universe or we are not. Both are equally terrifying."

TINY BUT TOUGH

Lions, tigers, and water bears! Oh my!

The tardigrade, also known as a water bear, a moss piglet, or a slow walker, is a tiny invertebrate that can inhabit almost any place on Earth. They measure around half a millimeter and have four little pairs of legs with claws on each end. These claws give them the appearance of a bear, lending them the nickname *water bear*!

Tardigrades are extremophiles, meaning they can survive in the most extreme living conditions most other organisms wouldn't have a chance in. From freshwater to salt water to the moist moss in your backyard, water bears can thrive in temperatures ranging from near absolute zero (−460°F/−273°C) to a balmy 248°F (120°C)!

These miniscule creatures have the ability to enter a stage called cryptobiosis, where they dry up, curl up into a ball, create a hard outer shell, and stay like that for more than 100 years. They rehydrate themselves when living conditions improve. Can you say nap royalty?

BONE MUSIC

During a time when plastic vinyl was hard to come by and music was heavily censored, Soviet-era Russians would share and play tunes off of exposed X-ray film.

Before CDs, MP3s, and streaming, vinyl records were once the most popular way to enjoy music (and have made quite the comeback). To play music, vinyl records are covered in thin grooves that are translated into sound by delicately placing a needle into the channels and then spinning the record on a turntable.

The X-ray records work in the same way, but instead of using the black plastic of typical vinyl records, *stilyagi* used exposed X-ray film scavenged from hospital dumpsters. The *stilyagi* were a Soviet-era subculture of young Russians fascinated by Western pop culture, which was heavily censored by the government. Illegal copies of songs were etched into the X-ray film, which would then be cut into a circle and then burned with a cigarette in the middle so the record could be placed on a turntable. And no matter what genre of music was copied onto the makeshift record, that's pretty punk.

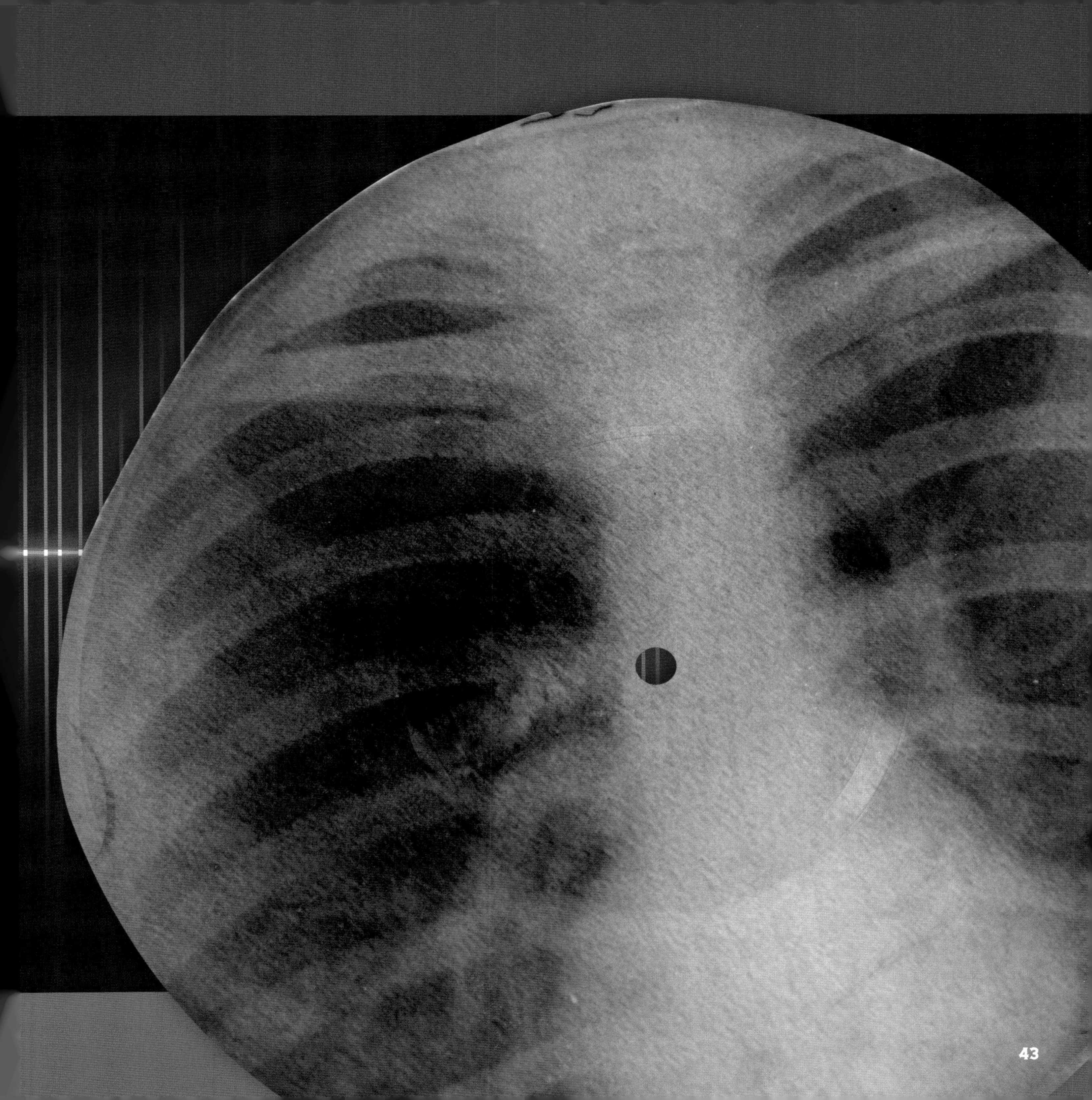

Believe It or Not! **. . . An onion has a genetic code five times longer than that of a human being!**

FIGHTING BACK THE TEARS

Why is it that onions make you cry when you begin to mercilessly dissect them? It's fairly unlikely that it's because you've formed an emotional bond with your onion and are sad to see it chopped up into little pieces—so it must boil down to some rather curious chemistry.

Onions belong to a group of vegetables that absorb high quantities of sulfur compounds from the soil. These are converted by the onion plant into other compounds that can readily transmogrify into a gas.

Murdering an onion splits open cells that release enzymes and these gas-prone compounds—combining the two forms into a jarringly named gas, syn-propanethial s-oxide, which quickly reaches your eyes. Detecting this chemical irritant, your eyes send a signal to your central nervous system, which in turn causes your eyes to weep in an attempt to wash it out.

Unfortunately, it wouldn't be a good idea to genetically modify onions to remove these pesky compounds: They're actually partly responsible for making onions so tasty in the first place.

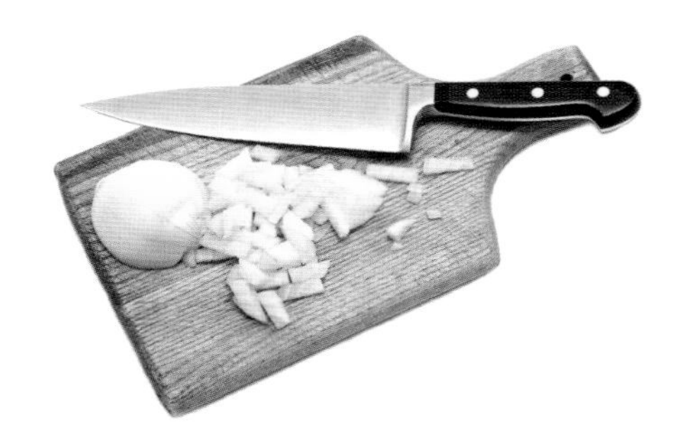

Believe It or Not! . . . **A raisin will bounce up and down continuously when dropped in a glass of champagne!**

PHYSICS

RAISE A GLASS

A popping champagne cork produces freezing jets of carbon dioxide and, unexpectedly, shock waves like the ones released by fighter jets.

Before a bottle of champagne has been opened, a mixture of pressurized carbon dioxide and water in gaseous form lies trapped beneath the cork in the bottle's "headspace," or neck. With the use of high-speed cameras, a group of researchers have found that when the cork flies off, that trapped gas is released, cooling down and condensing in the process, which forms a jet of dry ice that whooshes out of the bottle faster than the speed of sound.

Meanwhile, the process creates something known as a Mach disk, the kind of shock wave you'd see in the exhaust streams whizzing out of rockets and jets. The Mach disk exits the bottle in the plume of CO_2 and water vapor, vanishing in a mere millisecond. The researchers noted that it is safer to uncork a bottle gently with a "subdued sigh" to avoid eye-related incidents, but concede that a dramatic pop is more fun.

SALTY REFLECTIONS

Stretching for 4,086 sq mi (10,582 sq km) across the country of Bolivia, Salar de Uyuni is the world's largest mirror—eight times the size of New York City!

About 30,000 to 40,000 years ago, a giant prehistoric lake called Lake Minchin went through a series of transformations alongside several other vast lakes. When it dried, it left behind two bodies of water and major salt deserts. During the rainy season, the salt flat is covered with a thin sheet of water due to the floods and overflow from the neighboring lakes. It reflects light, creating a mirror effect under the vast open sky. Many people refer to it as "the place where Heaven meets Earth."

Salar de Uyuni sits 11,995 ft (3,656 m) above sea level, making it easily visible from space due to its bright white color and enormous size.

Believe It or Not! **. . . NASA and other space agencies sometimes use this salt flat's surface to calibrate satellite orbits.**

TALK TO THE HAND

Stringing together letters or symbols to create a coherent thought is part of the communication process. The ability to understand one another's thoughts is fundamental to a shared language.

But what if you were never exposed to language? Could you be taught something you never knew existed? In 1970, Susan Schaller, an American Sign Language interpreter in Los Angeles, California, did just that.

While interpreting at a community college, Schaller met Ildefonso, a 27-year-old student who was born deaf. After introducing herself, instead of signing back to Schaller with his own name, he copied her movements. He recognized her movements as commands to be mimicked instead of representations of abstract concepts, such as a wave to mean "hello."

Because Ildefonso thought every symbol was commanding him to do something, teaching him basic sign language was out of the question. So Schaller ignored him. During their sessions, she taught to an invisible student in an empty chair while Ildefonso watched from the sidelines. Schaller role-played as both the student and the teacher, hopping into the chair to mimic a student understanding the language.

After weeks of lessons, something clicked inside Ildefonso's mind as he realized every object, person, and movement has a name. At 27 years old, Ildefonso learned language.

STRIPES? ON. MOSQUITOES? OFF!

It might not be the most dignified look in the world, but a new study has found it might be worth painting your cows to look like zebras.

Experiments have shown that horseflies tend to avoid black-and-white striped surfaces, while other studies have suggested that the stripes may cause a kind of motion camouflage targeted at the insects' vision, confusing them much in the way that optical illusions confuse us.

To find out whether this can be applied to cows, Japanese researchers painted white stripes on a group of black cows and black stripes (on black bodies) on another, leaving another group of cows unpainted as control moos.

The cows were then observed for fly-repelling behaviors (head throws, ear beats, leg stamps, skin twitches, and tail flicks), and the number of flies landing on their bodies was counted. The zebra-cows were found to have more than 50 percent fewer biting flies on their bodies and a 20 percent decrease in fly-repelling behaviors versus the black-striped cows and the control group.

The researchers posit that painting stripes on livestock would not only be great for cow health but could also help reduce the need for pesticides. Sounds like a win-win (and a fashionable one at that).

Believe It or Not! **. . . Some species of mosquitoes fly up to 40 mi (64 km) to find a meal of blood!**

UPSET STOMACH

On June 6, 1822, 28-year-old Canadian fur trapper Alexis St. Martin was accidentally shot at short range in the stomach by a duck hunter, an injury that would have left most people of the time dead as a doornail. He lucked out and survived, but at a cost.

Dr. William Beaumont was able to save St. Martin, but he ended up with a gaping 2.4-in (6-cm) hole, or "gastric fistula," in his side when the hole in his stomach fused to the opening in his abdomen as he healed. But it wasn't all bad news, as Beaumont was able to observe digestion in real time by tying a silk string to pieces of beef, chicken, bread, and cabbage, and dangling them through the hole into St. Martin's stomach.

St. Martin's stint as a medical guinea pig lasted for about three decades, as he frequently returned to Dr. Beaumont for experiments in exchange for money and the promise that the hole would be sealed. The latter never happened, and the men parted ways when St. Martin asked for more money than Beaumont was willing to pay.

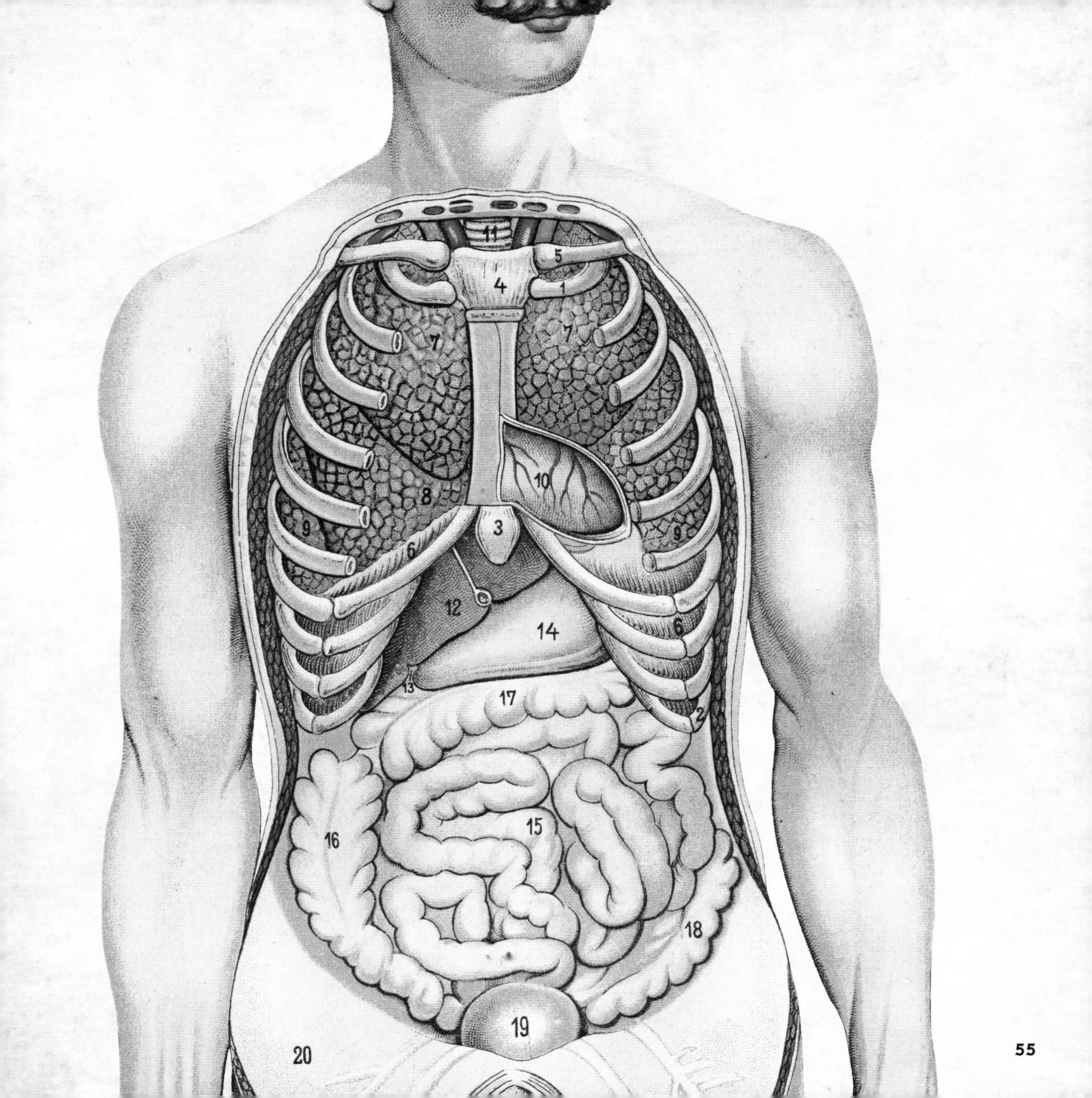
11
5
4
1
7
7
10
8
9
3
9
6
12
14
6
13
17
2
15
16
18
19
20

UNITED STATES OF AMERICA

THE UNITED STATES' DOOMSDAY PLANE

Should nuclear war break out, one of the safest places to shield yourself from the fallout is aboard a plane. More specifically, the U.S. Air Force's E-4B, or the Doomsday Plane.

Used to shuttle the Secretary of Defense from place to place, the E-4B is a modified Boeing 747 that comes in at nearly six stories tall. It boasts 18 bunks, six bathrooms, a battle staff work area, executive quarters, enough space for a 112-strong crew, and more. It can stay in flight for days at a time and refuel midair. There are no windows or digital touch screens. Instead, analog technology is used because it is less vulnerable to electromagnetic pulses. On top is a "ray dome" that houses about 60 satellite dishes and antennas that can be used to communicate with ships, subs, aircraft, and landlines around the world. And that's just what the public knows—most of its capabilities are classified.

As safe as E-4Bs may be against man-made disaster, apparently they are no match for mother nature. In 2017, a tornado struck the Offutt Air Force Base in Nebraska, leaving two of the four flying behemoths nonoperational for months.

LYRE LIAR

The Australian lyrebird can mimic the songs of as many as 25 other bird species, as well as imitate animal sounds and a whole range of human noises, including chainsaws, car engines, trains, car alarms, fire alarms, rifle shots, camera shutters, human voices, crying babies, and cell phone ringtones.

The superb lyrebird's ability to mimic almost any sound it hears is thought to stem from the makeup of its vocal organ, or syrinx. Whereas other songbirds have four pairs of syringeal muscles, the lyrebird only has three, making it more flexible.

Nobody really knows why the lyrebird needs such a vast repertoire. Some experts believe it uses its song simply to intimidate rivals in the forest. And believe it or not, the lyrebird's name does not come from its musical abilities, but rather the shape of the male's tail when spread in its courtship display.

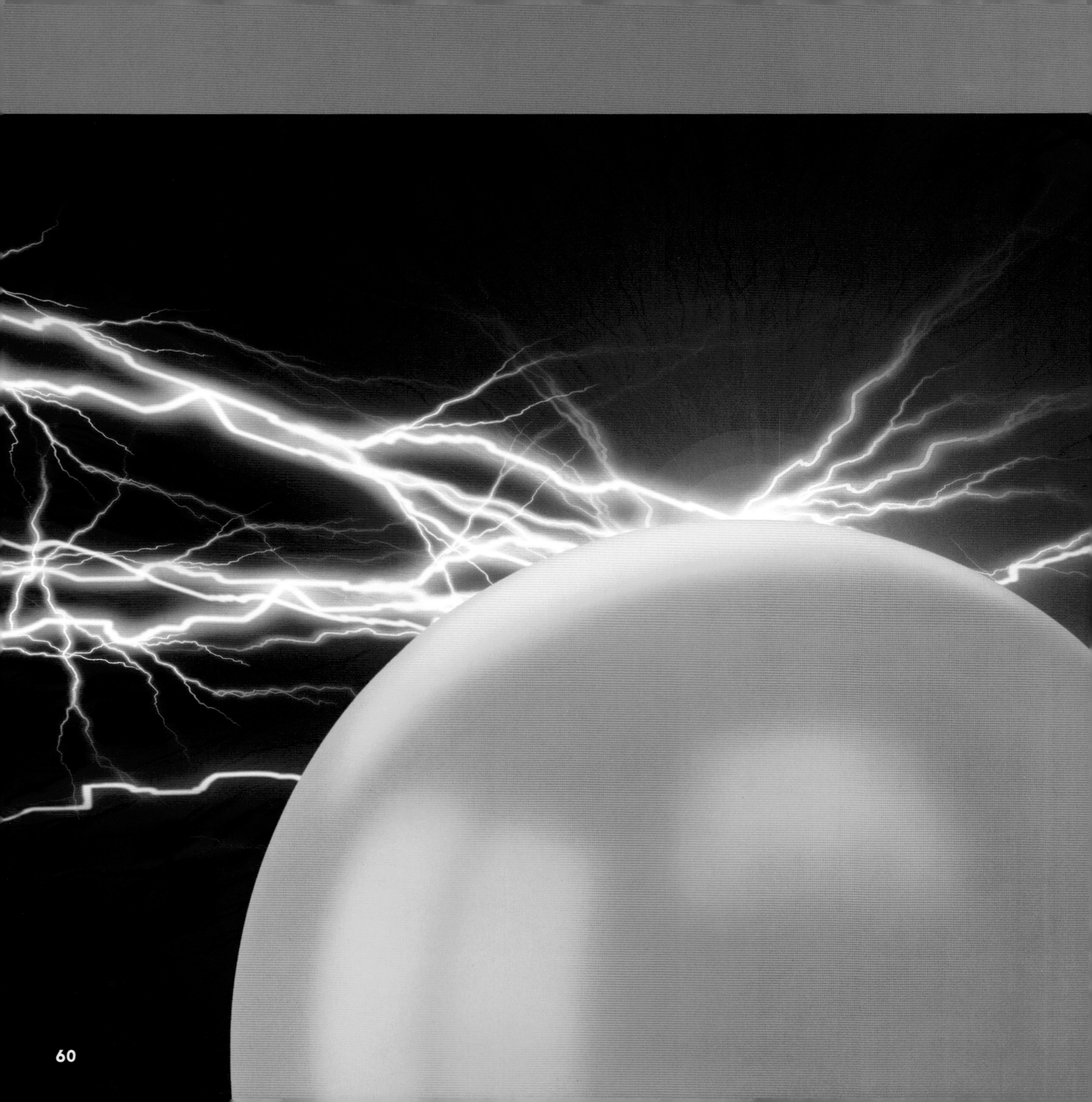

THE SHOCKING TRUTH

If you have ever rubbed a balloon on your head and watched your hair stand on end, received a small shock from touching metal after rubbing socked feet along the carpet, or seen small sparks when brushing fur in the dark, then you've experienced static electricity!

We know that rubbing two objects together creates static electricity, but scientists have finally uncovered the reason why it is created. Even on a microscopic level, no material is perfectly smooth, and parts of the surface protrude. These protrusions are bent by the force of rubbing them against another objects, which results in the "flexoelectric effect," or the charge that emits from them under stress. Shocking.

STAINING SPECIMENS

People who prepare animal specimens for museums and schools—as well as for personal collections—can make snakes, frogs, mice, and other small animals into scientific works of art called "diaphonized specimens." This technique, also known as "clearing and staining," helps people understand the internal anatomy of an animal in a unique way.

The process is complicated, involves somewhat dangerous chemicals, and takes a lot of training to perfect. In one step of the lengthy process, a preparator must soak the dead animal in a chemical called trypsin, which destroys a color-creating protein called casein. No casein, no color. After this part of the process, only a transparent version of the original animal remains.

Next, the preparator colors the specimen with types of dye that are attracted to certain substances in the body. As a result, depending on what dyes are used, collagen-rich bones usually turn red or pink, and the remaining cartilage can turn blue. The result is a colorful, mystical-looking specimen that is both artistic and educational.

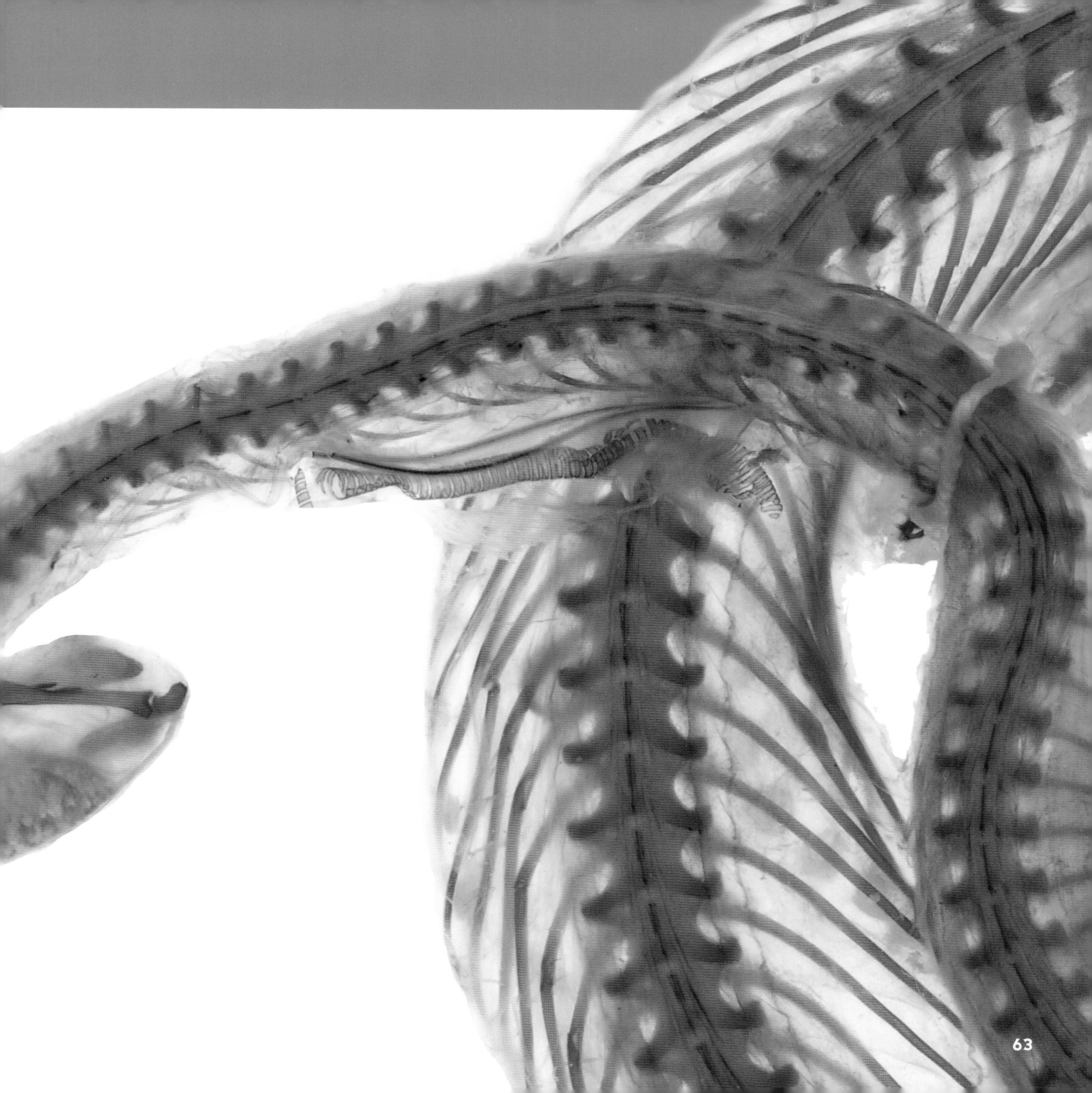

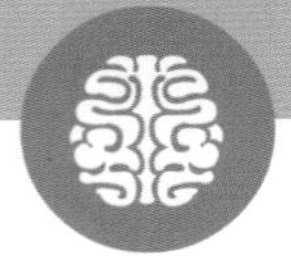

WAKING NIGHTMARE

Nightmares and dreams occur when the body is deep in REM (Rapid Eye Movement) sleep, where muscle functions are turned off. But if you are unable to move your body when falling asleep or just waking up, that phenomenon is called sleep paralysis.

Considered a parasomnia, an episode of paralysis is involuntary and occurs when the brain regains consciousness prior to your body catching on. These episodes can last anywhere from several seconds to several minutes. Paralysis usually ends on its own, but can also be interrupted by making an intense effort to move or by someone touching or speaking to you.

Sleep paralysis can inhibit your ability to speak or move your hands, arms, feet, legs, and head. Your breathing functions are normal and you are fully aware of your surroundings, but that doesn't make it any less terrifying. Common symptoms are feelings of anxiety and fear, but many cases describe hallucinations of hearing or seeing things that aren't real or the feeling of another person standing in the room.

It is possible that this 1781 painting, *The Nightmare* by Henry Fuseli, is an interpretation of sleep paralysis. Sufferers often report feeling a heavy weight or seeing evil creatures sitting on their chests.

***Believe It or Not!* . . .** Sleep paralysis is a common explanation for people who claim to have been abducted by aliens in their sleep.

BETTER OUT THAN IN

While humans just vomit the contents of their stomach up the way they came in, a few animals vomit their entire stomach instead of hurling. Known as stomach eversion, it's a thorough—if inelegant—way to clean your insides.

Many species of frogs will vomit out their own stomach. Some can even be seen giving their stomach a quick scrub with their feet. After pulling any remnant food off of their stomach, they swallow their organs, as if nothing happened at all. This process is normally incredibly quick, taking less than half a second.

Sharks also exhibit this stomach-churning tactic. Bones, feathers, turtle shells—anything that a shark should not have consumed—must also be ejected this way. Additionally, if a shark feels it is in danger, it will react by vomiting the contents of its stomach. With an empty belly, the shark can possibly swim more quickly to safety.

Believe it or not, some gluttonous sharks will vomit simply so they can eat more. Sharks feeding on baleen whale carcasses are known to vomit once full and then immediately return to eating. Maybe that's why they've been banned from buffets.

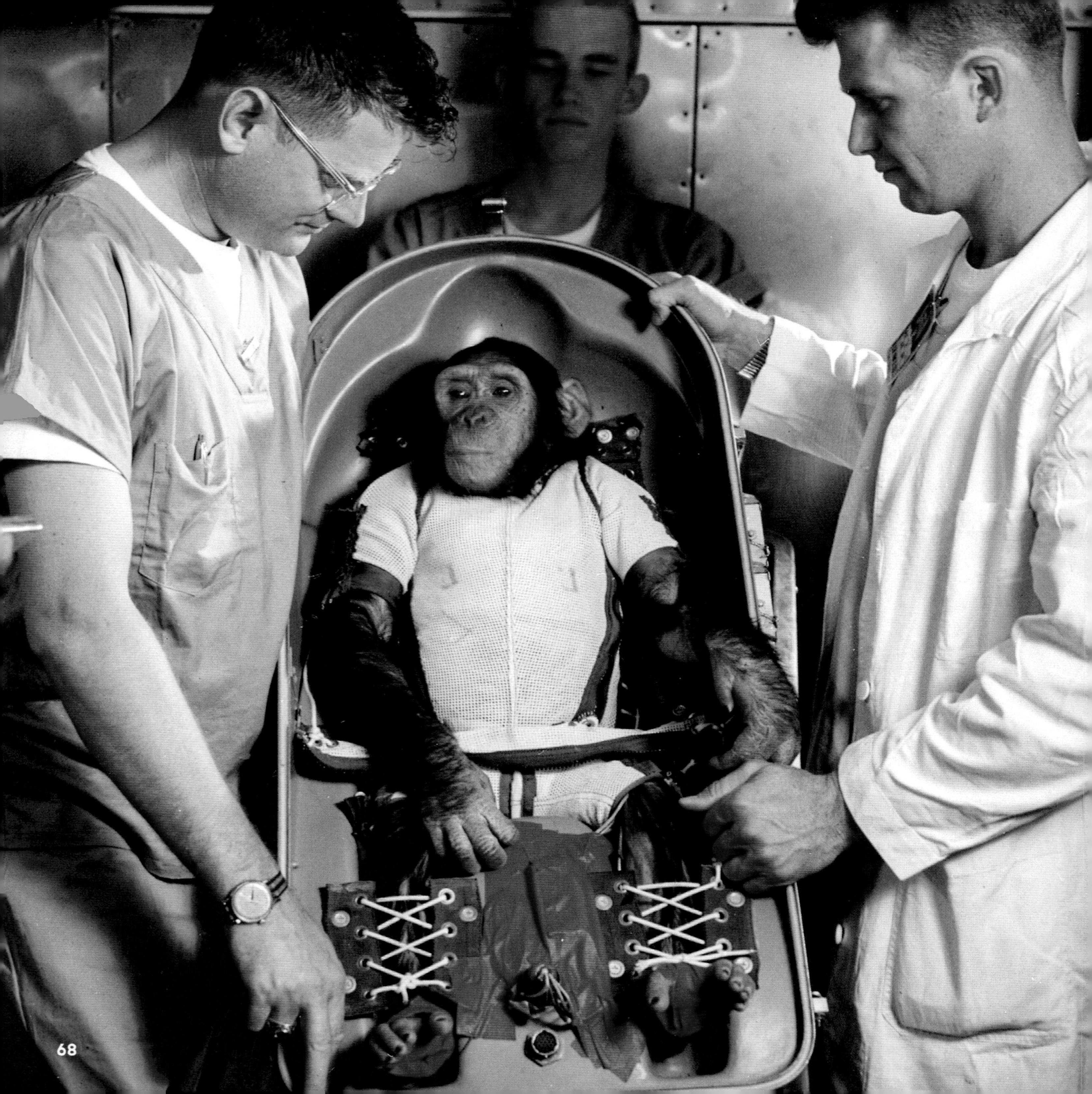

HAM THE SPACE CHIMP

Three months before Alan Shepard became the first American human in space, the United States launched a chimpanzee astronaut. His name was Ham.

For two years, number 65, as he was known (officials were worried that bad publicity might result from the death of a named chimp), was given intensive training at Holloman Air Force Base, New Mexico. He was taught to push a lever within five seconds of seeing a flashing blue light.

On January 31, 1961, the chimp, dressed in a mini space suit, was launched aboard a Mercury-Redstone rocket from Cape Canaveral, Florida. During his suborbital flight, computers on the ground measured normal vital signs, letting mission control know their brave chimp was alive.

He performed his tasks admirably, and his capsule touched down safely in the Atlantic at the end of the 16-minute flight. Though he pulled his lever just slightly slower in space than he did on Earth, this feat proved that human motor control was possible in space. Only when he had safely returned to Earth with nothing worse than a bruised nose was he renamed Ham.

VIRTUALLY UNWRAPPED

In 79 CE, as Mount Vesuvius rained down hell on the towns of Pompeii and Herculaneum below, a fine set of scrolls laid in a private library near the coastline. Along with the towns and their people, the scrolls were carbonized through a blast of hot volcanic debris, searing them into lumps of brittle carbon that are too fragile to unravel.

Collectively known as the Herculaneum papyri, the texts are thought to be the only surviving library from antiquity that exists in its entirety. Now, almost 2,000 years later, a team of researchers say they finally have the technology to decipher the papyrus text.

Scientists from the University of Kentucky have employed the help of high-energy X-rays to pick up on subtle hints of ink that are invisible to the naked eye. They will then use artificial intelligence to "fill in the gaps." The texts that have been successfully studied namely contain writings of a philosophical nature that provide insight into the world of the Roman Empire.

Professor Brent Seales, director of the Digital Restoration Initiative at the University of Kentucky.

BIKINI ATOLL IS THE BOMB

Bikini Atoll might sound like an idyllic island getaway, but any visitors would be better off wearing a biohazard suit than swimwear, as the nuclear fallout from tests carried out by the U.S. military more than 60 years ago has left parts of the Marshall Islands more radioactive than the infamous Chernobyl.

Between 1946 and 1958, the United States conducted almost 70 nuclear bomb tests in the Marshall Islands, a chain of atolls and volcanic islands in the central Pacific Ocean. The largest of these detonations released the equivalent of 15 megatons of TNT in Bikini Atoll on March 1, 1954. The explosion completely vaporized a nearby artificial island and left a crater measuring 1.2 mi (2 km) in diameter and 250 ft (76 m) in depth. Now that's a spicy meatball.

Believe It or Not! . . . Goosebumps are caused by tiny muscles attached to each and every hair follicle on your skin!

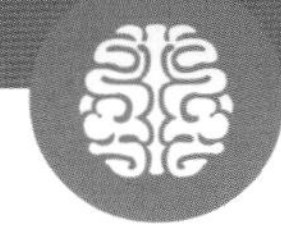

CAREFUL WHISPERS

It might seem like just another weird corner of the internet, but ASMR, short for Autonomous Sensory Meridian Response, has become incredibly popular on sites like YouTube. On these platforms, ASMRtists aim to trigger ASM responses in listeners by doing things like speaking softly; making quiet, repetitive sounds (like turning pages in a book); and performing mundane tasks.

Only some people appear to experience ASMR, and they describe it as a pleasant tingling that starts at the crown of the head and runs down the neck, usually sparked by watching or listening to certain stimuli.

It's not a new thing, either. The internet has made it easier to create a virtual community around ASMR, but some believe there is a reference to the sensation in Virginia Woolf's 1925 novel *Mrs. Dalloway*: "... with a roughness in her voice like a grasshopper's, which rasped his spine deliciously and sent running up into his brain waves of sound which, concussing, broke."

Scientists have recently looked at the psychological underpinnings of these "brain tingles," and it turns out they are actually pretty good for you. Along with decreasing levels of stress and sadness, ASMR was even shown to decrease people's heart rates.

MOLTEN MELTDOWN

When the roof of reactor 4 at the VI Lenin Nuclear Power Plant in Ukraine blew off in an uncontrolled explosion on April 26, 1986, around 57 metric tons of uranium were ejected into the atmosphere. The effects of such intense radiation displaced more than 300,000 people within the 18.6-mi (30-km) stretch of the Chernobyl Exclusion Zone. At least 237 people suffered acute radiation sickness, and the World Health Organization expects 4,000 have died or will die due to radiation effects.

The area that received the most intense dose of radiation was the Red Forest. Pine trees died out quickly due to the hot nuclear fuel burning their leaves, but deciduous plants that could drop their leaves survived the blast. Within two years after the disaster, the mammal population steadily increased. The lack of human threat and hunting has allowed animal populations to flourish.

If you want to bring a little piece of Chernobyl home, scientists from the United Kingdom and Ukraine have developed Atomik Vodka, made from radioactive grain from the Chernobyl Exclusion Zone!

***Believe It* or *Not!* . . .** This cooled molten mass of radioactive material, known as "the Elephant's Foot," once flowed like lava and emitted deadly levels of ionizing radiation, which is what distorted this photo.

Believe It or Not! . . . Cheddar cheese contains more tryptophan than turkey!

ASIAGO A DAY

Great news: cheese, mmm cheese, might actually protect you from some of the perils associated with eating too much salt.

While we all need to consume a bit of salt to keep our bodies ticking, too much can lead to high blood pressure, heart disease, strokes, and even dementia. In a world filled with fast food and processed meals, avoiding salt can be tricky, but new research suggests that eating dairy might help counteract its effects.

The results of a small study of 11 people with salt-sensitive blood pressure suggest "that people who consume the recommended number of dairy servings each day typically have lower blood pressure and better cardiovascular health in general," according to Lacy Alexander, Professor of Kinesiology at Penn State and co-author of the study.

However, before you start feasting on salty foods with a side of cheese thinking you're being healthy, there are a few caveats to take note of. First, no matter how much dairy you eat, it's best to keep your salt intake nice and low at the recommended 1,500 mg per day. And while cheese is both delicious and a great source of calcium, it can be high in saturated fat and salt. Everything in moderation—even fondue.

MIGHTY MONSTERS

Though a vast majority of the ocean floor has yet to be explored, this metallic and malicious creature may have you thinking twice about dragging your feet. *Eunice aphroditois*, commonly known as the bobbit worm, is a bristle worm that inhabits burrows it creates on the sea floor. The bobbit worm is only about 1 in (2.5 cm) wide but can grow anywhere from 4 in (10 cm) to 10 ft (3 m) long!

Once inside its sandy burrow, this ambush predator uses five antennae to sense moving prey and strikes with sharp, powerful mandibles—sometimes splitting a fish in half! The bobbit worm injects prey with a toxin, making it easier to digest. This bristle worm is typically found in warmer waters and hunts in a stationary position under soft silt or among coral reefs. Unfortunately for professional and hobby aquarists alike, bobbit worms have also been known to invade aquariums, hiding and surviving inside rocks collected from the ocean used to recreate the sea environment. The aquarists usually don't realize the worm is there until their fish start mysteriously disappearing.

OUR FILTHY HABITS

Online video streaming makes up 60 percent of the world's data traffic and generated more than 300 million tons of carbon dioxide during 2018—and nearly a third of it was porn.

Carbon emissions are produced by the electricity needed to power the consumption and production of digital equipment, including everything from data centers to your smartphone. According to a study by French think tank The Shift Project, porn makes up around 27 percent of the word's video streaming. That means it pumps out around 100 million tons of carbon dioxide each year—more than the total annual output of Belgium. Maybe next time just use your imagination, for the sake of the environment.

THROWING RED ROCKS IN GEL HOUSES

To avoid drastically altering Mars's atmosphere in order to make it livable for humans, a team of researchers instead propose encasing enormous areas of Mars in an actual greenhouse made from silica aerogel.

Aerogels are formed of interconnected nanoscale clusters surrounding pockets of gas. Being 97 percent porous, aerogel is exceptionally light but also an excellent insulator. It's already used to insulate the rovers from the dangerous cold of the Martian night.

Silica aerogel has several features that make it particularly suited for the task of colonizing Mars. It blocks ultraviolet light but lets visible wavelengths through, so it would allow enough radiation to reach the Martian surface for plants to grow. Meanwhile, it is so light that the shield could be built on an unthinkable scale. Laboratory testing suggests that when exposed to radiation matching Martian sunlight, just 1 in (2.5 cm) of aerogel can warm the area beneath by 150°F (65°C), close to the difference between Mars and Earth.

This approach would also avoid some of the ethical problems with terraforming Mars, potentially supporting millions of people while leaving most of the planet in its pristine state.

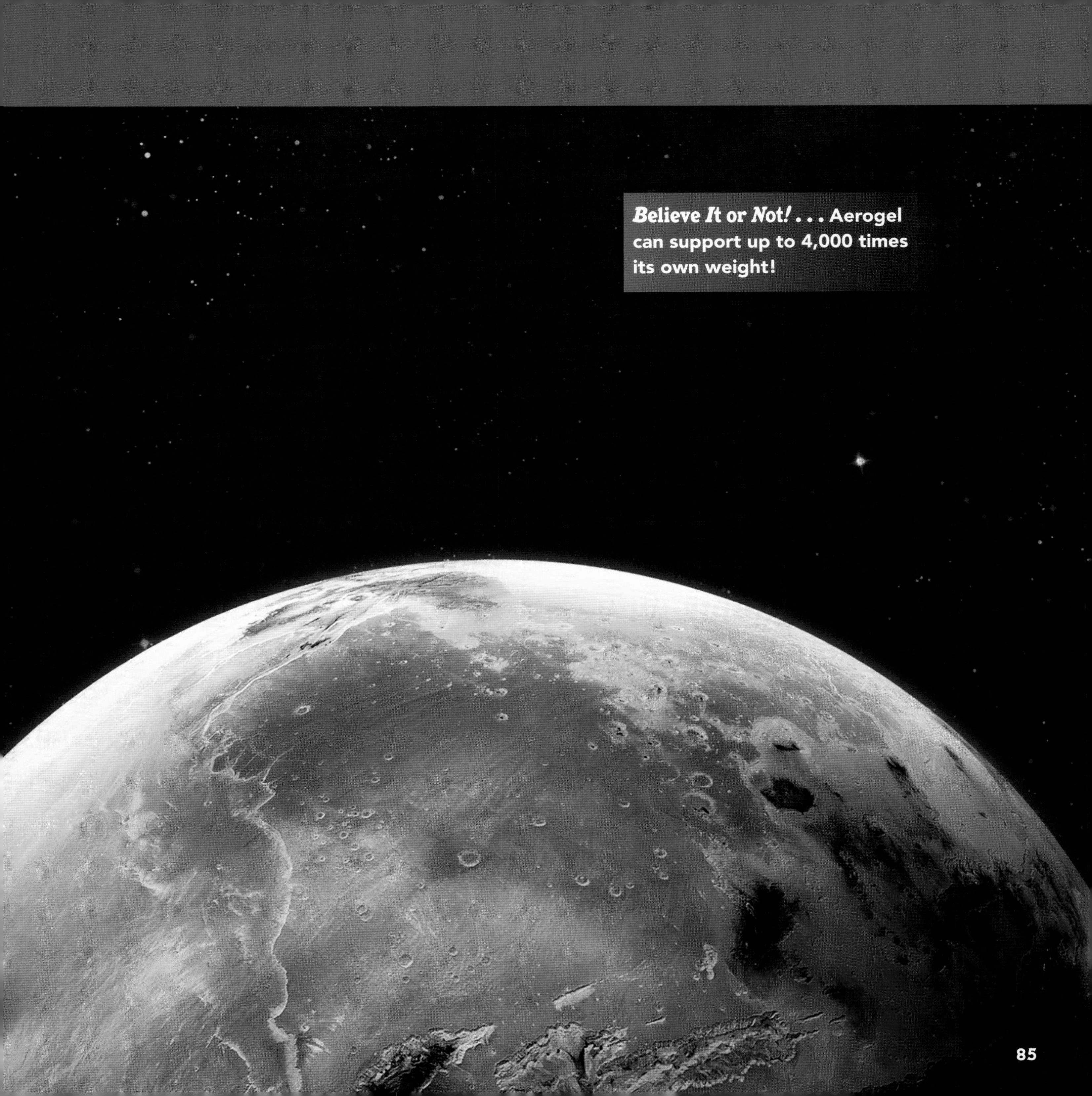

Believe It or Not! **. . . Aerogel can support up to 4,000 times its own weight!**

THE SOUND OF FACES

From the guy who does the voice-over for movie trailers to the announcers on the subway, our lives are full of faceless voices. And while most of us are content to build a mental image of these disembodied orators, a group of MIT researchers has created an artificial intelligence system that can reconstruct people's faces just by listening to their voice.

The application, called Speech2Face, is a deep neural network that was trained to recognize the correlation between voices and facial features by observing millions of YouTube videos with people talking. In doing so, it learned to associate different aspects of the audio waveform with a speaker's age, gender, and ethnicity, as well as certain cranial features such as the shape of the head and the width of the nose.

When the researchers then fed the system audio recordings of people's voices, it was able to generate an image of each speaker's face with reasonable accuracy. However, some improvements are still needed, as the images created by Speech2Face often only bear a general resemblance to the speaker. Nevertheless, faceless voices are one step closer to becoming a thing of the past, which should have major implications for prank callers, at least.

Believe It or Not! **. . . Two-thirds of the deaths in the Civil War were due to disease!**

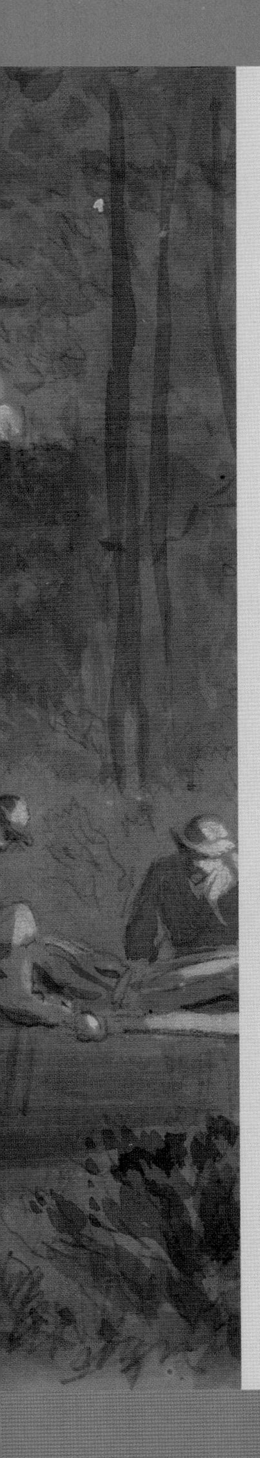

LET IT GLOW

During the Civil War, the Battle of Shiloh produced more than 23,000 casualties and was the bloodiest battle in American history at the time. Surviving soldiers were then stuck sitting in the dirt and mud for two straight days, waiting for medics to arrive. During a time when the smallest cut or scrape could become infected and kill you, lounging around with battle wounds was not the most sanitary.

When night fell, some of the soldiers noticed their wounds emanating a soft blue glow. Even though a glowing injury would send most of us running for the nearest emergency room today, the soldiers noticed that those with the blue glow had a higher survival rate, prompting this phenomenon to be called "Angel's Glow."

The cause of this heavenly luminescence? Nematodes! A type of roundworm, nematodes are typically a parasitic worm that burrows into larvae bodies and regurgitates bacteria that kills the host from the inside out. This bacteria is called *Photorhabdus luminescens*, and it has a soft blue radiance. The *P. luminescens* was responsible for attacking and killing the harmful germs and bacteria from the mud the soldiers were covered in, which is why they had a higher survival rate!

WARNING: OBJECTS ARE LARGER THAN THEY APPEAR

A stroke can have strange and unusual effects on people's perceptions, from changing their sense of smell to hallucinations. In a particularly curious instance of this perception-twisting effect, a man suffered from a stroke and developed micropsia, a visual disorder in which objects are perceived to be smaller than they actually are, like a miniature model.

As reported in a recent case study published in the journal *Neurocase*, a 64-year-old man was admitted to a hospital in the Netherlands with weakness in his left arm. He had also experienced a temporary loss of vision 11 days prior. Shortly after this incident, the man reported looking in the mirror and perceiving himself as 70 percent of his actual size.

The man also told doctors that he thought his clothes would not fit him anymore because they appeared to be too small. The effect was so severe he often worried whether certain corridors were too small for him to fit through.

The researchers weren't certain why this man acquired such an acute form of micropsia. However, they concluded the man sustained damage to his brain's visual processing hub during his stroke. In an attempt to rectify the damage and maintain some constancy in his perception, the visual system of his brain over-compensated and created this effect.

THE MANY COLORS OF LIBERTY

The Statue of Liberty as we know her is a distinctive and iconic blue-green color, but she wasn't always that way.

Believe it or not, when France gifted Lady Liberty to the United States in 1885, she was a brilliant and shiny shade of copper. Over the course of a few decades, a combination of oxidation and pollution caused her to change color. First, the copper reacted with the oxygen in the air to turn into the pinkish-red mineral cuprite. The cuprite continued to oxidize over time into tenorite, which is black in color. When water and sulfur in the atmosphere started mixing with those copper oxides, the statue began to turn her signature green, helped in part by chloride from the sea spray. Now fully oxidized and chemically stable, the Statue of Liberty has been her iconic blue-green color for more than 100 years.

Believe It or Not! **. . . The Statue of Liberty was used as the United States' first electric lighthouse from 1886 to 1902, when it was decommissioned, as it wasn't bright enough!**

THE RAREST EVENT EVER RECORDED

At a dark matter detector in Italy, scientists were lucky enough to observe the radioactive decay of a xenon-124 atom, a process that takes an unfathomably long time.

The detector, called XENON1T, is located deep within a mountain, where dark matter can theoretically permeate but interfering cosmic rays cannot. If any dark matter collides with even just a single atom making up the 7,716 lb (3,500 kg) of liquid xenon housed inside of it, XENON1T is advanced enough to detect it. And even though it wasn't built for it, apparently it is also sensitive enough to notice when a single atom decays.

According to Ethan Brown, a co-author of the report on the rare observance, "It's the longest, slowest process that has ever been directly observed, and our dark matter detector was sensitive enough to measure it."

Believe It or Not! **. . . The Xenon-124 isotope has a half-life of around 18 sextillion (18,000,000,000,000,000,000,000) years—or about 1 trillion times longer than the age of the universe.**

SWAT
OIL

MAY CONTAIN SMALL PARTS

There have been many selfless sacrifices made over the centuries in the name of science. One of the more recent, but not exactly heroic, examples was when a group of doctors swallowed LEGO pieces in order to study the health effects they could have on children.

In 2018, six doctors with the *Journal of Paediatrics and Child Health* each swallowed a LEGO minifigure head and monitored their digestive health. None reported any problems and passed the heads in an average of 1.7 days.

Taking into account the Found and Retrieved Time (FART) score and Stool Hardness and Transit (SHAT) score, they feel comfortable telling worried parents of toy-hungry children to just "wait and see" when a LEGO is swallowed. They do tell parents, however, to make sure nothing is caught in their child's throat and to seek medical attention if the object is sharp.

FELINE FERTILIZER

In ancient Egypt, mummified cats were considered a reverent gift to the gods. Literally millions of felines were raised for the sole purpose of mummifying them. Later, many of the sacred objects were turned into dirt to fertilize crops.

In 1888, a farmer digging in the sand found an enormous deposit—hundreds of thousands of cats! This was clearly a place for leaving sacrifices. But what should a person do with such a massive collection of cat mummies? A single body may have important information or collector's value, but when there are too many of one item on the market, the item loses value. (This was before Western civilization began to appreciate the cultural and historical value of mummies.)

So, some of the nicest-looking mummies were collected and sold, going to museums and private collections. However, about 180,000 of the cats were sent to Liverpool, ground up, and put into the earth to fertilize crops. The bodies and even wrappings were filled with nutrients that microorganisms could eat and turn into rich soil.

However, it appears this feline-to-fertilizer conversion was a one-time occurrence, as it resulted in a cholera outbreak when the mummies were contaminated in transit to Europe—a mummy's curse, perhaps?

Believe It or Not! **. . . In the 19th century, it was common to hold mummy unwrapping parties!**

TURNING TO STONE

Decorated with teddy bears, bicycles, and other souvenirs, Mother Shipton's petrifying well has an unusual quality—it can turn objects to stone!

According to lore, Mother Shipton was born Ursula Southhell in 1488, in a Knaresborough, England, cave. She was said to be a witch and an oracle, associated with many tragic events in the area and predicting, in prose, the horrors that were to doom the Tudor reign. She is to blame for bewitching the well.

The well's petrifying properties can also be explained by modern science. When the well water flows over objects, its unusually high mineral content hardens them—similar to how stalactites and stalagmites form in caves. Astoundingly, objects are hardened in just three to five months!

Believe It or Not! . . . Not all Swiss cheese has holes in it!

CAN'T BE BEAT

According to researchers in Switzerland, not only does music affect the flavor of maturing cheeses, but hip hop produces the best.

Sound bonkers? Well, yes. But, also, not so fast. Sonochemistry is a real field of scientific exploration looking at the influences of sound waves and the effect of sound on solid bodies, using ultrasound to alter chemical reactions. And cheese is essentially a chemical reaction, so perhaps sound waves can have some kind of influence.

To test out this theory, researchers and a cheesemaker placed nine 22-lb (10-kg) Emmental cheese wheels in individual wooden crates in a cheese cellar, and each was played a different 24-hour loop of one song using a mini transducer that directed the sound waves directly into the cheese.

Six months later, the cheeses were analyzed by food technologists, followed by a blind taste test by a panel of culinary experts. The result? Hip-hop cheese topped them all in terms of fruitiness and was the strongest in smell and taste—with the panel also concluding that a clear difference could be discerned between the cheeses. No word on if leaving a speaker on in your fridge will make those processed slices taste any better, though.

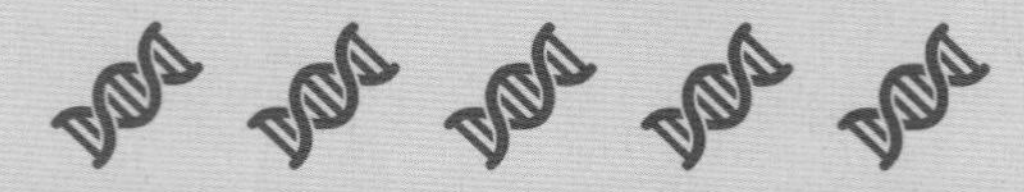

SHARP DIET

Pica is the name given to a wide variety of eating disorders that involve the ingestion of items with no nutritive value, such as soil, hair, wood, and metal. The umbrella term covers a range of conditions, including acuphagia, which refers to the eating of sharp objects.

A recent, and extreme, example of acuphagia is Bhola Shankar, who turned up at a hospital in the northwest Indian state of Rajasthan in May 2019 complaining of stomach pains. An initial X-ray revealed a mass of nails lodged in the 43-year-old's stomach, which were then surgically extracted the following day.

There were a total of 116 iron nails removed, each 2.5 in (6.5 cm) long. Shankar was unable to explain why he had eaten them. Usually, doctors first test for a deficiency in iron, which can lead to a compulsive drive to compensate for this by eating metal. However, in many cases, the condition is driven by psychological rather than nutritional causes, and a range of different therapies are needed to treat it.

Believe It or Not! **. . . There are estimated to be more trees on Earth than stars in our galaxy!**

TWINKLE, TWINKLE, LITTLE NOPE

If you left the Earth's atmosphere and looked at the stars, they wouldn't twinkle. That's because that signature shimmer isn't a property of stars—it's a property of our own atmosphere.

There's even a technical term for it: astronomical scintillation. Our atmosphere is made up of several different layers, each with its own temperatures, densities, and other variables that cause the light from faraway stars to bend and refract. Planets don't appear to twinkle from our point of view on Earth because they are much closer to us and appear larger, making the changes in light caused by our atmosphere not visible to the human eye.

POSITIVELY RADIANT

Believe it or not, radioactive uranium glassware was once all the rage. Collectors today search for these glassware pieces, commonly known as Vaseline glass due to its pale yellow-green color. This uranium glass was made with anywhere from 2 to 25 percent of uranium oxide.

When viewed under a black light, the glassware glows bright green! Don't worry, it doesn't glow based on how radioactive it is; the glass radiates simply because it's made with uranium. The levels of uranium are low enough to make the glass safe enough to handle, but you wouldn't want to eat or drink anything out of it!

ENVIRONMENT

OCEANIC DIAMONDS

Some diamonds have salt water trapped inside them. The origin of that water has been theorized but never tested—until now. A group of researchers in Germany mimicked extreme conditions in a lab, bolstering the theory that the salt water inside some diamonds comes from marine sediment.

The theory holds that when parts of the seafloor rapidly glide under a continental plate (a process called subduction), sediment on the seafloor drops hundreds of miles into the Earth's crust, where high temperatures and intense pressure compound the minerals into small crystals. These then melt in the ancient mantle at temperatures of more than 1,500°F (800°C). These small carbon-fixed stones mix with volcanic magma and spout back onto the Earth's surface as diamonds. Basically, the planet eats the seafloor and then spits out diamonds.

IF YOU'RE HAPPY AND YOU KNOW IT

Tyrannosaurus rex is terrifying in *Jurassic Park*, yes, but what about those sad, stumpy little arms? Well, it looks like Rexy will get the last laugh, as research suggests those arms may have been much more useful (and dangerous) than once thought.

Scientists from Stockton University theorize T. rex's feeble arms were much, much more flexible than we've long thought. T. rex (and other theropods) were probably able to rotate their palms upward and inward, with a range of motion great enough to allow them to perform a clapping motion. Applause might be a concept lost on dinosaurs (with the exception of Barney, of course), but this is still super impressive.

It may not sound like very much, and it's speculative, but there's potential for this to be a huge dino-deal. One possible conclusion to be drawn here is that the ability to rotate the arms and bring them inward toward the chest actually was key in gripping and biting prey.

Believe It* or *Not! **. . . More time separates the *Stegosaurus* from the *Tyrannosaurus rex* than the T. rex from humans.**

I WANT TO BELIEVE

We finally have the first absolutely 100 percent confirmed sighting of a fully functional flying saucer. A team of scientists and engineers in Romania has developed a first-of-its-kind, hyper-maneuverable flying saucer.

Demonstrating an ADIFO (All-DIrection Flying Object) prototype, the team says a full-scale model would create "a new and revolutionary flight paradigm," and fly like the UFOs depicted in fiction for decades.

At low altitudes and speeds, the saucer uses ducted fans, as you'd see in a normal quadcopter. At higher speeds and altitudes, it uses jet engines loaded at the rear of the saucer. The vehicle also has lateral nozzles, which allow it to perform sudden vertical or horizontal movements at high speeds, much like flying saucers in sci-fi movies. They claim that by using all the methods of thrust simultaneously, ADIFO can perform unique maneuvers "superior to any known aircraft," including sudden stops at speed while maintaining altitude, and full maneuverability while flying upside down.

THE LOST AND FOUND REMAINS OF JOSEPH MERRICK

After nearly 130 years, the remains of Joseph Merrick, also known as "The Elephant Man," have been found—somewhat thanks to infamous Victorian killer Jack the Ripper.

Merrick was born in Leicester in 1862. He started to develop unusual symptoms at five years old, characterized by large abnormal growths across much of his skin and bone, possibly caused by a combination of Proteus syndrome and neurofibromatosis. At the age of 17, he joined a "freak show" that toured across Europe as part of a circus.

Merrick died on April 11, 1890, aged 27, after becoming asphyxiated by the weight of his own head, apparently after trying to lie down. His skeleton has been stored at the Royal London Hospital ever since, but the location of his soft tissue was never officially logged.

While carrying out research for her biography about Merrick, *Joseph: The Life, Times & Places of the Elephant Man*, author Jo Vigor-Mungovin noticed the link between Jack the Ripper and Merrick. She noted that many of Jack the Ripper's 1888 victims were killed in the same district of London where Merrick died two years later. This led her to the records of the City of London Cemetery and Crematorium, where two of the Ripper's victims were laid to rest. Vigor-Mungovin searched the cemetery's records, found Merrick's name, and was able to narrow her research down to a single unmarked grave, where she is "99 percent certain" the Elephant Man's remains were laid to rest.

BABIES... IN SPACE!

Scott Solomon, Professor of Evolutionary Biology at Rice University, has speculated that if human beings ever procreate in space, the resulting offspring might look like your typical Hollywood alien.

In order to spare the child bearer's zero-gravity-weakened bones, space babies would likely be delivered via Caesarean sections. And since the size of our heads is restricted by the size of the birth canal, the increased use of C-sections could lead to our descendants' heads being larger due to the lack of restriction.

Gravity, and the lack thereof, also affects the fluids in our bodies. Normally on Earth, all of the fluids in our bodies are pulled downward. Since this is not possible in space, space babies might develop bloated bodies and puffy faces. Their blood pressure would also increase in the upper body due to zero gravity, causing their eyes to bulge.

On top of all this, space babies might also have a new type of skin pigment. Without Earth's protective ozone layer, radiation from the sun could have disastrous impacts on humans' health, especially our skin. This could lead to a potential change of skin color as evolution tries to counteract the harmful cosmic rays.

All of these factors combined leave us with a baby looking something like the alien emoji.

BLUE BLOODS

Thanks to a natural immuno-response in horseshoe crab blood, biologists have been able to test medicine and health care equipment for contamination since the 1970s.

Having crawled this Earth for more than 400 million years, horseshoe crabs are considered living fossils. They've been around for so long, they actually predate the first dinosaurs by about 200 million years.

Their circulatory system is completely open, meaning their blood doesn't pass through veins or capillaries but circulates around the entire cavity of their body. Horseshoe crabs don't have white blood cells to fight off infection. Instead, their blood is able to detect toxins and bacteria, and then form a robust gel casing around anything harmful.

While most animal blood is red due to a reliance on iron, horseshoe crab blood is rich with copper, making it blue. In the 1970s, scientists developed a way to use their blood to validate the purity of medicine and equipment. Prior to this, infections caused by attempts at medical care were sometimes worse than the injury itself. Nowadays, there is a synthetic substitute for horseshoe crab blood, which may soon make horseshoe crab milking obsolete.

Believe It or Not! **. . . The rarest blood type is RH-Null, or "golden blood." Less than 50 people in the world have it!**

BOLD MOLD

Slime mold, despite its name, is not actually a mold, a fungus, a plant, an animal, or a bacterium. It belongs to a kingdom of life called Protista that contains any single-celled organism that is not an animal, plant, or fungus.

One species of slime mold is called *Physarum polycephalum*, which means "many-headed slime." It's not a single creature but rather a collection of unicellular organisms that can band together in a single form. They can be chopped into many pieces, only to fuse back together within a few hours. If they come across any other slime molds along their travels, they will join together.

There is neither a male nor a female of the species, but more than 720 different sexes. It can creep from place to place at up to 1.6 in (4 cm) per hour by extending stringy fingerlike protrusions.

To get even weirder, slime mold has neither a brain nor a central nervous system, nor any neurons. Nevertheless, some scientists argue they exhibit intelligence because they can "learn" from experience and change their behavior accordingly.

If artificial intelligence doesn't overtake mankind, slime mold just might.

THE MIGHT OF LIGHT

Light might have no mass, but it can still push things around. This is known as radiation pressure. Light particles (photons) carry a momentum with them, but how this momentum is transferred is not exactly clear. However, new research has come up with a way to actually study these interactions between light and matter.

An international team constructed a very special experiment to study the momentum of light. Photons carry a tiny momentum, and their effect can only be studied cumulatively. Still, there were no devices sensitive enough to measure the effect. This is why it has been so difficult to study how radiation pressure is converted into force or movement.

The team built a mirror fitted with acoustic sensors. They shot laser pulses at the mirror and studied the effects. Then the sensors recorded the vibration generated by the photons. The elastic waves moved across the mirror like ripples on the surface of a pond. These observations finally confirm predictions regarding the transfer of momentum.

4
2
5
9
13
16
20
17
25
27
28
24
25
28

WHEN EVERY DAY IS UNFORGETTABLE

Think of a random date from your childhood onward. Can you remember what day of the week it was, what you were doing that day, and what news events occurred? Somebody with an ordinary memory would probably have trouble, especially if nothing significant transpired. But 34-year-old Joey DeGrandis of New York can almost definitely tell you within seconds.

DeGrandis is one of fewer than 100 people worldwide with Highly Superior Autobiographical Memory, or HSAM, a rare condition that typically allows them to recall life memories from specific dates with great accuracy and ease.

Take February 25, 2010. Your average person probably can't tell you about what they did on that exact day. But DeGrandis remembers that it was a Thursday (correct) and it was snowing in New York (also correct). He knows he went to Katz's Deli with his friends Jeff and Dan, and it was two days after he had gone on a job interview for a position he really wanted.

HSAM manifests itself differently in those who have it. Some view it as merely an interesting ability. Others say it has caused significant challenges in their daily lives. Some experts think HSAM could open new doors in the study of memory and potentially offer new insights into Alzheimer's disease and other memory loss issues.

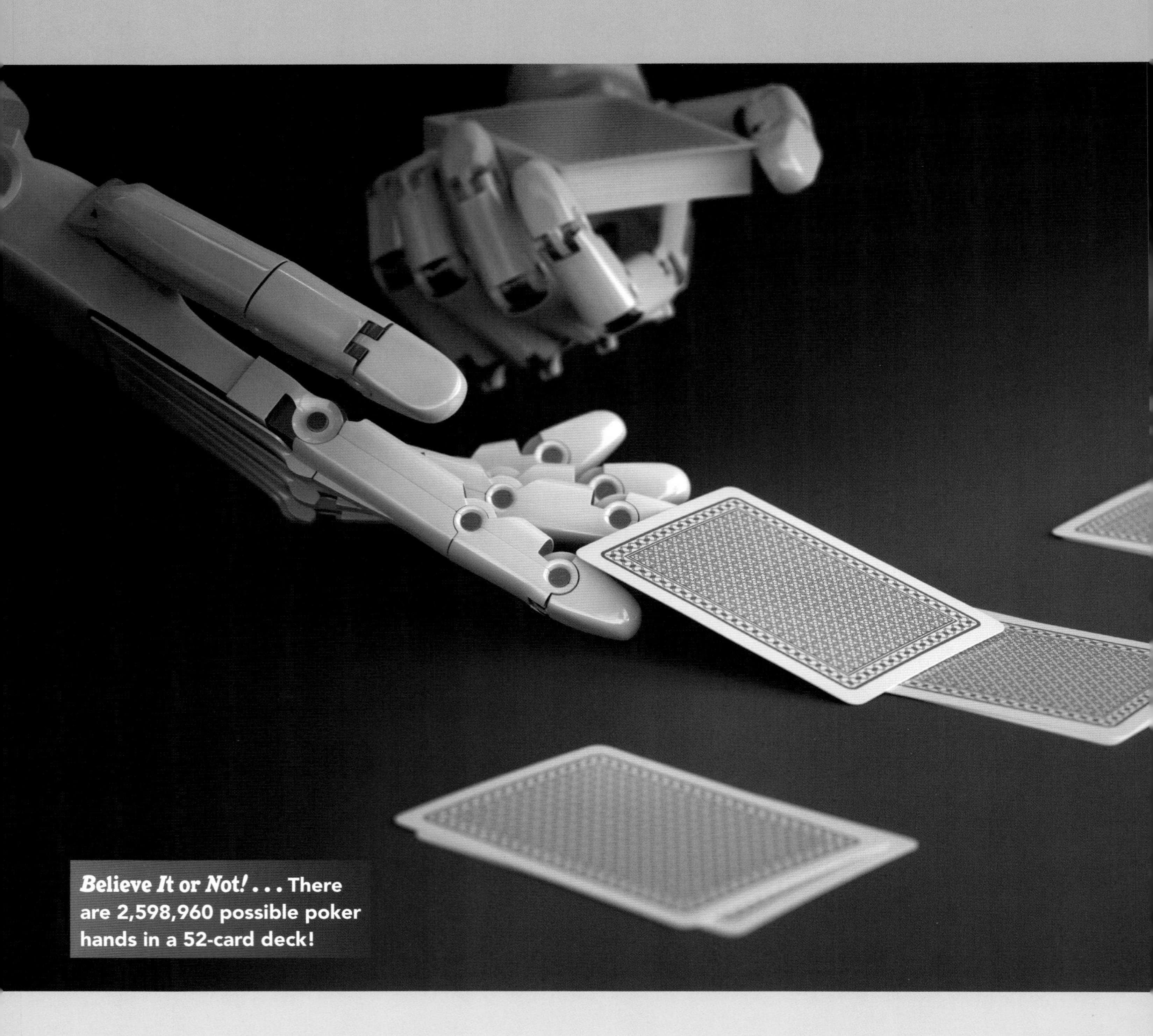

Believe It or Not! **. . . There are 2,598,960 possible poker hands in a 52-card deck!**

UPPING THE ANTE

Artificial intelligence can beat the world's best at chess, Go, Jeopardy!, and now six-player no-limit Texas hold 'em poker—showing it's well on track to become our almighty overlord in the not-so-distant future.

Programmers have developed a computerized poker champion that has successfully defeated Darren Elias (who holds the most World Poker Tour titles), Chris "Jesus" Ferguson (winner of six World Series of Poker events), and more than a dozen pros who, between them, have won over $1 million from the game.

One thing that makes this triumph so special is the secretive nature of poker. In chess and Go, both players can see everything that goes on the board. In poker, they can't—cards in play aren't always visible and players can bluff. This, the researchers say, makes it a trickier game to play for a machine built on logic and probabilities.

The machine, "Pluribus," uses a limited-lookahead search algorithm, enabling it to predict the strategy its opponents will use in the next two to three plays (as opposed to the entire game). Pluribus also thrives on unpredictability. After all, it wouldn't get very far if it saved its bets for excellent hands only. The novel strategy makes AI more relevant to "real-world" problems, which often involve missing information and multiple players.

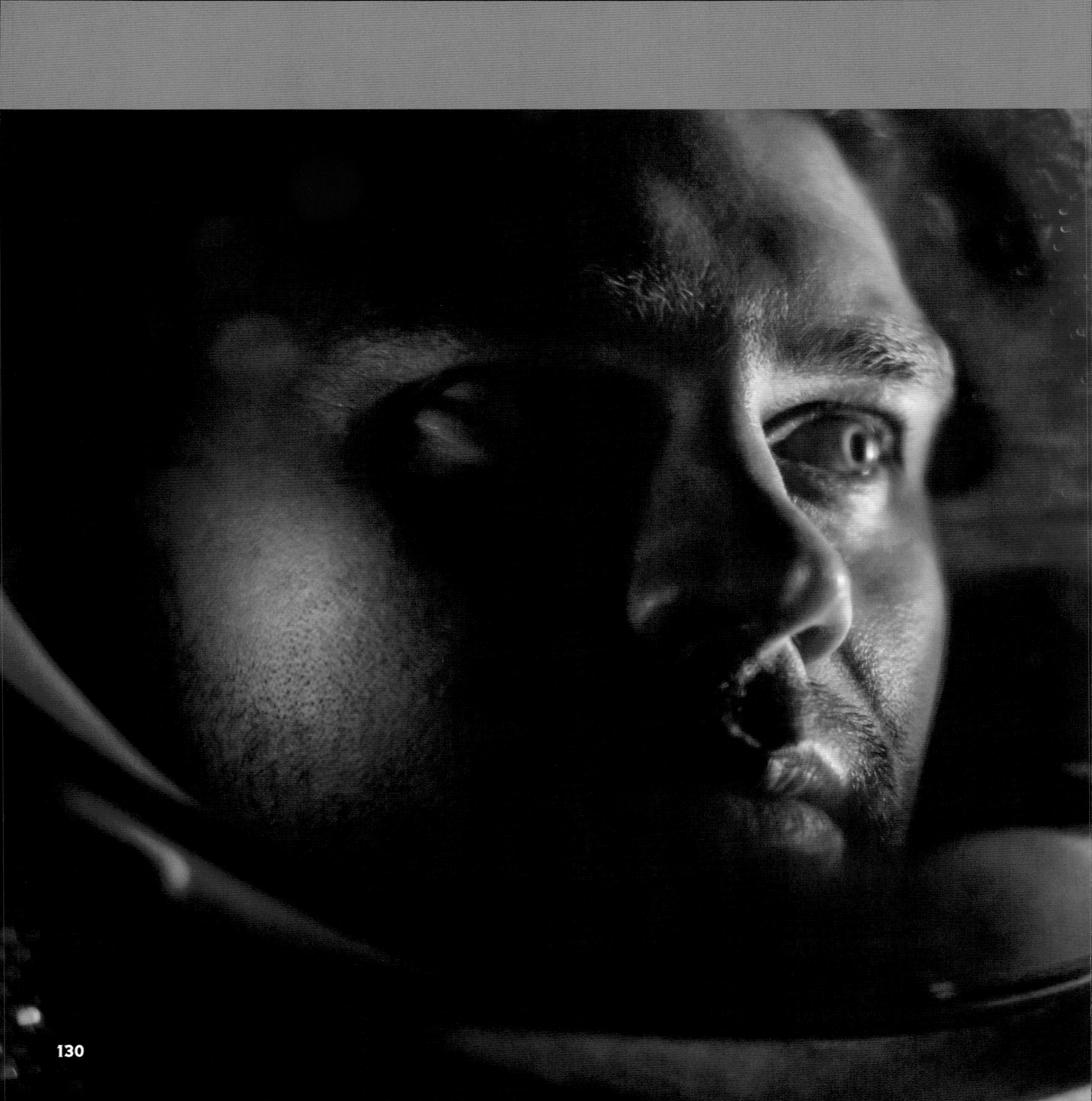

DON'T STRESS

Space travel may be out of this world, but the side effects can be unexpected and dangerous. Certain dormant viruses have been seen resurrecting inside astronauts' bodies after time spent in space. Specifically? The herpes virus.

NASA scientists have discovered that the herpes virus reactivates during longer stints of space travel. The virus has co-evolved with humanity and only wakes up during times of high stress or illness. Immuno-suppressing stress hormones, like cortisol and adrenaline, surge during spaceflight, simulating a high-stress environment for the dormant virus to resurface.

Four of the eight herpes viruses known to infect humans have been identified in astronauts, such as the ones responsible for chicken pox and mono. Once infected, the astronauts stay contagious for up to 30 days after returning from space!

INVINCIBLE INSECTS

It is often said that cockroaches could survive a nuclear apocalypse—they can't. But that doesn't mean they are easy to get rid of. And, lucky for us, these creepy crawlies are only getting harder and harder to kill.

Researchers recently tested out different treatments of three insecticides in numerous cockroach-infested apartments across Indiana and Illinois over six months. Regardless of the different chemical cocktails, the researchers were unable to reduce the size of the cockroach populations. (Some even got larger.) Even scarier, some populations developed resistance to the insecticides within a single generation.

While cockroaches are still not immune to a good foot stomping, this new study does suggest that humans need to wise up when it comes to pest control. The researchers say their findings highlight the need for combining chemical treatments with traps, improved sanitation, and vacuums to control cockroaches, rather than just relying on insecticides.

DEADLY DIET

It is said that you should eat everything in moderation, but "everything" probably shouldn't include microplastics. The average American consumes 1,314,000 calories, almost 80 lb (36 kg) of sugar, and more than 74,000 microplastic particles every year. These particles are micro-sized pieces of plastic from larger pieces that have been broken down.

Researchers have reviewed 26 studies analyzing the number of microplastics found in fish, shellfish, added sugars, salts, alcohol, tap or bottled water, and air to find out how much microplastic we really consume. Varying factors, such as age, sex, and dietary preferences affect the overall number, but the general estimate? Anywhere between 74,000 and 121,000 particles a year. If you like to drink bottled water, add an extra 90,000! The food we eat is responsible for 39,000 to 52,000 particles, while we inhale the rest throughout the day.

Though these numbers may sound alarming and negative side effects are possible, scientists say there is no need to worry about imminent danger.

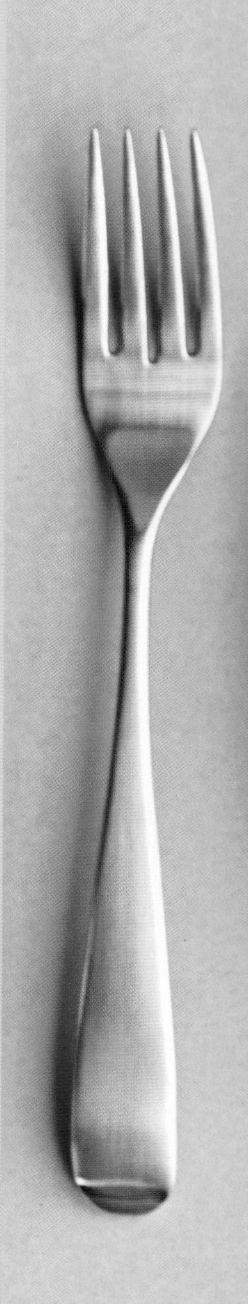

A GLOWING LEGACY

Famous physicist and chemist Marie Curie made significant contributions to science, including coining the term "radioactivity," but if you want to handle her personal manuscripts, you'll have to wear protective clothing and sign a liability waiver.

The Polish-French scientist worked extensively with radioactive substances before the dangers of radiation were understood. She even walked around with bottles of polonium and radium—elements she and her husband, Pierre, discovered—in her pockets and kept bottles of them on her shelves, admiring the dim glow they gave off in the night.

Curie passed away in Savoy, France, on July 4, 1934, from aplastic anemia, thought to have been caused by her excessive exposure to radiation. Her papers will remain radioactive for more than 1,000 years and are currently housed in lead-lined boxes at the Bibliothèque Nationale in France.

***Believe It or Not!* . . .** **Marie Curie was the first person to receive two Nobel Prizes—first in physics, then later in chemistry.**

BEANS ARE GO

SPACE SUPERSTITIONS

You wouldn't think that the world's foremost scientific agency would be very superstitious, but NASA has some long-standing traditions that they live and breathe by.

Before every launch from the Kennedy Space Center, astronauts eat a meal of steak, eggs, and cake, no matter the hour, and must play poker until the commander loses. They typically also bring along a stuffed animal. Not only is the plush considered lucky, but its fluffy body is a safe enough object to signal when gravity shifts and objects start floating.

And it's not just the astronauts. Launchpad engineers believe it's bad luck for astronauts to see the rocket before launch day and take great measures to ensure none of them see their ride during the sometimes days-long journey to the launch pad. And back at mission control, every shuttle launch is celebrated with a round of baked beans.

Cosmonauts have their rituals as well. Every single person launched into space from Baikonur Cosmodrome in Kazakhstan has peed on a bus tire just before takeoff. This unpeelievable tradition started after Yuri Gagarin—the first man to orbit the Earth—took an emergency pit stop on a bus tire in 1961.

THE POISON GARDEN
THESE PLANTS CAN KILL
THESE PLANTS CAN KILL

FOR YOUR EYES ONLY

Alnwick Castle in Northumberland, England, plays host to the small but deadly Poison Garden—filled exclusively with around 100 toxic, intoxicating, and narcotic (illegal) plants.

Surrounded by the beautiful 12-acre Alnwick Garden, the boundaries of the Poison Garden are kept behind intricate black iron gates. The only way to see the garden is on a guided tour, during which visitors are strictly prohibited from smelling, touching, or tasting any plants. (Although some people still occasionally faint from inhaling toxic fumes while walking in the garden.)

The garden contains exotic plants like the *Brugmansia* of Brazil, which can cause paralysis and death, along with common English plants like laurels, whose smell can render people unconscious. Other toxic plants featured include hemlock, castor beans, and deadly nightshade. The garden also contains a variety of illicit drugs, including cannabis, coca, and poppy.

The garden is the brainchild of Jane Percy, Duchess of Northumberland, who was tasked with finding something to do with unused castle grounds. Despite its royal origins, this is one garden where you *don't* want to stop and smell the flowers.

THE FIRST CYBORG ARTIST

Neil Harbisson was born with achromatopsia—a rare visual condition that results in total color blindness. To him, the world is a constantly dreary plane of grays, black, and whites. But since 2003, the eccentric artist has had an antenna poking out of his hair that allows him to "hear" colors and gives him the distinction of being the world's first cyborg artist.

His head-mounted antenna is able to detect the wavelengths of light reflected off whatever is in front of the sensor and then convert these data into sound, with different wavelengths corresponding to different sound frequencies. The Belfast-born, Catalan-raised artist's antenna is permanently attached to his skull and delivers the sound waves to his inner ear through bone conduction.

Purples and indigos are perceived as a high-pitched beep, with the colors becoming lower pitched as the spectrum shifts from blues to greens, then yellows to oranges, and so on. After years of practice, Harbisson can now perfectly recognize colors purely based on the pitch and tone of sound they create.

***Believe It or Not!* . . .** **Neil's antenna allows him to perceive infrared and ultraviolet colors!**

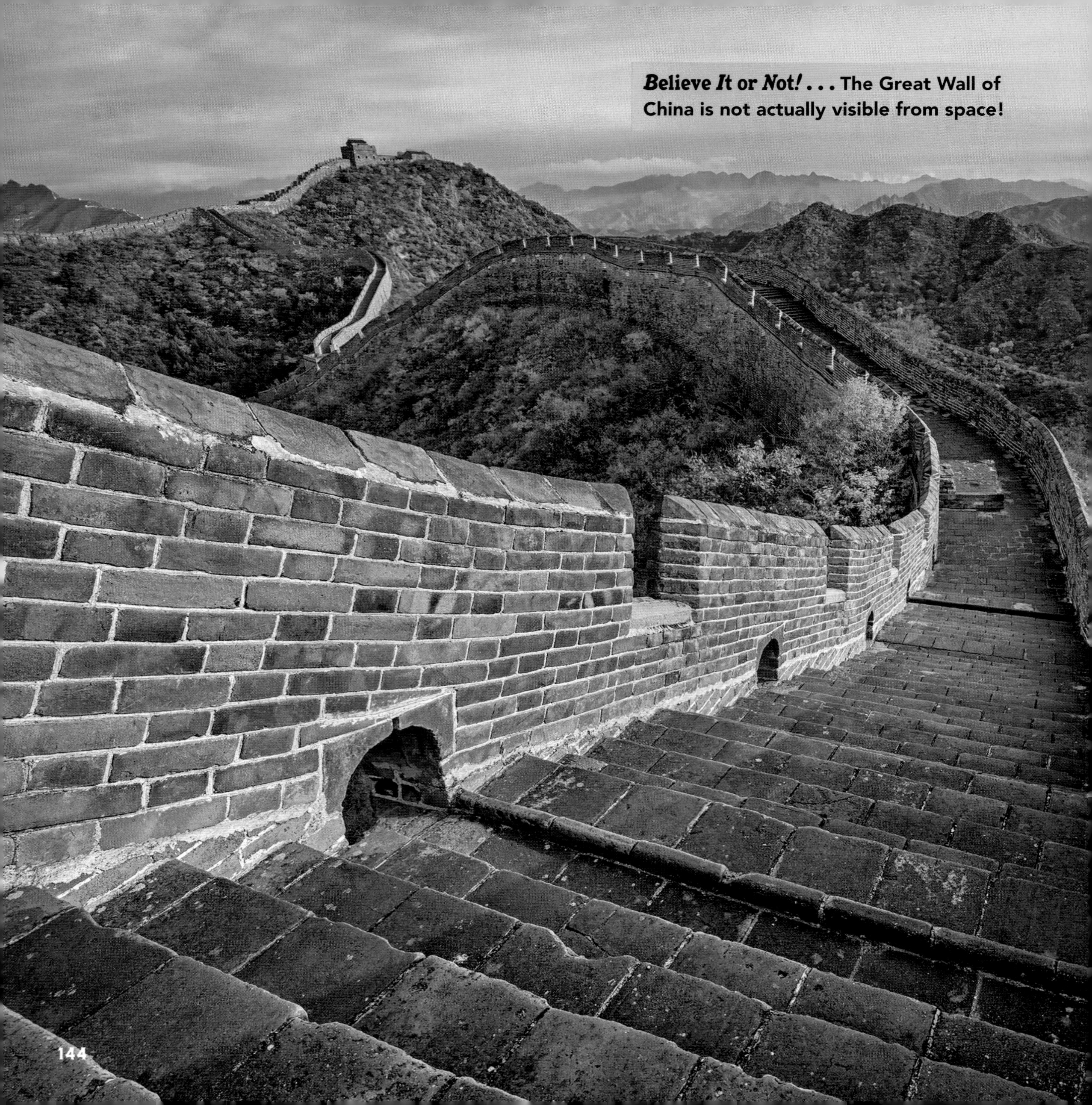

Believe It or Not! **. . . The Great Wall of China is not actually visible from space!**

BRICK BY BRICK BY GRAIN

Centuries-old portions of the Great Wall of China are still standing thanks to a powerful mortar created with an unexpected ingredient—sticky rice!

In one of the greatest technological innovations of the Ming Dynasty (1368–1644), workers developed sticky rice mortar. They crafted it from a mixture of slaked lime—a standard ingredient in mortar—and sweet rice flour. The result was the first composite mortar in history, a potent mix of inorganic and organic ingredients.

A team of researchers from Zhejiang University investigated the chemical composition of Ming-era mortar and found that the legendary strength of rice-lime mortar comes from amylopectin. When amylopectin (the organic portion of the mortar recipe) comes into contact with calcium carbonate (the inorganic part), a complex interaction occurs. Acting as an inhibitor, the amylopectin controls the growth of the calcium carbonate crystal.

The result is a more tightly bonded mixture with three key advantages: First, it's highly water resistant. Second, it shrinks less and holds its shape. Third, the key chemical reaction in the mortar continues over time. Put another way, the mortar gets stronger as the years go by!

R.I.P.

WHERE SATELLITES GO TO DIE

Have you ever wondered what happens when a spacecraft launched into space shuts down and begins falling toward Earth? They don't just drop randomly; otherwise, the thousands of satellites, landing modules, experimental spacecraft, and space stations would be coating us with debris every week.

Located 2,500 mi (4,023 km) off the coast of New Zealand, a spacecraft graveyard lies in what's officially called the South Pacific Ocean Uninhabited Area (SPOUA).

SPOUA has been designated as entirely void of human life; it contains no islands and very few shipping lanes. Scientists determined it is the least likely place for an incoming spacecraft to harm a human being. At the center of SPOUA lies Point Nemo, the exact place on Earth that is farthest from any land mass. Out of sight, out of mind, right?

NO MORE ICE, ICE, BABY

Nothing makes mornings worse than they already are quite like having to scrape a night's worth of ice off of your windshield.

So, if you don't want to waste energy using a scraper or waste time with that defroster heating up your windshield, then science has got a quick and cheap solution for you!

The solution is an actual chemistry solution—a mixture of one part water and two parts rubbing alcohol that will dissolve the frost from the windshield rapidly and effortlessly. Isopropyl (rubbing) alcohol has a freezing point of –128°F (–89°C), so the solution not only doesn't freeze, it actually helps lower the freezing point of water and melts the frost away.

Looks like whoever owns this car is going to need a lot.

SUDDENLY SAGE

Sudden savant syndrome, also known as an acquired savant, is the inexplicable onset of astonishing new abilities at a gifted or prodigal level. There is no scientific explanation for why this occurs.

One such case of a sudden savant is a 28-year-old man from Israel. His only musical experience was memorizing a major and minor chord, without fully understanding how musical scales worked. While playing random keys at a piano in a mall, he suddenly began playing popular songs just from his memory. He knew every chord and scale, how the notes worked together, and how to recognize harmonies.

With no history of a neurological disorder or brain injury, this man became a sudden musical savant. Other cases of sudden or acquired savant syndrome have seen people become prolific painters, photographers, and even mathematical geniuses. Some of these instances were preceded by head injuries, but we don't recommend trying to recreate them in hopes of becoming the next Mozart. Just practice like the rest of us.

URINE FOR A SURPRISE

Despite repeated assertions in popular culture and across online forums throughout the years, your pee isn't actually sterile.

This "fact" sprang from the development of urinary tract infection tests by epidemiologist Edward Kass. He began testing surgery patients' urine and cleared them if they got a "negative" for bacteria. This led many people—even doctors—to believe that healthy urine is completely free from bacteria. This, however, was an oversimplification of the test; a negative result doesn't mean there aren't any bacteria at all, but instead that the bacteria falls below a certain threshold. Everything in or on the human body is contaminated with microbes.

But don't worry—just because your pee contains microbes doesn't make it dangerous. Much of the bacteria in the human body is essential to our bodily functions, especially digestion. So despite containing germs, your pee is not dangerous unless you have something like a urinary tract infection, but we still wouldn't recommend drinking it.

***Believe It* or *Not!* . . .** **Almost all animals take the same amount of time to empty their bladders—about 21 seconds!**

mazda3
JND-43-76

ENVIRONMENT

OH, HAIL NO

A freak hailstorm in Guadalajara, Mexico, on June 30, 2019, left residents of at least six neighborhoods to find the streets, and their vehicles, buried in up to 5 ft (1.5 m) of ice. It was all the more shocking because up until then, the city had been basking in temperatures of 88°F (31°C).

Seasonal hailstorms have been known to occur, but nothing on this scale has been seen in recent memory. While people seemed to enjoy the novelty of a snow day in Guadalajara, not everyone was pleased. At least 200 homes and businesses reported hail damage, and it's thought at least 50 vehicles were swept away by ice running down from the hills or were buried under hailstones, too.

QUANTUM CANVAS

Humans love art. From frescos in the Sistine Chapel to doodles on notepads, we are constantly letting out our artistic side. And now art can enter a new frontier: the quantum world. Researchers have developed a way to "paint" tiny masterpieces on a special state of matter called a Bose-Einstein Condensate (BEC).

The BEC happens when a diluted gas of certain particles—in this case, rubidium atoms—is cooled down to a few billionths of a degree above absolute zero. Under these conditions, where most atoms are in their lowest possible state, microscopic quantum phenomena suddenly become macroscopic.

And on this quantum blob of matter, researchers were able to project an image using a laser to create a "light stamp." They were able to create micro-copies of paintings such as the *Mona Lisa* and *The Starry Night* by Van Gogh. These pieces of art are tiny but not atom-sized. They are roughly 100 microns across, which is more or less the width of a human hair.

WARNING: ZOMBIES AHEAD

We may not have to worry about a zombie virus infecting humans, but gastropods, such as snails, should keep their antennae up.

The *Leucochloridium* is a parasitic flatworm ingested by snails in the form of eggs found in bird droppings. Once consumed, the eggs hatch into larvae and "infect" the snail by forcing it to move into an unsafe environment, such as a sunny area or higher ground. The worm moves into the snail's transparent eyestalks and pulsates, mimicking a caterpillar, to attract hungry birds.

The snail may not want to be eaten, but the worm has other plans. Once inside the bird's gastrointestinal tract, the zombie snail infects it with the *Leucochloridium* larvae that then mature and release eggs. After the bird excretes these eggs, the cycle continues once again.

Believe It or Not! **. . . The victim snail will often survive this horror show, as a hungry bird usually just plucks off the offending eyestalks, leaving the snail to regenerate the lost body parts and potentially become part of a parastic flatworm's life-cycle once again.**

BIG BANG BUZZ

Some of the static on analog TVs and FM radio stations is from the Big Bang!

According to the theory, the universe began its life around 13.8 billion years ago, when literally everything erupted from a singularity, causing a massive release of energy. You might think that energy would disappear over time, but since the universe contains literally everything that exists, it just bounces around the cosmos.

Now it can be observed as background radiation called the Cosmic Microwave Background (CMB). About 1 percent of the static between channels on analog TVs and the white noise on empty radio stations is caused by the afterglow of the Big Bang. The switch to digital TVs and streaming music has made experiencing the CMB in these ways a much rarer occurrence.

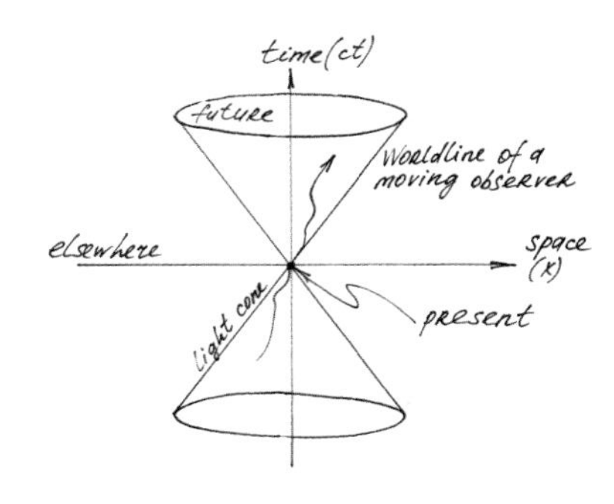

TECHNOLOGY

A DIFFERENT KIND OF CATCALLING

In 1929, two Princeton University researchers were able to turn a living cat into a working telephone.

In an effort to learn more about how the auditory nerve perceives sound, Professor Ernest Wever and his research assistant Charles Bray removed part of a sedated cat's skull and attached one end of a telephone wire to the feline's right auditory nerve and another to a telephone receiver. With Wever 50 ft (15 m) away in a soundproof room with the receiver, Bray talked into the cat's ear and, astonishingly enough, Wever was able to hear him loud and clear!

Although some aspects of the experiment were later disproven, it is believed their work inspired research that helped develop the cochlear implant—a device that stimulates the auditory nerves of deaf individuals by converting sound into electrical signals.

***Believe It or Not!* . . .** **The World Chess Boxing Organization motto is "Fighting's done in the ring, and war's waged on the board."**

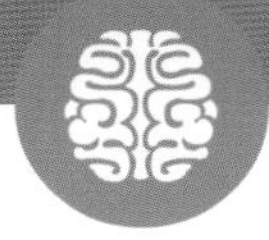

BRAINS AND BRAWN

There is no finer sport that matches wits and fists than chess boxing. Whether you choose to call it a hybrid fighting sport or hybrid board game, chess boxing is exactly what you think it would be. Two opponents play a game of chess for one round, box for another, and then repeat.

The match lasts 11 rounds and begins with chess. The combatants square off in a timed game of chess for six minutes, then switch right over to fighting. Once the boxing round ends, they are back at the board continuing their ongoing chess match. Separate referees typically monitor the chess match and boxing.

Athletes only have a short 60 seconds while the board is being removed from the ring to take a break. A win is decided by a checkmate or knockout. If the chess match ends in a tie, the match is decided by technical points, and if that's a tie, the black chess player wins.

SCALY BANDAGES

In 2016, doctors in Brazil successfully treated severe burns by covering them with dressings made of fish skin.

The skin comes from the abundant and disease-resistant tilapia fish. The alternative bandages go through a process that removes the scales, muscle tissue, possible toxins, and fishy smell before it is stretched, laminated, and cut into strips. These strips can then be placed on damaged skin, such as burn victim Maria Ines Candido da Silva, who was the first patient to receive this treatment. The flexible and moist nature of the fish skin makes it the perfect material for dressing burns and has been increasing in usage.

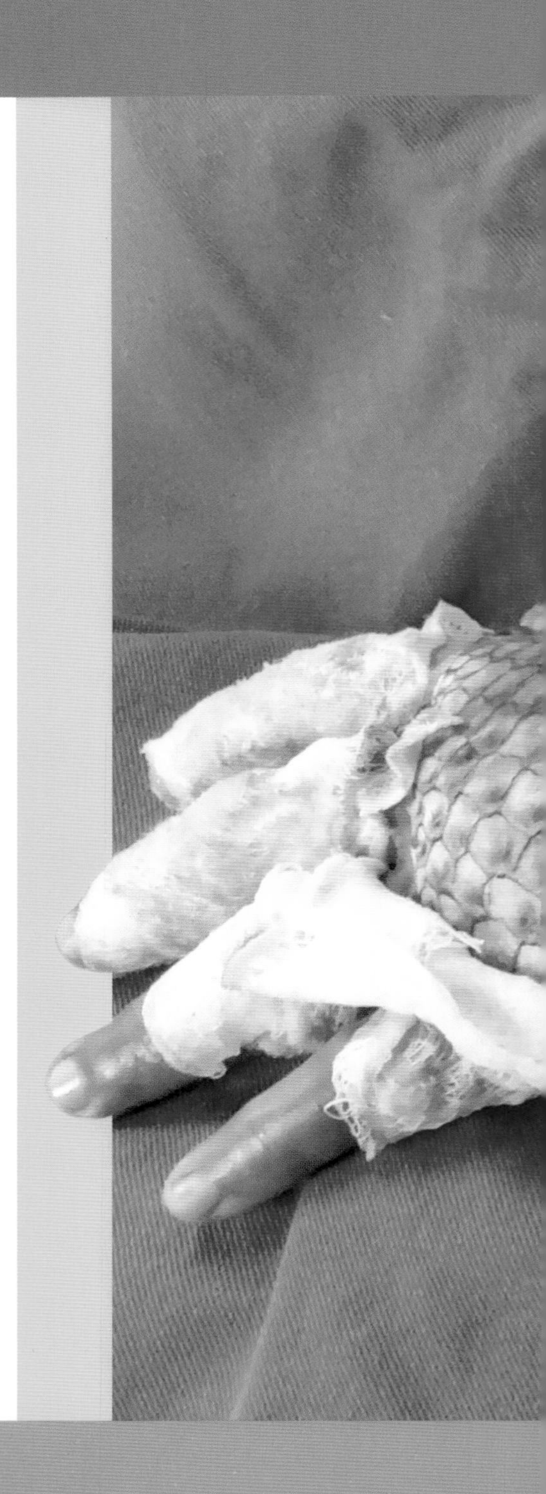

WHY CAN'T WE WALK THROUGH WALLS?

The question looks like an easy one and the answer fairly straightforward. You are solid. Walls are solid. Therefore, you can't walk through them.

But things get a little more complicated when you look at it on a microscopic level. We—and everything else in the universe—are really just an assemblage of atoms, and atoms are almost entirely empty space. To be pedantic, they are 99.99999 percent empty space. So if this is the case, why can't we walk through walls?

It comes down to the principle that no two fermions (a group of subatomic particles that includes electrons, protons, and neutrons) can be in the same state or same configuration at any one time. Electrons are constantly swarming haphazardly around an atom's nucleus at such a speed that it is as if they are taking up all of the empty space at once. Also, the electrons of one atom repel the electrons of other atoms, so that each atom remains distinct.

This means that if you were to walk through a wall, two electrons (yours and the wall's) would have to coexist in the same space—something that is just not possible. Therefore, despite the fact that we are almost entirely empty space (a mind-boggling fact in itself), we cannot walk through walls—or any other solid material, for that matter.

KELLY
STS-124
HAM
NYBERG
CHAMITOFF
HOSHIDE
きぼう
NOWAK
WILSON
FOSSUM
SELLERS
REITER
UF-1
ОНУФРИЕНКО WALZ BURSCH
CULBERTSON ДЕЖУРОВ ТЮРИН

SPACED OUT

We have been sending people into outer space since 1961. But what do we really know about what happens to the human body during space travel? Researchers followed the lives of astronaut Scott Kelly and his twin brother Mark, a retired astronaut, to examine what happens to your genetic makeup in space.

During Scott's 340 days on the International Space Station, 10 studies were conducted on both twins. The results? Scott Kelly's genetic expression, bone density, immune system responses, and telomere dynamics were altered.

One of the more intriguing differences between the twins was a shift in Scott's gut bacteria, with an increased production of good bacteria. These levels returned to normal when he was back on Earth. Scott also had longer telomeres—"caps" on the end of chromosomes related to aging—while he was in space, even though they typically shorten as a person ages. After about six months back on Earth, these also returned to normal.

Human DNA chemical compounds remained unchanged during the mission, which makes public space travel a growing possibility!

Astronaut twins Mark (left) and Scott Kelly (right).

FALLING FOR YOU

While the death of a whale can be a sad sign of polluted waters, food scarcity, or human violence, the gargantuan bodies left behind by these majestic creatures can create a hotbed for life.

Sometimes called a whale fall, carcasses that sink to the deep depths of the ocean's abyss are an important transmission vector for nutrients to an otherwise static part of the ocean.

Over the course of months, the soft tissue is completely eaten away by fish, sharks, shrimp, eels, and crabs. The detritus and material of the whale don't just provide direct sustenance, however. The nutrients that make it into the soil give rise to plant life and bacterial mats, which in turn are a new food source for the whole biological community.

Even the remaining skeleton can become a basis for colonization, with microorganisms living off the chemical reaction of its decomposition. Anemones specific to whale falls, as well as unique bone-eating zombie worms, call the rotting carcass home. These organisms can be supported for decades from a single whale carcass.

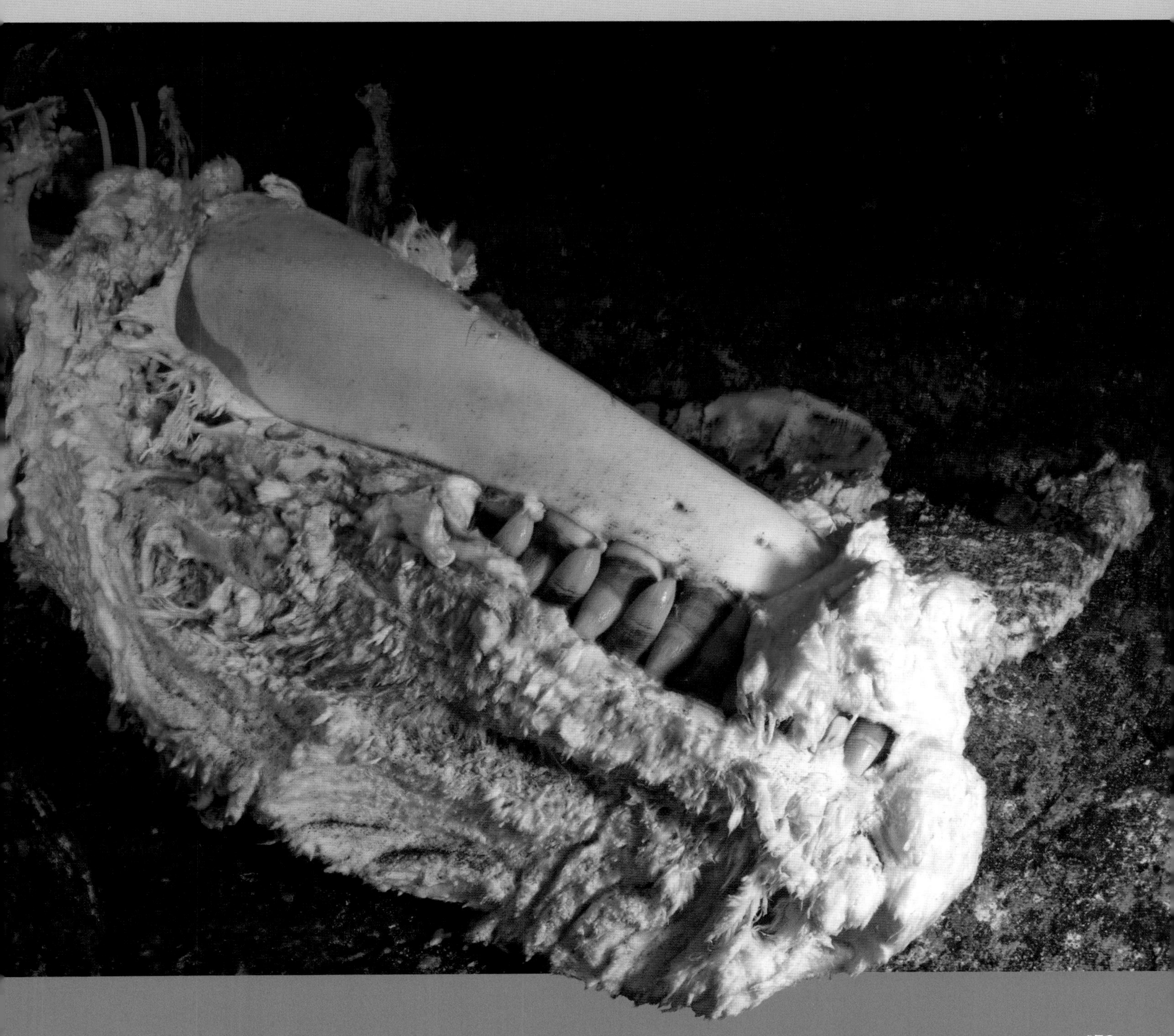

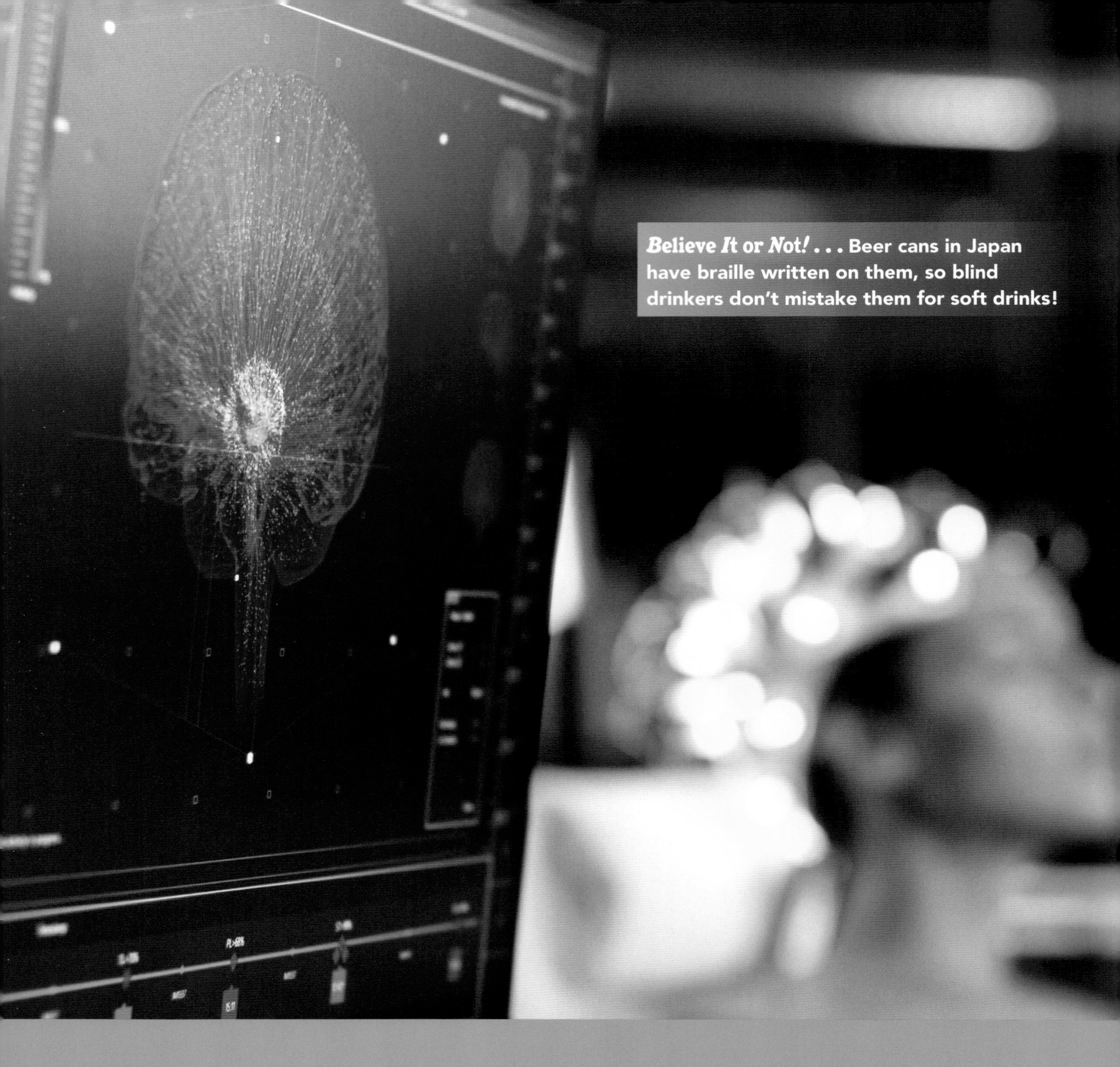

Believe It or Not! **. . . Beer cans in Japan have braille written on them, so blind drinkers don't mistake them for soft drinks!**

DO YOU SEE THAT SOUND?

It's often said that as you go blind, your other senses will be heightened. There has been growing evidence that in blind people, the part of the brain that processes vision repurposes itself to process sound!

A study was conducted that monitored the brain activity of both blind and sighted people as they listened to three different audio recordings. One was perfectly clear, the second was slightly distorted, and the third was almost unrecognizable. While the monitors showed activity in the auditory sections of the brain in both groups, blind subjects showed increased activity in the visual sectors. Researchers argue that the visual parts of the brain are, in fact, being used to process sound!

CREATURES OF THE DEEP

The ocean is a deep, dark, and mysterious place. It's so mysterious that scientists aren't capable of explaining every phenomenon they come across, especially abyssal gigantism!

Stories of mythical sea serpents, such as Jörmungandr of Norse mythology or the Loch Ness monster, have been told for centuries. These supersized aquatic creatures aren't too difficult to fathom when you take a look at abyssal gigantism, when deep-sea creatures grow much larger than their shallow-water family members.

Isopods, a type of crustacean, have been found measuring from just a few micrometers to the size of a small dog! Japanese spider crabs, another type of crustacean, can have a leg span of up to 15 ft (4.6 m)!

Oarfish, the animal that most likely inspired tales of the Loch Ness monster, is the longest bony fish in the sea. It can measure up to 56 ft (17 m) in length!

And fear of the kraken, an enormous fabled cephalopod, is likely based on the giant squid, which wasn't caught on camera until 2004. Believe it or not, they can grow up to 40 ft (12 m)—that's the size of a school bus!

789879
123213
789879
567657
12102
789879

ARE YOU SMARTER THAN A COMPUTER?

Computers certainly aren't dumb. However, for all their brainpower, machines are still surprisingly clunky and awkward in the art of conversation, especially when it comes to answering questions.

To overcome this weakness, computer engineers at the University of Maryland generated a collection of more than 1,200 questions that completely bewilder even the best computer answering systems today, despite being comparatively easy for people to answer, hoping they will become better trained at communicating with humans using language. Here are a select few examples of the trivia questions:

- Name this European nation that was divided into Eastern and Western regions after World War II.
- Identify this metal that is used for decorative coatings and many musical instruments.
- Name this South African leader who became president in 1994 after spending 27 years in prison.

But how can a computer be foiled by such simple questions? The reason has much more to do with language than knowledge. It's notable that the questions are worded in a slightly odd way. That's because they're laced with six different language phenomena that consistently stump computers but don't tend to phase humans.

OH, SNAP!

Did you know that a single strand of spaghetti is referred to as a spaghetto? If you try to snap a spaghetto in half, you'll end up with three unequally sized pieces.

Why can't they break into two equal halves? Once snapped, the strands send a violent ripple backward and cause additional breakage. How can you remedy this aggressive shockwave? You twist it!

Scientists from MIT, Cornell University, and the University of Aix in Marseille have created a device that rotates the spaghetto a full 360° before pushing clamps together to cause a break. The reverberations then release through the unwinding of the pasta, preventing further shattering!

TECHNICALLY THE TALLEST

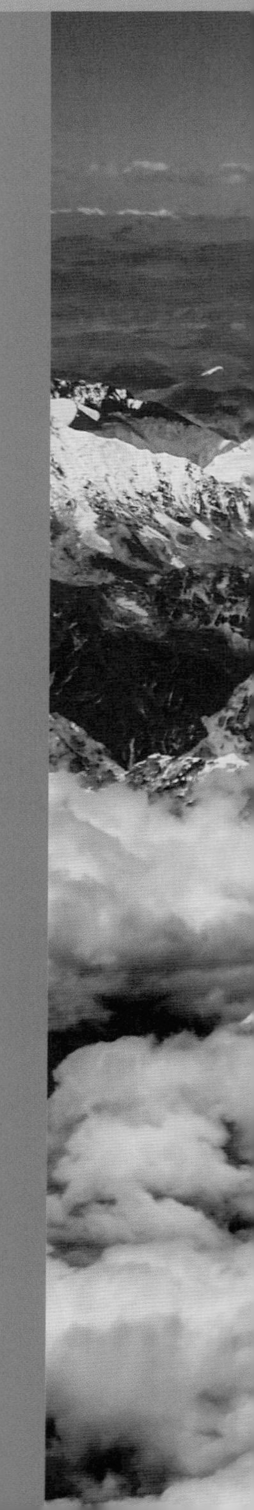

It's common knowledge that Mount Everest is the tallest mountain on Earth, but what does "tallest" even mean? Height above sea level? Greatest distance from base to peak? What about distance from space? The answers to all of these questions change which mountain earns the tallest mountain title.

Mount Everest stands a proud 29,029 ft (8,848 m) above sea level. But that status delicately hangs on the way sea levels work. Sea levels vary all over the globe, and the elevation of Mount Everest is measured from the world average.

From its base to its peak, Mauna Kea measures more than 33,000 ft (10,000 m). Unlike Everest, the base of this Hawaiian mountain starts way below the Pacific Ocean. If its base were raised to sea level—where the base of Everest is measured—Mauna Kea would stand about a mile taller.

At 20,548 ft (6,263 m), Mount Chimborazo is the tallest mountain in Ecuador. It is also very close to the equator. As the Earth spins, it pushes out around the equator, becoming somewhat disc-shaped. Because of this planetary centrifugal force, Chimborazo is about 1.3 mi (2.1 km) closer to space than Everest.

Believe It* or *Not! . . . It is estimated that climbers leave a combined 26,500 lb (12,020 kg) of human waste on Mount Everest every year.

THE WRIGHT WAY

Brothers Orville and Wilbur Wright achieved the first sustained flight with a heavier-than-air aircraft on December 17, 1903. Orville flew 120 ft (36.5 m) over a period of 12 seconds.

The Wright brothers paved the way for revolutionizing air travel, and on July 20, 1969—just 65 years, 7 months, and 3 days later—the *Apollo 11* spacecraft was sent to the Moon. In this short amount of time, air travel went from a single engine and propeller mechanism to the advanced technology of the *Saturn V* rocket.

The *Saturn V* rocket stood 363 ft (111 m) tall—taller than the Statue of Liberty—and had an on-board computer that guided it into Earth's orbit. NASA had large computers back on the ground to help with navigational corrections.

In between the creation of the first aircraft and the engineering of technologically advanced spacecrafts, airplane passengers in the 1930s sat in wicker seats! We just celebrated the 50th anniversary of the first Moon landing—who knows where we'll be flying off to next.

Believe It or Not! **. . . The Wright brothers' historic flight was initially reported in just four newspapers!**

CHEMISTRY

HOLD IT IN

Hold your cheeks together the next time you go under the knife, because a squeaky-bottomed Japanese woman recently ended up with burns to her legs and waist after her fart caught fire during surgery.

According to a Japanese newspaper, the lady was being treated at a hospital in Tokyo, where doctors were using a laser to perform a procedure on her cervix. A report into the incident explained that the laser ignited gases that leaked from her intestines, causing the surgical drape to ignite.

Farts contain a number of different gases that are released as by-products of our intestinal activities. Among these are hydrogen and methane, both of which are flammable and give our windy expulsions their combustible characteristics.

Believe It or Not! **. . . A sperm whale can detect a 1-ft-long (0.3-m) squid at a range of 1 mi (1.6 km) using sonar sound waves.**

CAN YOU HEAR ME NOW?

Brought to fame by Herman Melville's whale-hunting epic *Moby Dick*, sperm whales are some of Earth's most mysterious creatures. Even with the ability to dive thousands of feet deep, researchers still don't know what goes on below the water's surface.

What we do know about sperm whales is that they communicate by using a series of four different clicking noises. These clicks are used for both social communication and honing in on prey. When hunting, the sperm whale's noise reaches up to 230 decibels (dB)!

To put that in perspective, a normal conversation between two people is held at about 60 dB, a lawn mower is at about 105 dB, and a sports arena ranges from 120 to 130 dB. Any sound higher than 85 dB is considered harmful, but your eardrum can rupture at 150 dB!

OXYGEN
GENERATION
EFFICIENCY
74%
Plant Analyzer Unit
G7

THE FERTILE FRONTIER

If we are going to establish permanent bases on the Moon or Mars, we need to know that they can be self-sufficient. Once we figure out what we're going to live in and how we're going to breathe, what are we going to eat?

Not to worry, because researchers in the Netherlands have managed to produce crops in Martian and lunar mock soils developed by NASA. They found that it is possible to grow food for future astronauts directly in the soil of another world and that the crops grown can produce viable seeds that can then be replanted.

The simulated soils were mixed with organic matter to provide nutrients for the crops, and standard Earth soil was used as a control sample. The team attempted to cultivate 10 different crops: garden cress, arugula, quinoa, tomato, radish, rye, spinach, chive, pea, and leek. The results show that it's only bad news for the Popeye fans among the astronauts, because spinach was the only crop that didn't reach a point where the scientists could harvest edible parts.

ACKNOWLEDGMENTS

4-5 (bkg) © Dima Zel/Shutterstock **4** (bl) © Gerald Robert Fischer/Shutterstock, (tr) © 3Dstock/Shutterstock, (br) © zenstock/Shutterstock **5** (c) gameover/Alamy Stock Photo, (tr) © Vadim Sadovski/Shutterstock, (cr) © Lotus Images/Shutterstock, (br) © Pedro Bernardo/Shutterstock **6-7** © Natalia Barsukova/Shutterstock, (bkg) © Alona_S/Shutterstock **8** © grebcha/Shutterstock **10-11** Bailey-Cooper Photography/Alamy Stock Photo **11** © rangizzz/Shutterstock **12** © Valentyn Volkov/Shutterstock **13** © Peter J. Traub/Shutterstock **14** © Aedka Studio/Shutterstock **14-15** © vilax/Shutterstock **16-17** Media Drum World/Alamy Stock Photo **18-19** © Jan Cejka/Shutterstock **20-21** © fizkes/Shutterstock **22-23** Public Domain {{PD-US-expired}} via Rutgers University Libraries and Wikimedia Commons **23** © Picsfive/Shutterstock **24** © Somchai Som/Shutterstock **24-25** © SakuraPh/Shutterstock **26** © Olha Birieva/Shutterstock **28** (bkg) © Luisa Fumi/Shutterstock, (c) History and Art Collection/Alamy Stock Photo **30-31** © Suchota/Shutterstock **32-33** © Hoiseung Jung/Shutterstock **34-35** © tomertu/Shutterstock **36** Public Domain {{PD-US-expired}} George III by Johan Zoffany via the Royal Collection Trust **38-39** © Denis Belitsky/Shutterstock **40-41** © 3Dstock/Shutterstock **42-43** (bkg) © Titima Ongkantong/Shutterstock **43** Ripley Entertainment **44** © Sean Locke Photography/Shutterstock **45** © Denise Kappa/Shutterstock **46-47** © Africa Studio/Shutterstock **48-49** © Olga Kot Photo/Shutterstock **50** © Sergey Nivens/Shutterstock **52-53** (bkg) © aleks.k/Shutterstock, (l) © Potapov Alexander/Shutterstock **53** (c) © Arina_B/Shutterstock **54** Harris & Ewing Collection, Prints & Photographs Division, Library of Congress, LC-H2- B-7464 **55** (bkg) © Lukasz Szwaj/Shutterstock, (c) gameover/Alamy Stock Photo **56-57** © Davide Calabresi/Shutterstock **56** (l) © KREML/Shutterstock **58-59** (bkg) Dave Watts/Alamy Stock Photo **59** (tl) © Parilov/Shutterstock, (bl) © FamVeld/Shutterstock, (bc) © jgorzynik/Shutterstock **60-61** (bkg) © argus/Shutterstock, (b) © CHIARI VFX/Shutterstock **62** (b) © Gjermund/Shutterstock **62-63** © Pedro Bernardo/Shutterstock **64-65** {{PD-US-expired}} Accessed via Wikimedia Commons and Detroit Institute of Arts **66** © Tau5/Shutterstock **68** Public Domain {{PD-USGov-NASA}} **70-71** David Stephenson/Lexington Herald-Leader/Tribune News Service via Getty Images **72-73** © Everett Historical/Shutterstock **74** © Andrey_Popov/Shutterstock **77** Courtesy of U.S. Department of Energy **78-79** © HikoPhotography/Shutterstock **80** © xpixel/Shutterstock **81** © Gerald Robert Fischer/Shutterstock **82-83** © kudla/Shutterstock **83** © AG-PHOTOS/Shutterstock **84** © Vadim Sadovski/Shutterstock **86** (bkg) © Sergey Nivens/Shutterstock, (c) © robypangy/Shutterstock **88-89** Morgan collection of Civil War drawings; Waud, William, -1878; Prints & Photographs Division; Library of Congress; LC-DIG-ppmsca-21750 **91** © Marco Rubino/Shutterstock **92** {{PD-US-expired}} Accessed via Wikimedia Commons and Beinecke Rare Book & Manuscript Library, Yale University **92-93** © lunamarina/Shutterstock **95** © Oleksandr Kulichenko/Shutterstock **96-97** © Levent Konuk/Shutterstock **98-99** © Andrea Izzotti/Shutterstock **100-101** Mother Shipton's Cave **102** (bkg) © DmitriyRazinkov/Shutterstock, (c) © likekightcm/Shutterstock, (b) © JLwarehouse/Shutterstock **104-105** © krungchingpixs/Shutterstock **106-107** © Romolo Tavani/Shutterstock **107** © Astor57/Shutterstock **108-109** © antony cullup/Shutterstock **110-111** (bkg) © Deni_Sugandi/Shutterstock, © WhiteBarbie/Shutterstock **112-113** © Herschel Hoffmeyer/Shutterstock **114-115** ADIFO/Cover Images **115** © Javier Rosano/Shutterstock **116** (bkg) © Gill Copeland/Shutterstock **116-117** Universal History Archive/UIG via Getty images **119** (bkg) © Dima Zel/Shutterstock, (c) © Leo Blanchette/Shutterstock **120-121** Timothy Fadek/Corbis via Getty Images **122-123** CC BY 2.5 by frankenstoen **124-125** © SkillUp/Shutterstock **126** © Brian A Jackson/Shutterstock **128-129** © maxuser/Shutterstock **130-131** © Gorodenkoff/Shutterstock **132-133** © gan chaonan/Shutterstock **133** © Photoongraphy/Shutterstock **134-135** © zakalinka/Shutterstock **136** © Everett Historical/Shutterstock **136-137** © Lia Koltyrina/Shutterstock **138-139** Public Domain {{PD-USGov-NASA}} **140-141** Design Pics Inc/Alamy Stock Photo **142** © doomu/Shutterstock **143** CTK/Alamy Stock Photo **144-145** © Hung Chung Chih/Shutterstock **145** © SOMMAI/Shutterstock **146-147** (bkg) © Triff/Shutterstock **146** (bl) © koya979/Shutterstock **147** © Timofeev Vladimir/Shutterstock **148-149** © Pixelcruiser/Shutterstock **150-151** © Oleksandr Bilchuk/Shutterstock **153** © imging/Shutterstock **154-155** EFE News Agency/Alamy Stock Photo **156-157** University of Queensland/Cover Images **158-159** © D. Kucharski K. Kucharska/Shutterstock **159** © Mriya Wildlife/Shutterstock **160** (bkg) © Zakharchuk/Shutterstock, (c) © Fer Gregory/Shutterstock **161** © dmitro2009/Shutterstock **162-163** (bkg) © azazello photo studio/Shutterstock **163** (l) © Jagodka/Shutterstock **164-165** © Africa Studio/Shutterstock **166** © Lotus Images/Shutterstock **166-167** IJF BURNS UNIT/CATERS NEWS **168** (bkg) © fotorath/Shutterstock, (c) © Viorel Sima/Shutterstock **170-171** Public Domain {{PD-USGov-NASA}} Photographer: Robert Markowitz **172-173** Claudio Contreras via Minden Pictures **174-175** © Gorodenkoff/Shutterstock **176-177** © kikujungboy/Shutterstock **178** © HQuality/Shutterstock **180-181** © ugurv/Shutterstock **181** © stockphoto-graf/Shutterstock **182-183** © angela Meier/Shutterstock **184-185** (bkg) Public Domain {{PD-US}} Library of Congress Prints and Photographs Division Washington, D.C. 20540 USA http://www.loc.gov/pictures/item/00652085/, (b) © Alones/Shutterstock **185** (l) © Philip Arno Photography/Shutterstock **186** © seeyou/Shutterstock **186-187** © UfaBizPhoto/Shutterstock **188-189** © Willyam Bradberry/Shutterstock **189** © Elnur/Shutterstock **190-191** © Gorodenkoff/Shutterstock **191** © Zeeking/Shutterstock **Master Graphics** Courtesy of IFL Science

Key: t = top, b = bottom, c = center, l = left, r = right, bkg = background

Every attempt has been made to acknowledge correctly and contact copyright holders and we apologize in advance for any unintentional errors or